SERGIO ARAGONÉS the GROO™ LIBRARY

Writer/Artist
Sergio Aragonés

Wordsmith
Mark Evanier

Letterer
Stan Sakai

Colorist
Tom Luth

DARK HORSE MAVERICK™

[redacted]

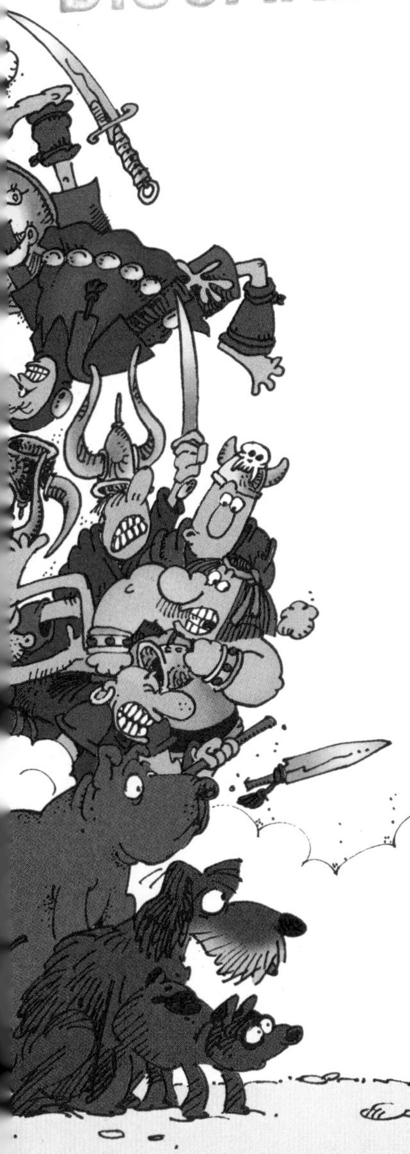

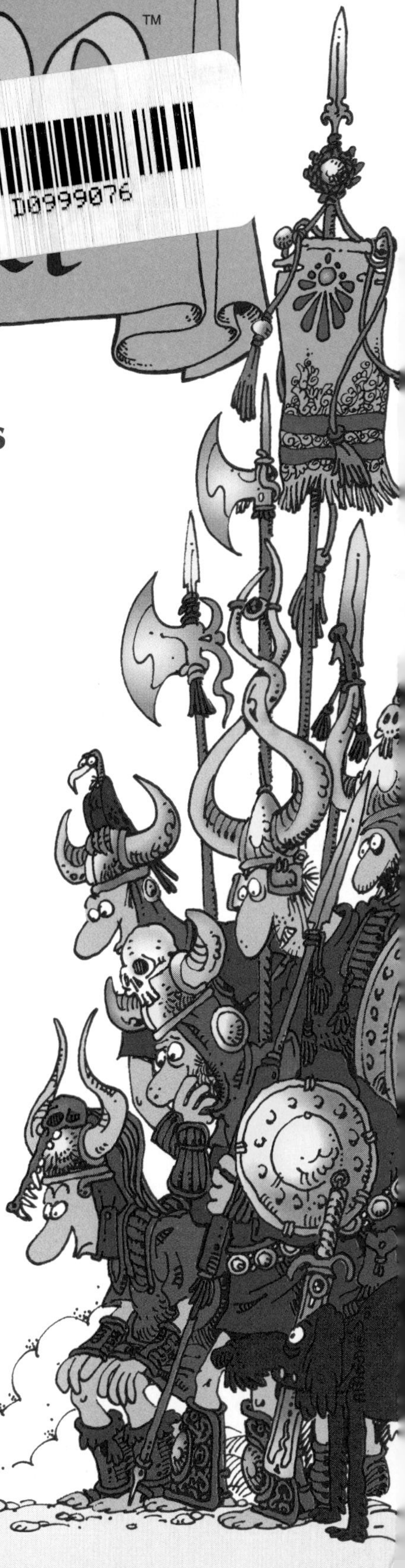

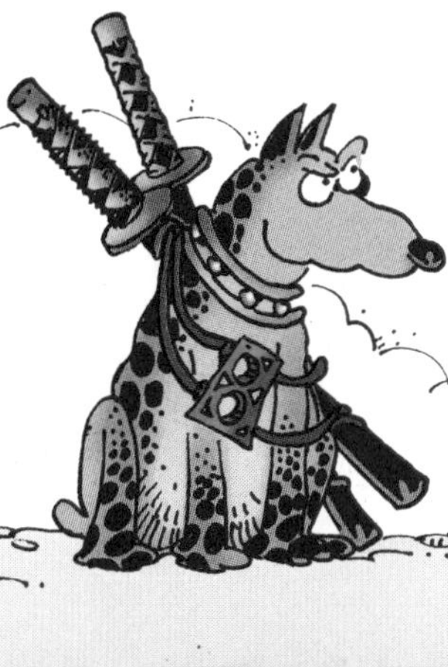

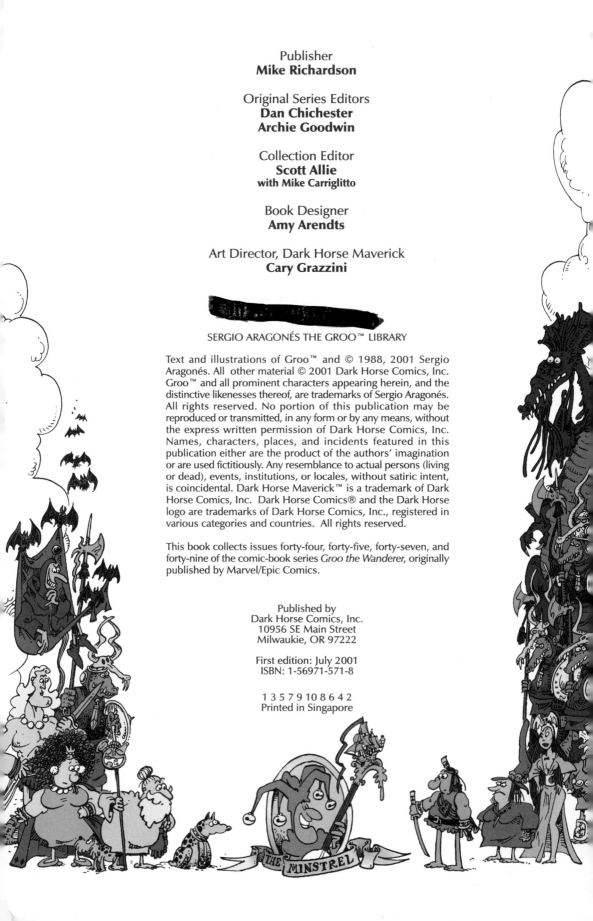

Publisher
Mike Richardson

Original Series Editors
Dan Chichester
Archie Goodwin

Collection Editor
Scott Allie
with Mike Carriglitto

Book Designer
Amy Arendts

Art Director, Dark Horse Maverick
Cary Grazzini

[redacted]

SERGIO ARAGONÉS THE GROO™ LIBRARY

This book collects issues forty-four, forty-five, forty-seven, and forty-nine of the comic-book series *Groo the Wanderer*, originally published by Marvel/Epic Comics.

Published by
Dark Horse Comics, Inc.
10956 SE Main Street
Milwaukie, OR 97222

First edition: July 2001
ISBN: 1-56971-571-8

1 3 5 7 9 10 8 6 4 2
Printed in Singapore

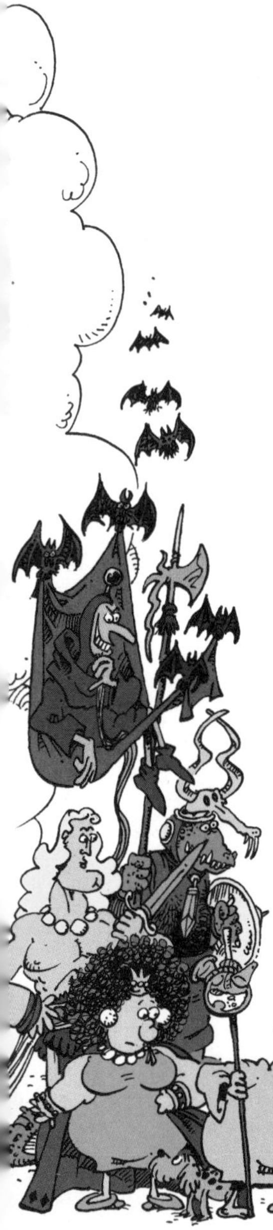

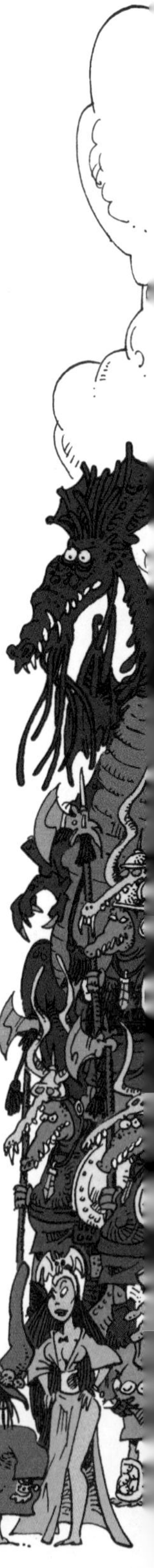

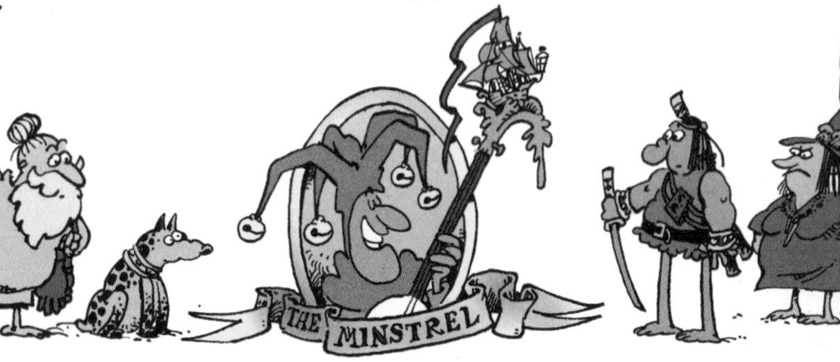
THE MINSTREL

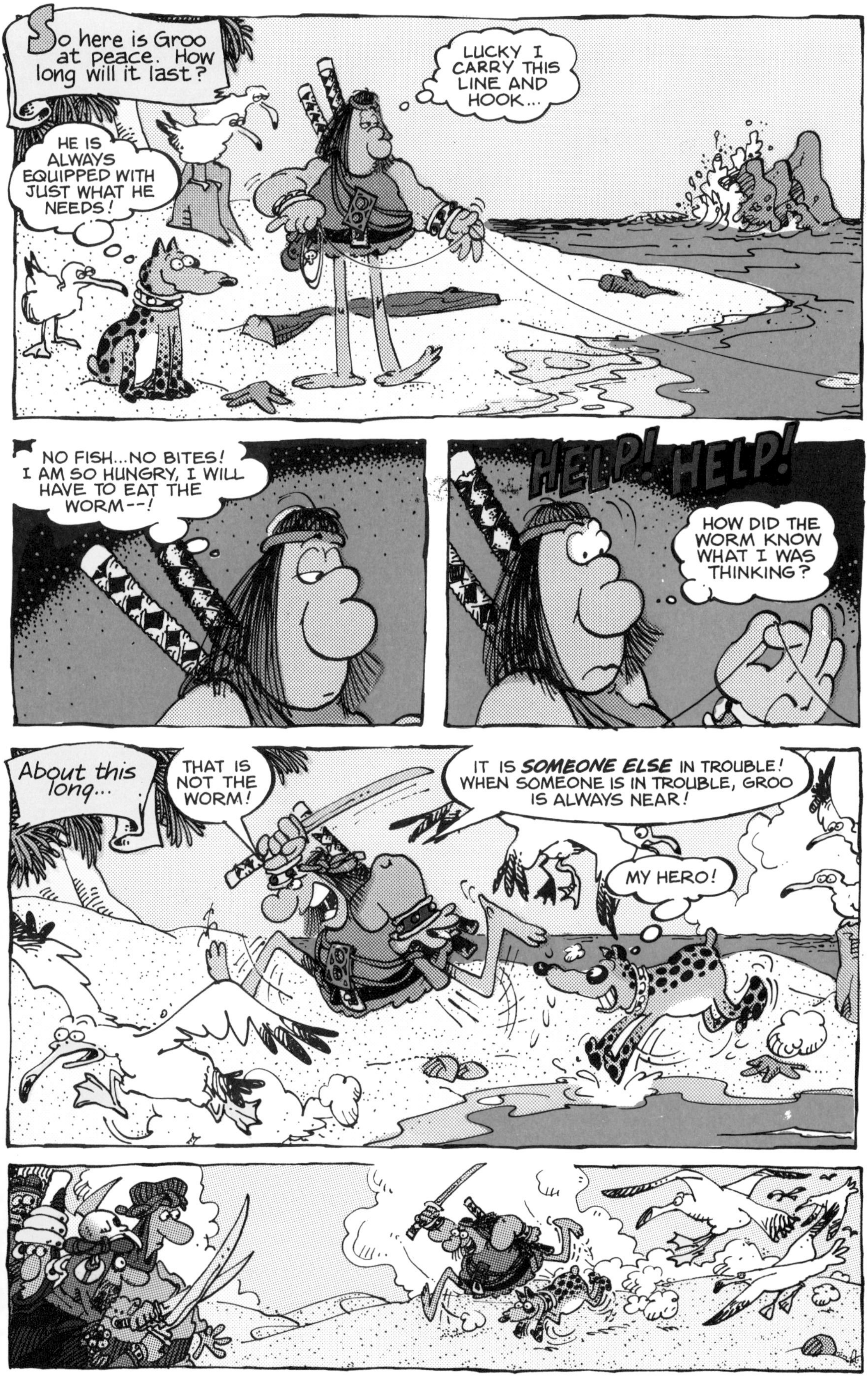
So here is Groo at peace. How long will it last?
LUCKY I CARRY THIS LINE AND HOOK...
HE IS ALWAYS EQUIPPED WITH JUST WHAT HE NEEDS!
NO FISH...NO BITES! I AM SO HUNGRY, I WILL HAVE TO EAT THE WORM--!
HELP! HELP!
HOW DID THE WORM KNOW WHAT I WAS THINKING?
About this long...
THAT IS NOT THE WORM!
IT IS SOMEONE ELSE IN TROUBLE! WHEN SOMEONE IS IN TROUBLE, GROO IS ALWAYS NEAR!
MY HERO!

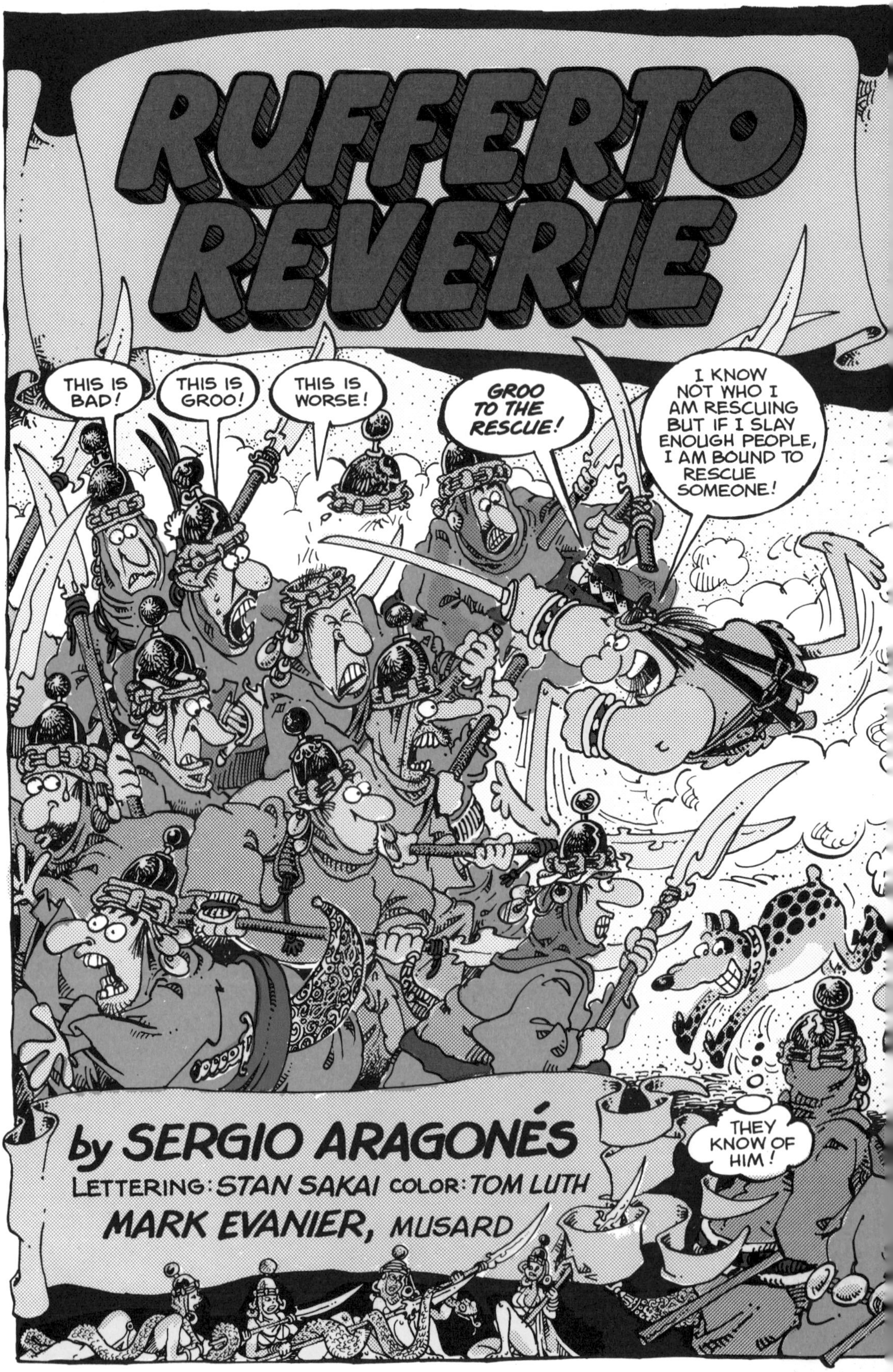
RUFFERTO REVERIE
THIS IS BAD!
THIS IS GROO!
THIS IS WORSE!
GROO TO THE RESCUE!
I KNOW NOT WHO I AM RESCUING BUT IF I SLAY ENOUGH PEOPLE, I AM BOUND TO RESCUE SOMEONE!
THEY KNOW OF HIM!
by SERGIO ARAGONÉS
LETTERING: STAN SAKAI COLOR: TOM LUTH
MARK EVANIER, MUSARD

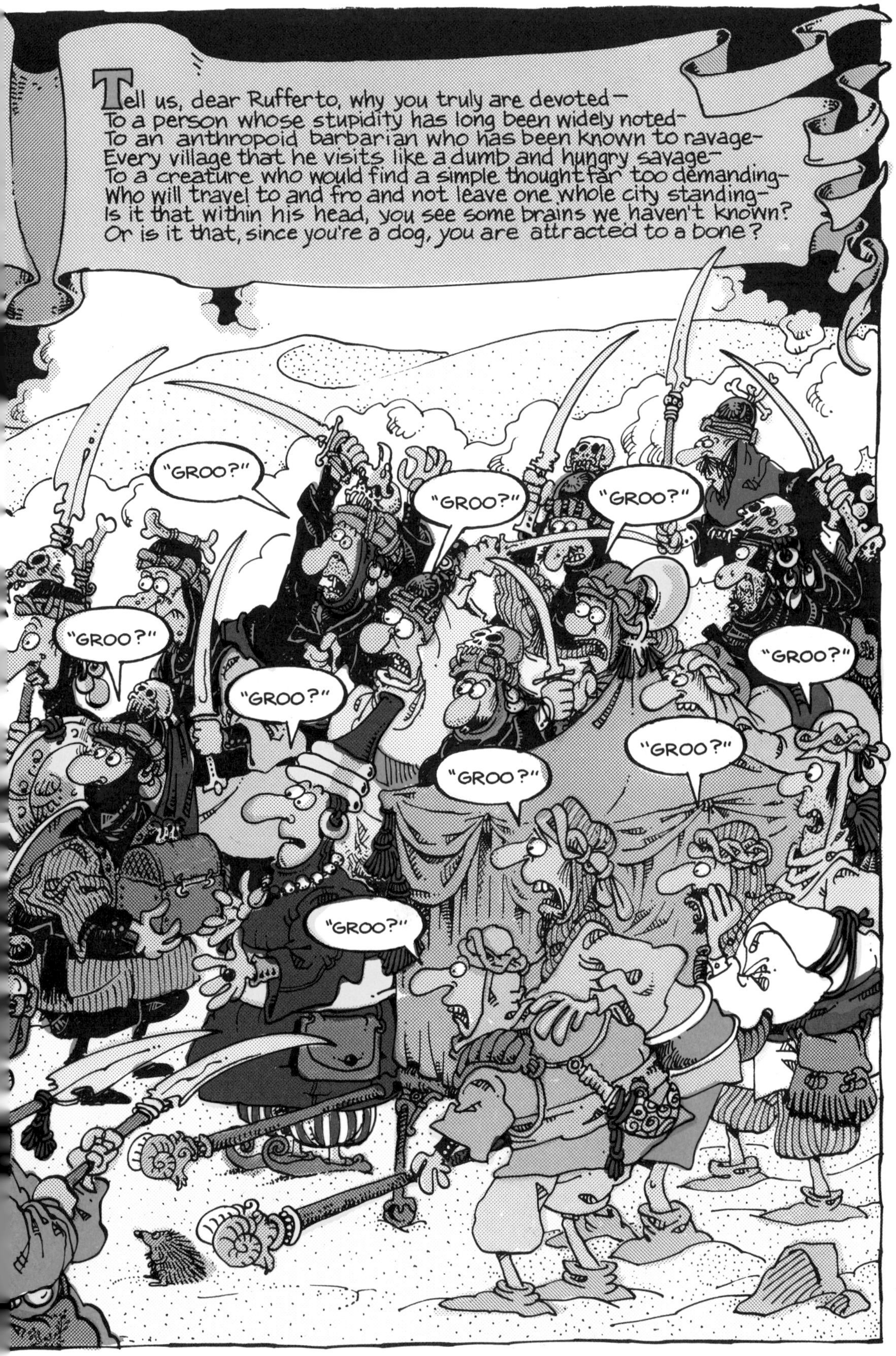
Tell us, dear Rufferto, why you truly are devoted—
To a person whose stupidity has long been widely noted—
To an anthropoid barbarian who has been known to ravage—
Every village that he visits like a dumb and hungry savage—
To a creature who would find a simple thought far too demanding—
Who will travel to and fro and not leave one whole city standing—
Is it that within his head, you see some brains we haven't known?
Or is it that, since you're a dog, you are attracted to a bone?
"GROO?"
"GROO?"
"GROO?"
"GROO?"
"GROO?"
"GROO?"
"GROO?"
"GROO?"
"GROO?"

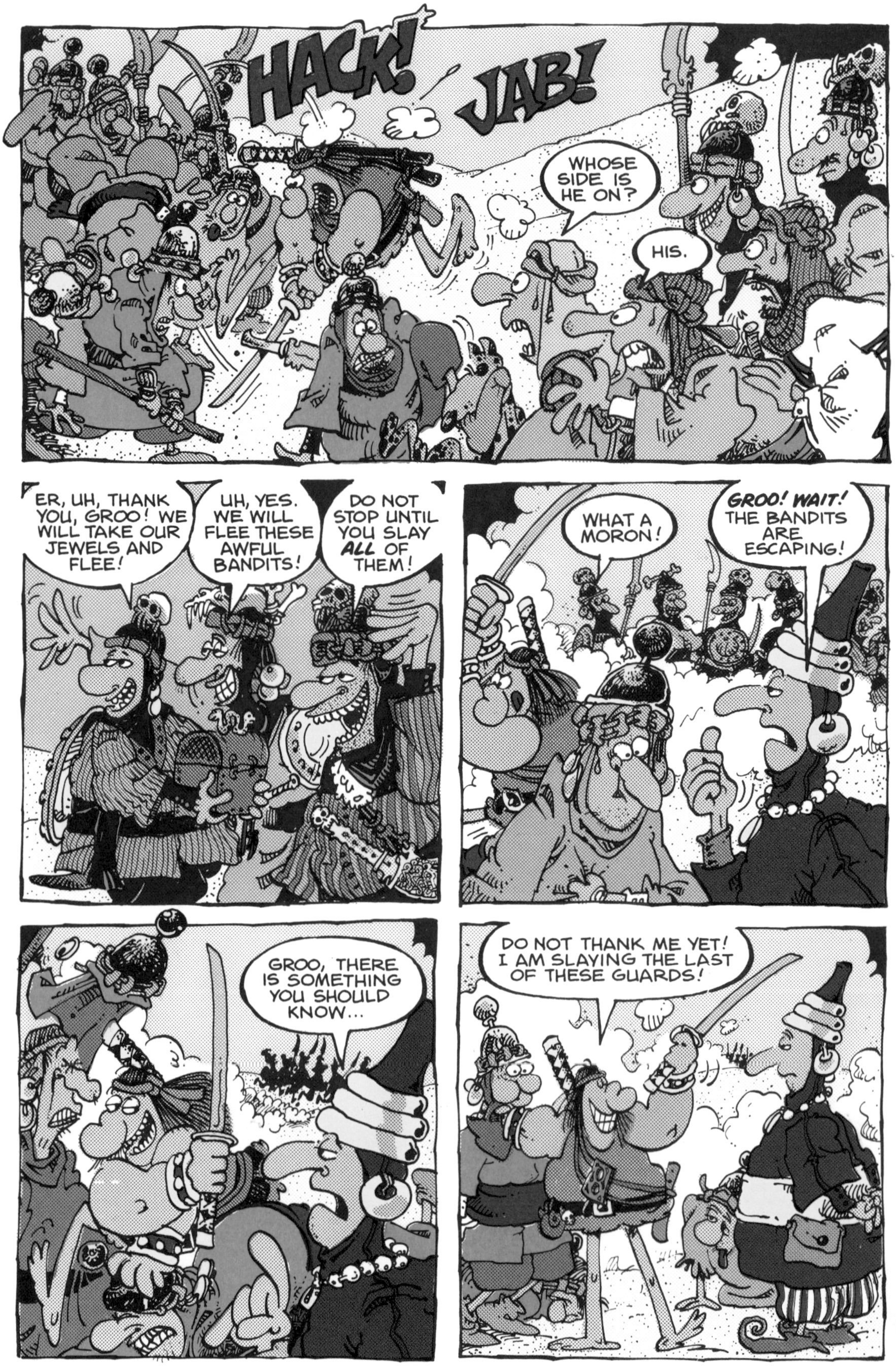
HACK!
JAB!
WHOSE SIDE IS HE ON?
HIS.
ER, UH, THANK YOU, GROO! WE WILL TAKE OUR JEWELS AND FLEE!
UH, YES. WE WILL FLEE THESE AWFUL BANDITS!
DO NOT STOP UNTIL YOU SLAY ALL OF THEM!
WHAT A MORON!
GROO! WAIT! THE BANDITS ARE ESCAPING!
GROO, THERE IS SOMETHING YOU SHOULD KNOW...
DO NOT THANK ME YET! I AM SLAYING THE LAST OF THESE GUARDS!

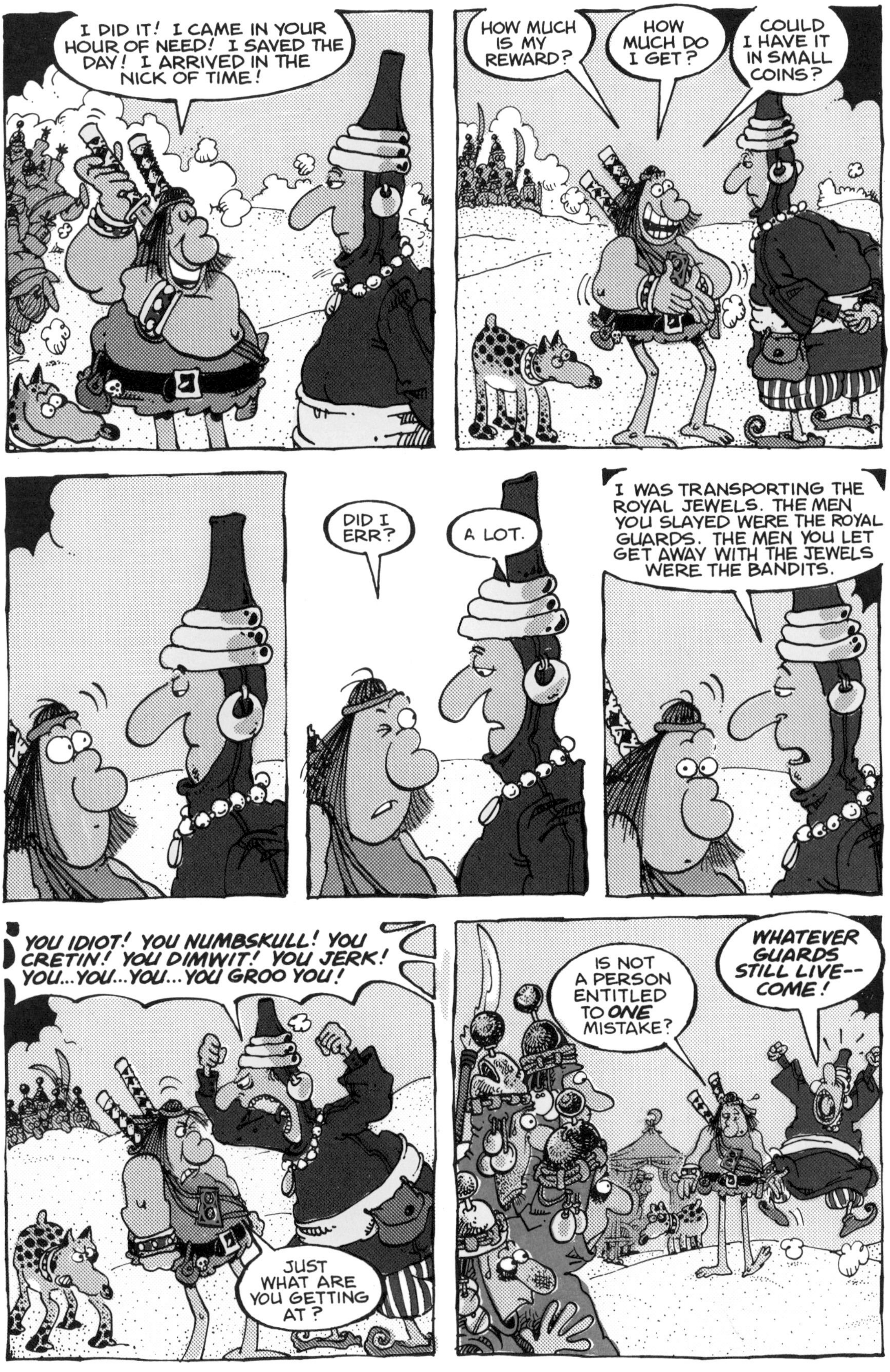
I DID IT! I CAME IN YOUR HOUR OF NEED! I SAVED THE DAY! I ARRIVED IN THE NICK OF TIME!
HOW MUCH IS MY REWARD?
HOW MUCH DO I GET?
COULD I HAVE IT IN SMALL COINS?
DID I ERR?
A LOT.
I WAS TRANSPORTING THE ROYAL JEWELS. THE MEN YOU SLAYED WERE THE ROYAL GUARDS. THE MEN YOU LET GET AWAY WITH THE JEWELS WERE THE BANDITS.
YOU IDIOT! YOU NUMBSKULL! YOU CRETIN! YOU DIMWIT! YOU JERK! YOU...YOU...YOU...YOU GROO YOU!
JUST WHAT ARE YOU GETTING AT?
IS NOT A PERSON ENTITLED TO ONE MISTAKE?
WHATEVER GUARDS STILL LIVE-- COME!

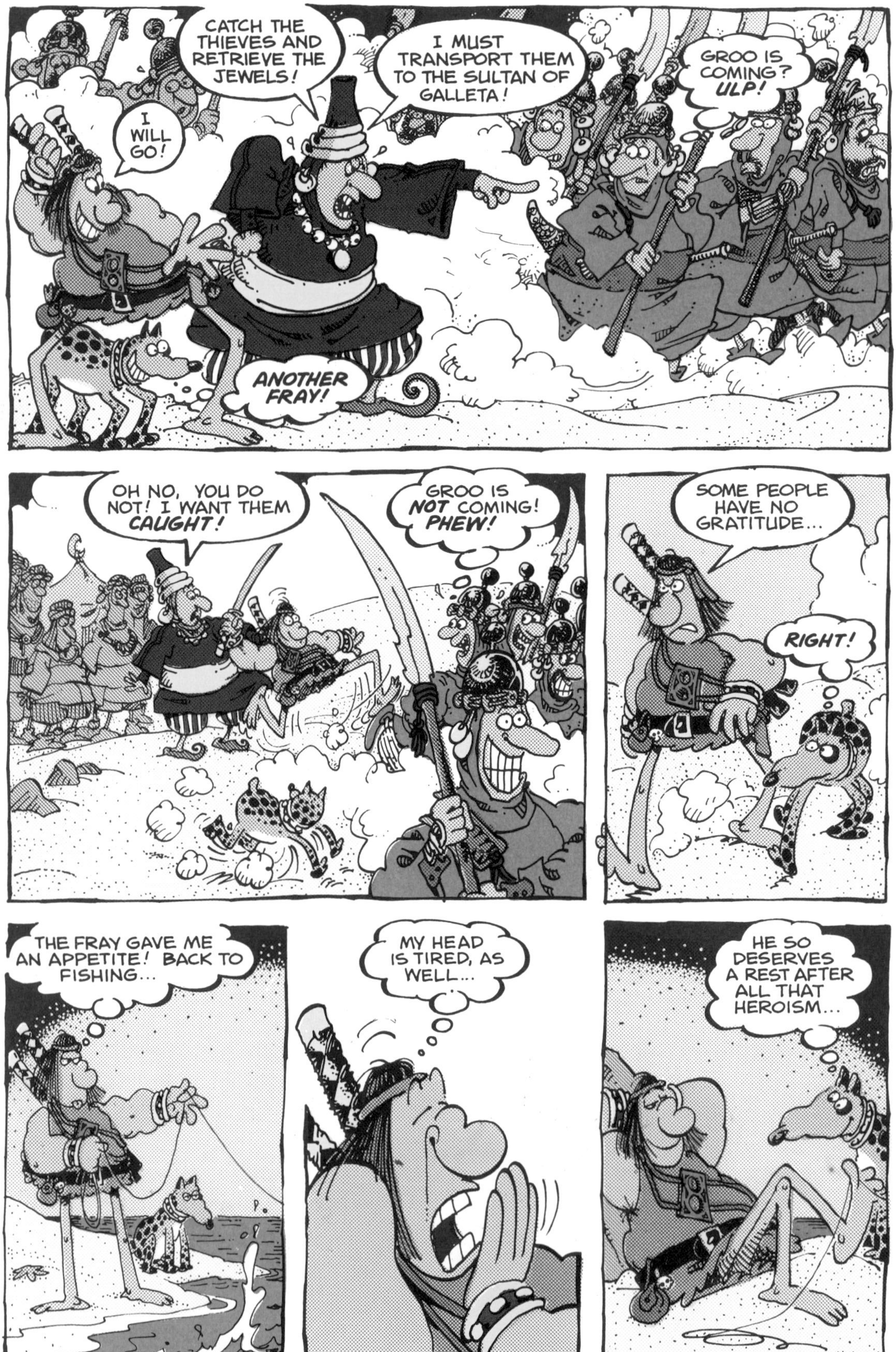
I WILL GO!
CATCH THE THIEVES AND RETRIEVE THE JEWELS!
I MUST TRANSPORT THEM TO THE SULTAN OF GALLETA!
GROO IS COMING? ULP!
ANOTHER FRAY!
OH NO, YOU DO NOT! I WANT THEM CAUGHT!
GROO IS NOT COMING! PHEW!
SOME PEOPLE HAVE NO GRATITUDE...
RIGHT!
THE FRAY GAVE ME AN APPETITE! BACK TO FISHING...
MY HEAD IS TIRED, AS WELL...
HE SO DESERVES A REST AFTER ALL THAT HEROISM...

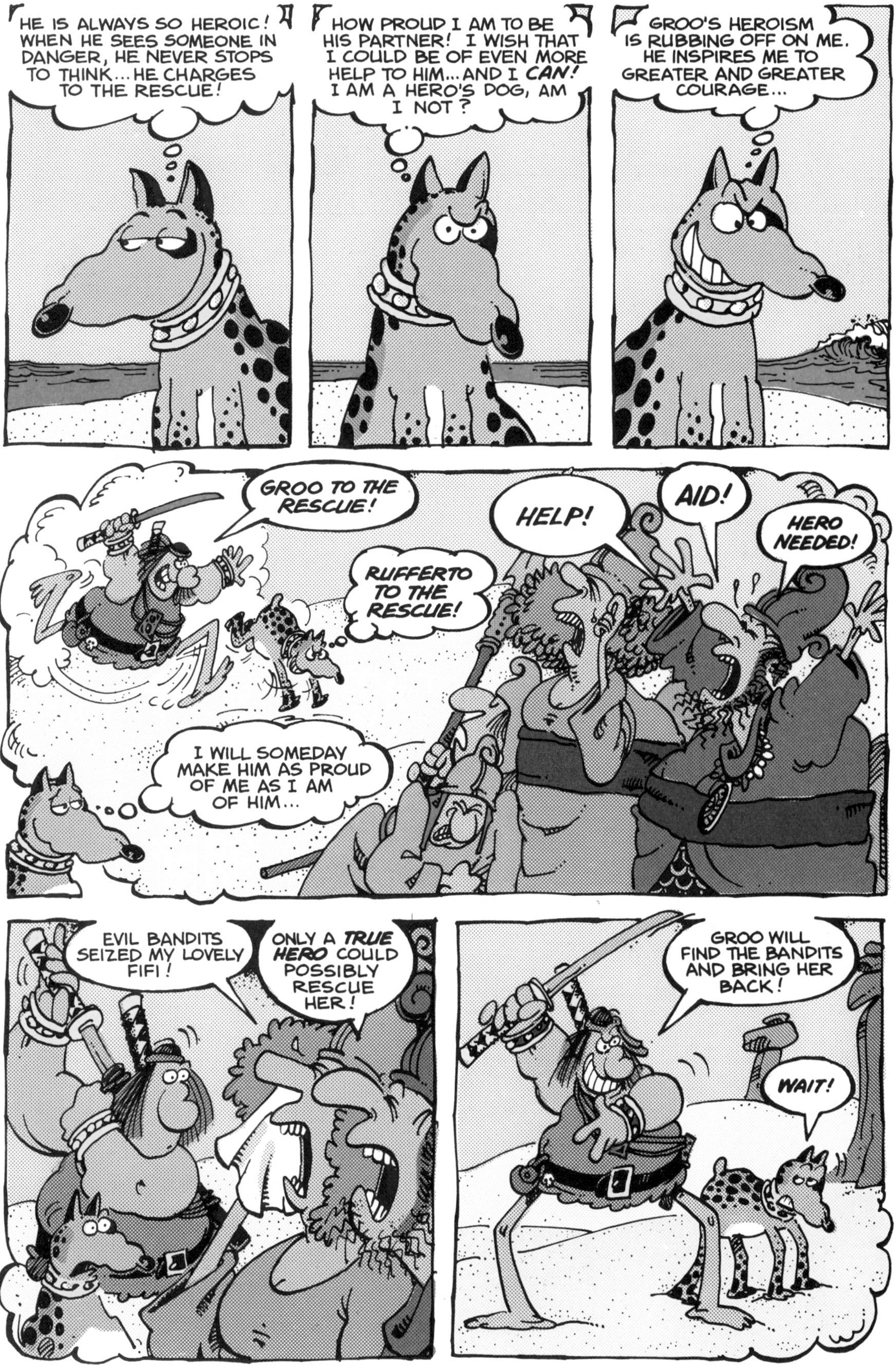

HE IS ALWAYS SO HEROIC! WHEN HE SEES SOMEONE IN DANGER, HE NEVER STOPS TO THINK... HE CHARGES TO THE RESCUE!
HOW PROUD I AM TO BE HIS PARTNER! I WISH THAT I COULD BE OF EVEN MORE HELP TO HIM... AND I CAN! I AM A HERO'S DOG, AM I NOT?
GROO'S HEROISM IS RUBBING OFF ON ME. HE INSPIRES ME TO GREATER AND GREATER COURAGE...
GROO TO THE RESCUE!
RUFFERTO TO THE RESCUE!
HELP!
AID!
HERO NEEDED!
I WILL SOMEDAY MAKE HIM AS PROUD OF ME AS I AM OF HIM...
EVIL BANDITS SEIZED MY LOVELY FIFI!
ONLY A TRUE HERO COULD POSSIBLY RESCUE HER!
GROO WILL FIND THE BANDITS AND BRING HER BACK!
WAIT!

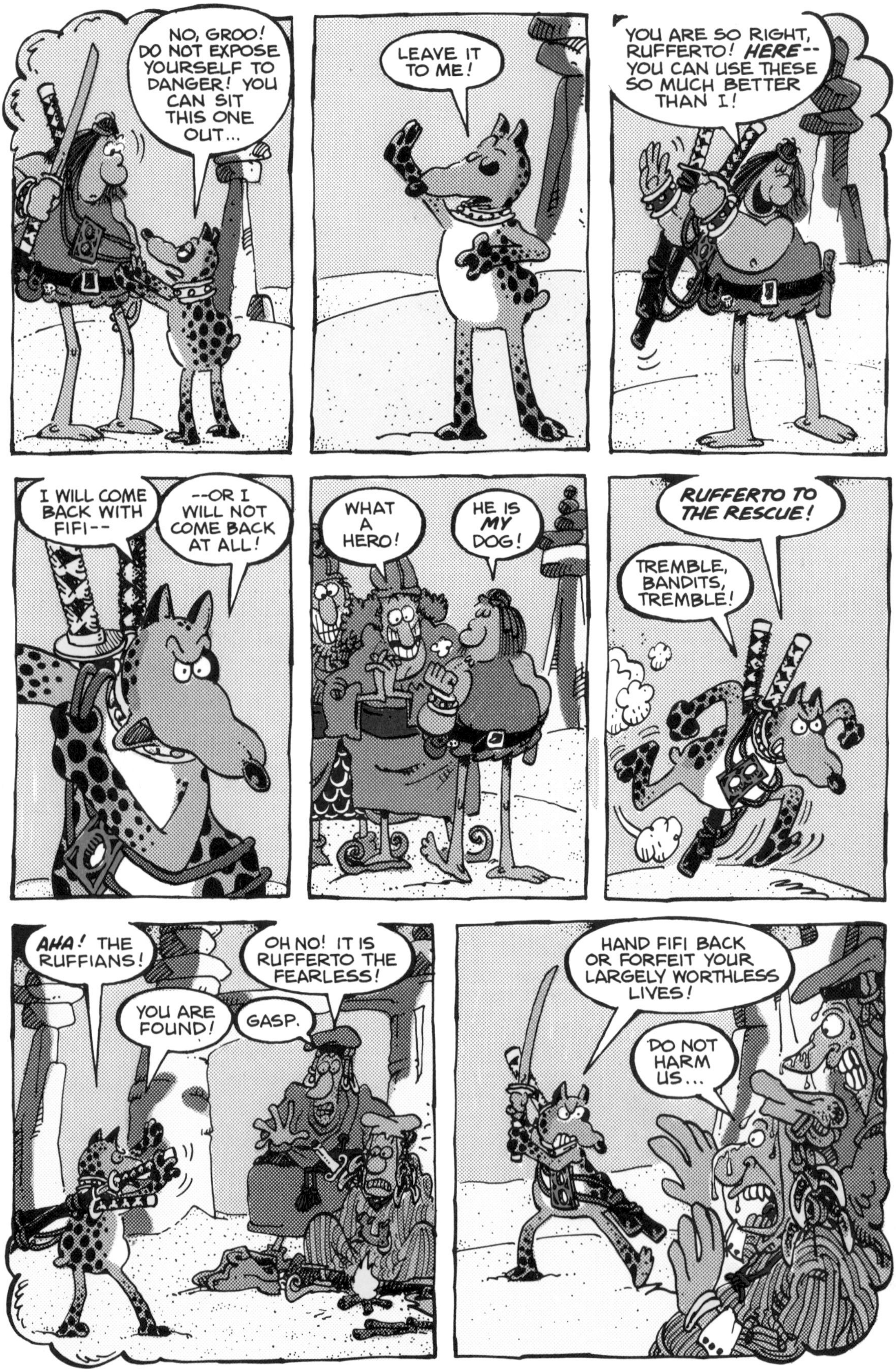
NO, GROO! DO NOT EXPOSE YOURSELF TO DANGER! YOU CAN SIT THIS ONE OUT...
LEAVE IT TO ME!
YOU ARE SO RIGHT, RUFFERTO! HERE-- YOU CAN USE THESE SO MUCH BETTER THAN I!
I WILL COME BACK WITH FIFI--
--OR I WILL NOT COME BACK AT ALL!
WHAT A HERO!
HE IS MY DOG!
RUFFERTO TO THE RESCUE!
TREMBLE, BANDITS, TREMBLE!
AHA! THE RUFFIANS!
YOU ARE FOUND!
OH NO! IT IS RUFFERTO THE FEARLESS!
GASP.
HAND FIFI BACK OR FORFEIT YOUR LARGELY WORTHLESS LIVES!
DO NOT HARM US...

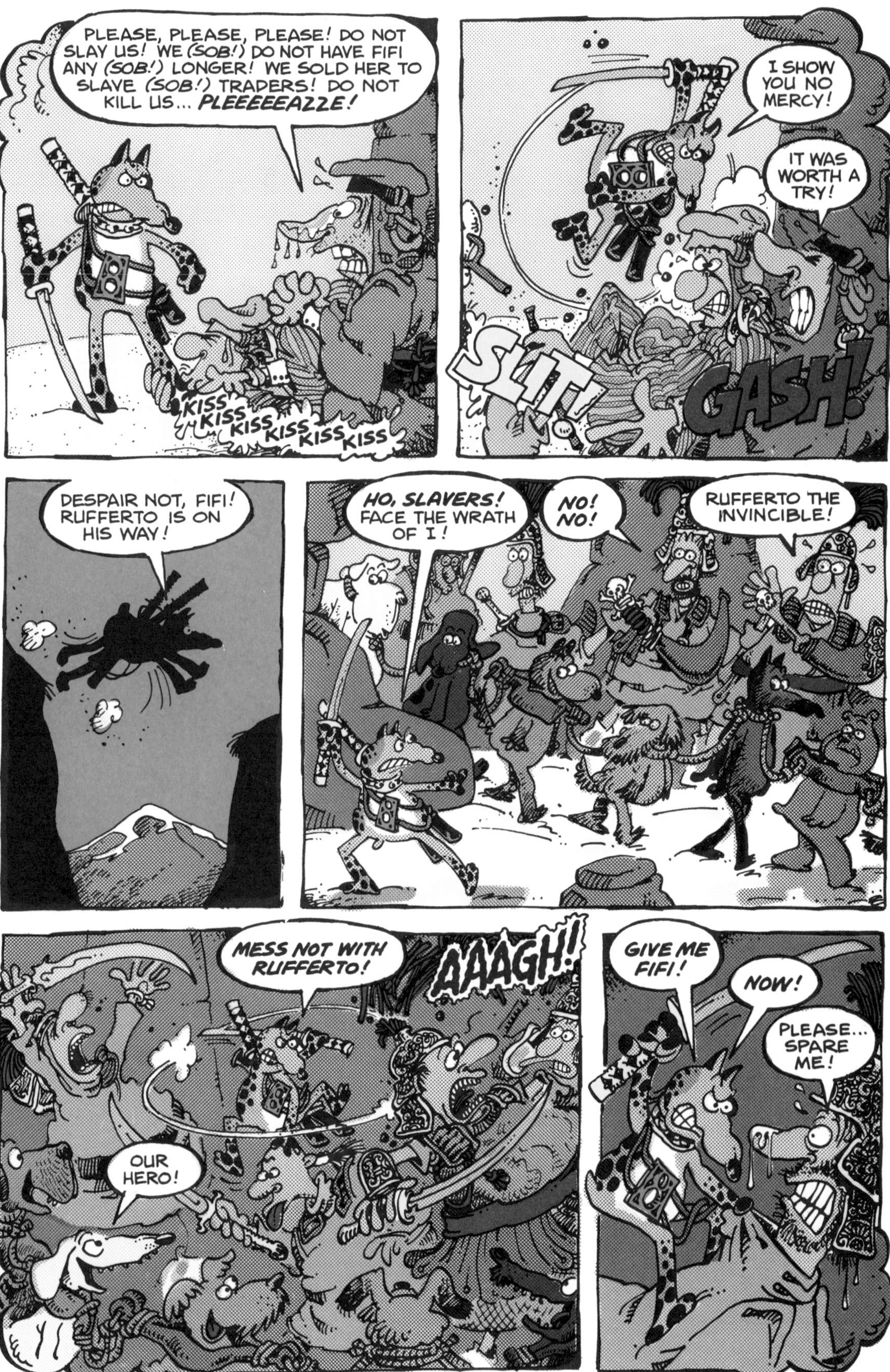
PLEASE, PLEASE, PLEASE! DO NOT SLAY US! WE (SOB!) DO NOT HAVE FIFI ANY (SOB!) LONGER! WE SOLD HER TO SLAVE (SOB!) TRADERS! DO NOT KILL US... PLEEEEEAZZE!
KISS KISS KISS KISS KISS KISS
I SHOW YOU NO MERCY!
IT WAS WORTH A TRY!
SLIT!
GASH!
DESPAIR NOT, FIFI! RUFFERTO IS ON HIS WAY!
HO, SLAVERS! FACE THE WRATH OF I!
NO! NO!
RUFFERTO THE INVINCIBLE!
MESS NOT WITH RUFFERTO!
AAAGH!
OUR HERO!
GIVE ME FIFI!
NOW!
PLEASE... SPARE ME!

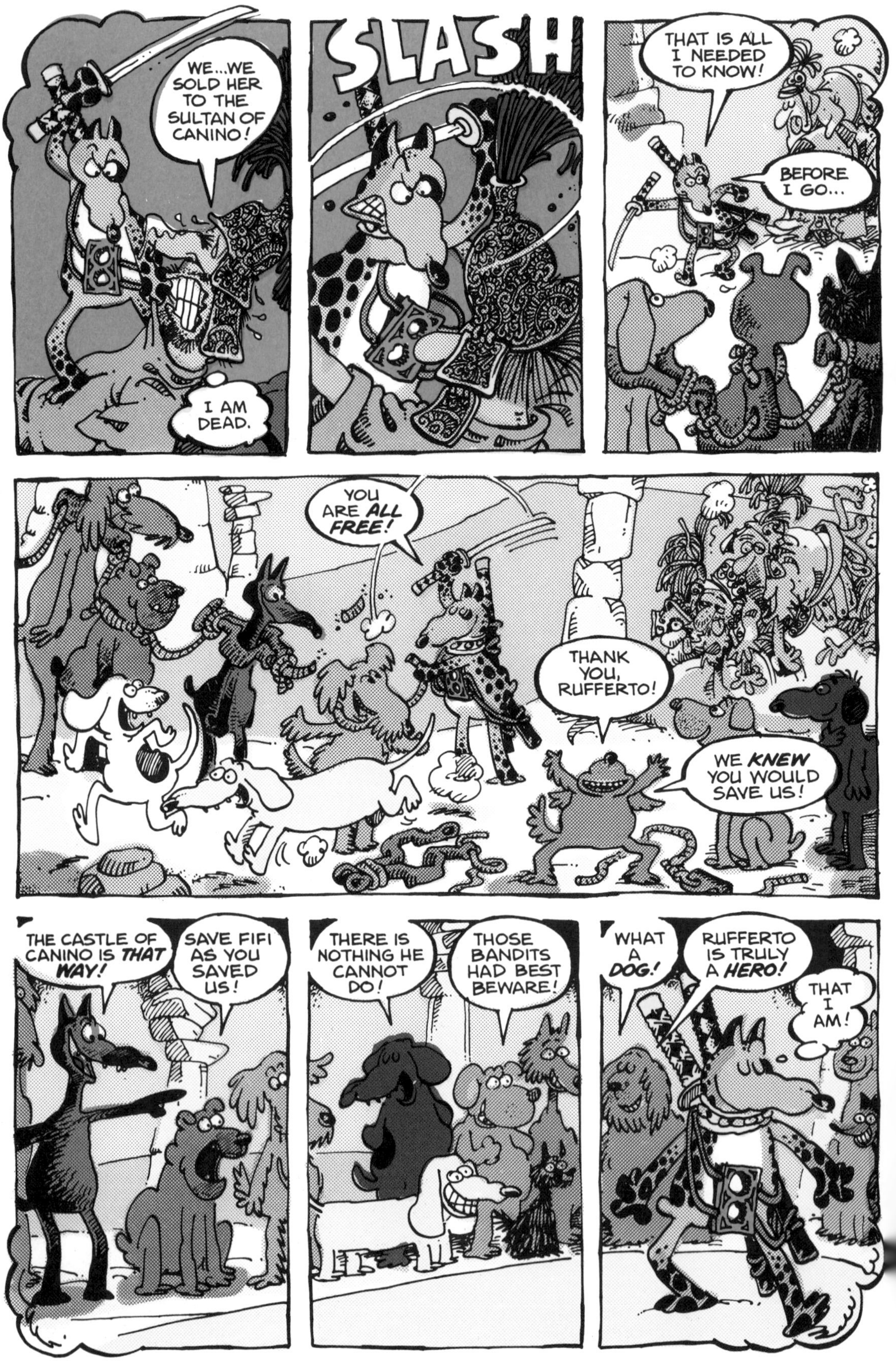
WE...WE SOLD HER TO THE SULTAN OF CANINO!
I AM DEAD.
SLASH
THAT IS ALL I NEEDED TO KNOW!
BEFORE I GO...
YOU ARE ALL FREE!
THANK YOU, RUFFERTO!
WE KNEW YOU WOULD SAVE US!
THE CASTLE OF CANINO IS THAT WAY!
SAVE FIFI AS YOU SAVED US!
THERE IS NOTHING HE CANNOT DO!
THOSE BANDITS HAD BEST BEWARE!
WHAT A DOG!
RUFFERTO IS TRULY A HERO!
THAT I AM!

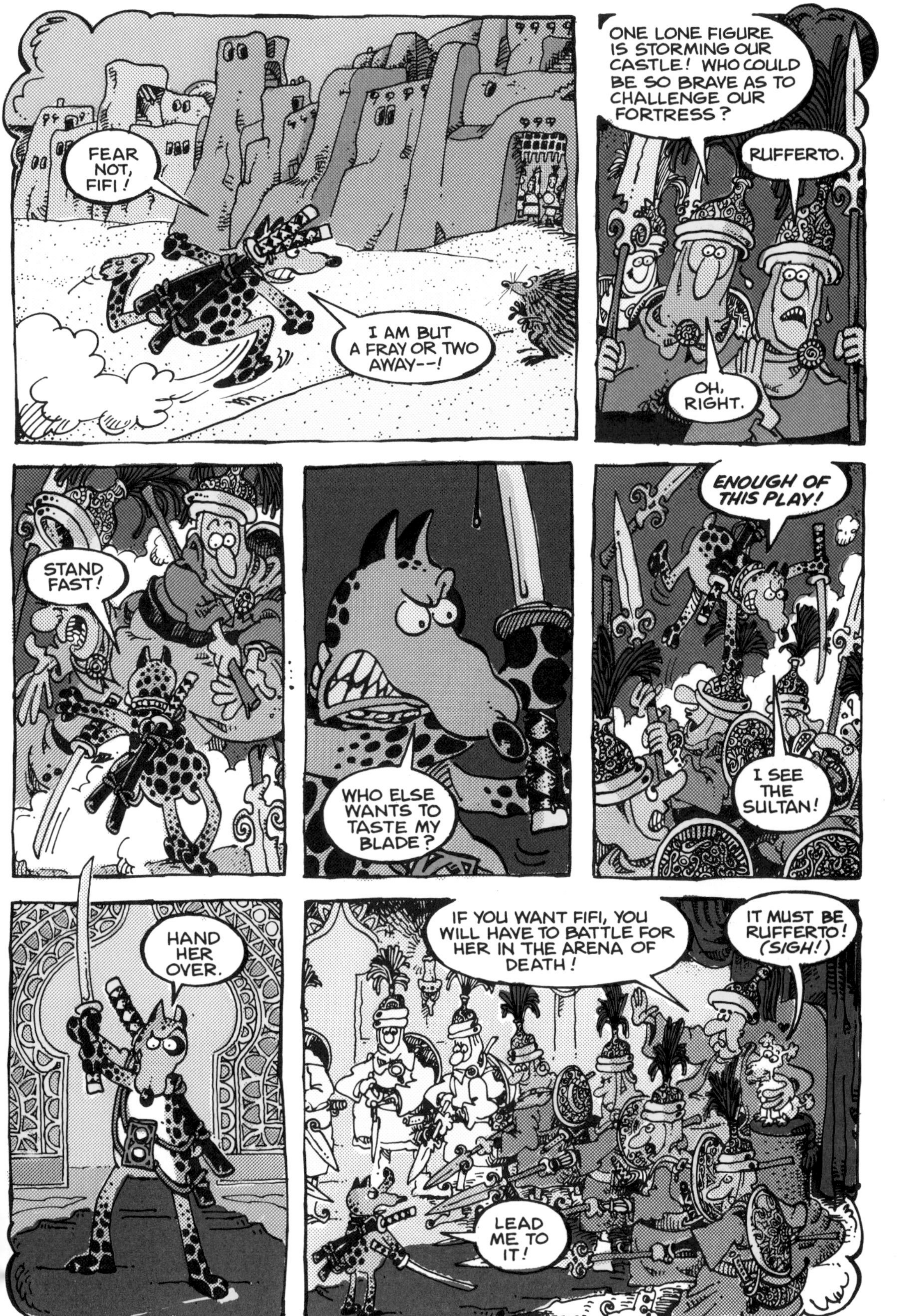
FEAR NOT, FIFI!
I AM BUT A FRAY OR TWO AWAY--!
ONE LONE FIGURE IS STORMING OUR CASTLE! WHO COULD BE SO BRAVE AS TO CHALLENGE OUR FORTRESS?
RUFFERTO.
OH, RIGHT.
STAND FAST!
WHO ELSE WANTS TO TASTE MY BLADE?
ENOUGH OF THIS PLAY!
I SEE THE SULTAN!
HAND HER OVER.
IF YOU WANT FIFI, YOU WILL HAVE TO BATTLE FOR HER IN THE ARENA OF DEATH!
IT MUST BE RUFFERTO! (SIGH!)
LEAD ME TO IT!

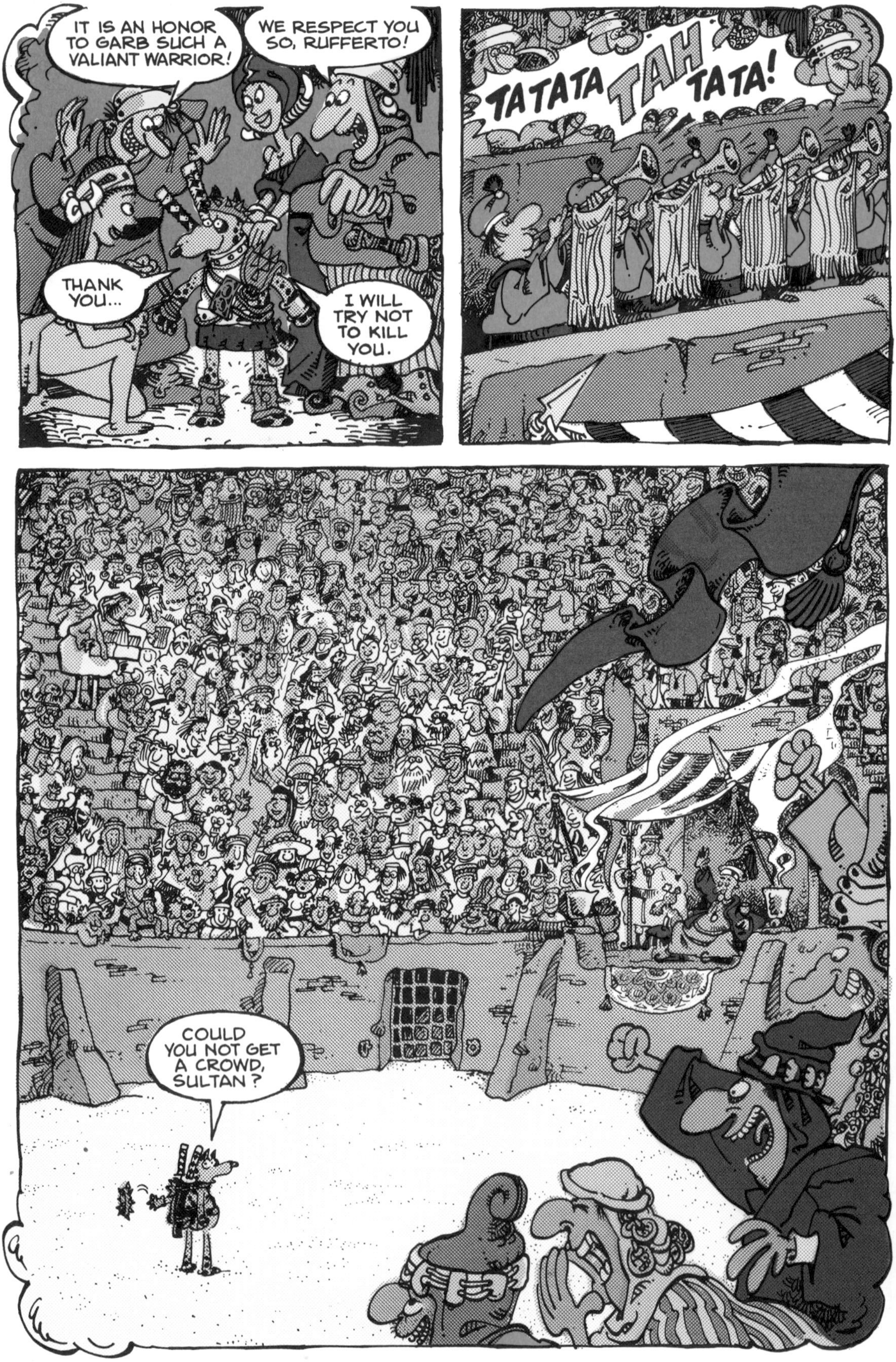
IT IS AN HONOR TO GARB SUCH A VALIANT WARRIOR!
WE RESPECT YOU SO, RUFFERTO!
THANK YOU...
I WILL TRY NOT TO KILL YOU.
TATATA TAH TATA!
COULD YOU NOT GET A CROWD, SULTAN ?

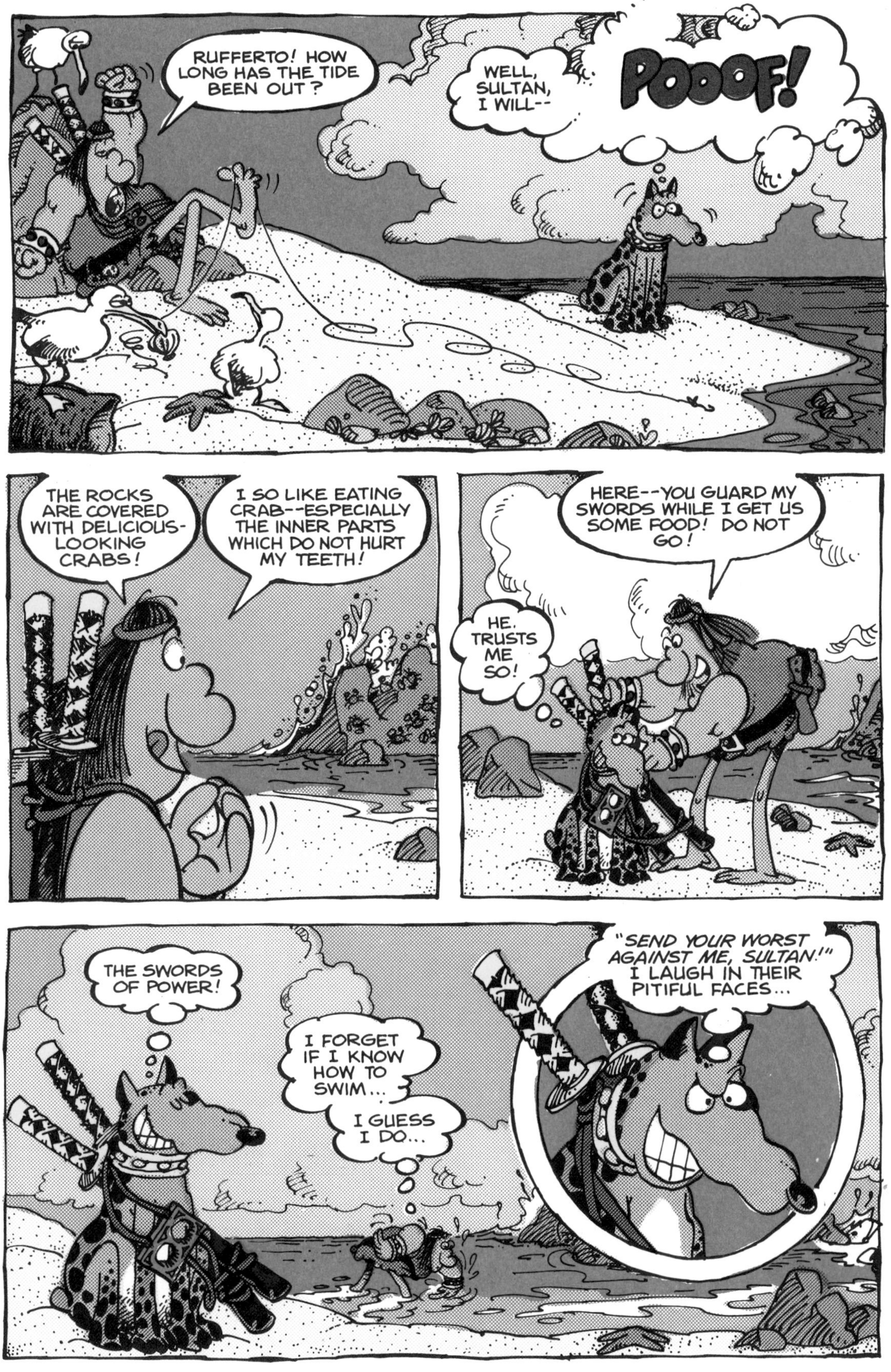
RUFFERTO! HOW LONG HAS THE TIDE BEEN OUT?
WELL, SULTAN, I WILL--
POOOF!
THE ROCKS ARE COVERED WITH DELICIOUS-LOOKING CRABS!
I SO LIKE EATING CRAB--ESPECIALLY THE INNER PARTS WHICH DO NOT HURT MY TEETH!
HERE--YOU GUARD MY SWORDS WHILE I GET US SOME FOOD! DO NOT GO!
HE. TRUSTS ME SO!
THE SWORDS OF POWER!
I FORGET IF I KNOW HOW TO SWIM...
I GUESS I DO...
"SEND YOUR WORST AGAINST ME, SULTAN!" I LAUGH IN THEIR PITIFUL FACES...

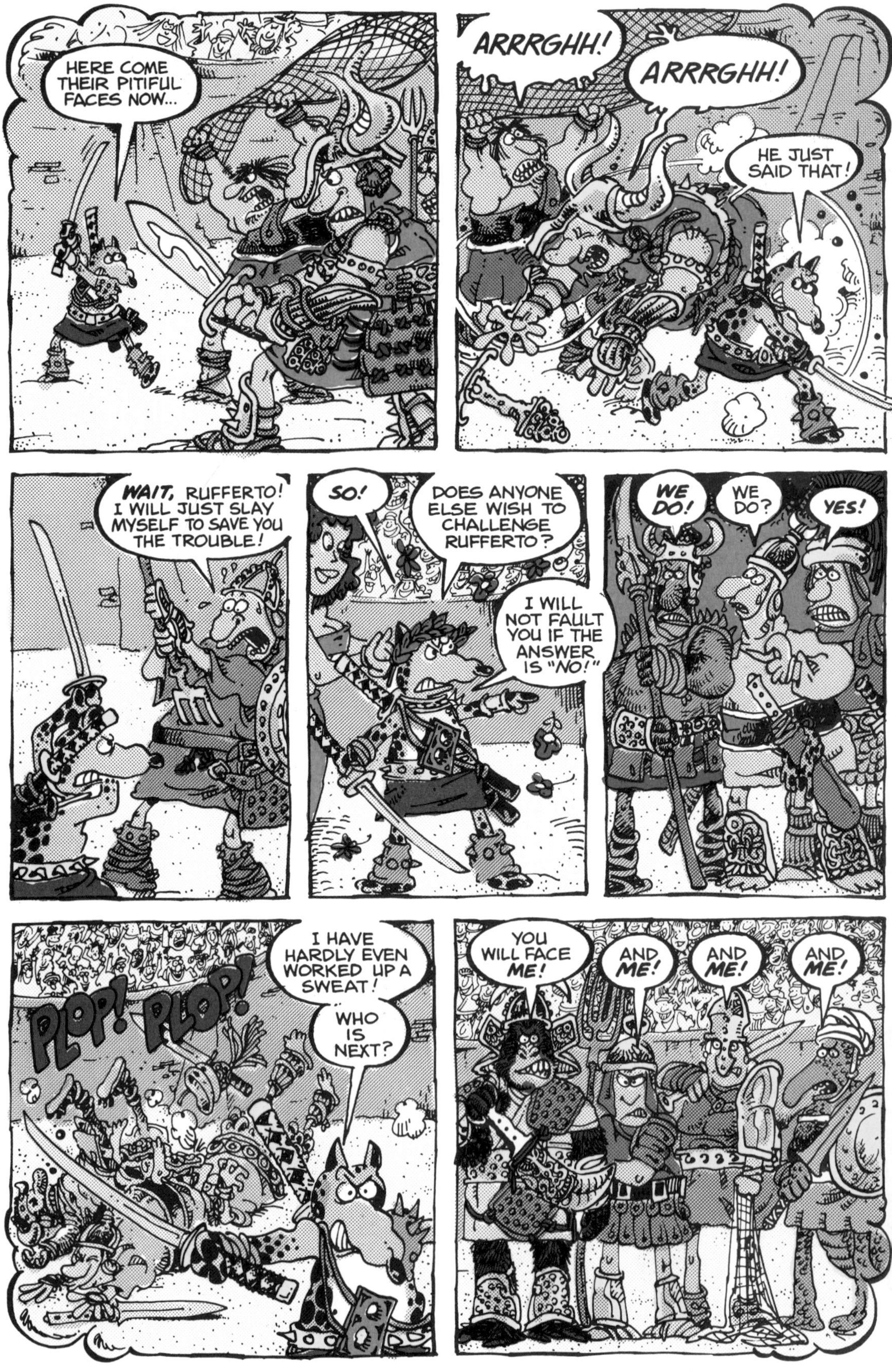
HERE COME THEIR PITIFUL FACES NOW...
ARRRGHH!
ARRRGHH!
HE JUST SAID THAT!
WAIT, RUFFERTO! I WILL JUST SLAY MYSELF TO SAVE YOU THE TROUBLE!
SO!
DOES ANYONE ELSE WISH TO CHALLENGE RUFFERTO?
I WILL NOT FAULT YOU IF THE ANSWER IS "NO!"
WE DO!
WE DO?
YES!
PLOP! PLOP!
I HAVE HARDLY EVEN WORKED UP A SWEAT!
WHO IS NEXT?
YOU WILL FACE ME!
AND ME!
AND ME!
AND ME!

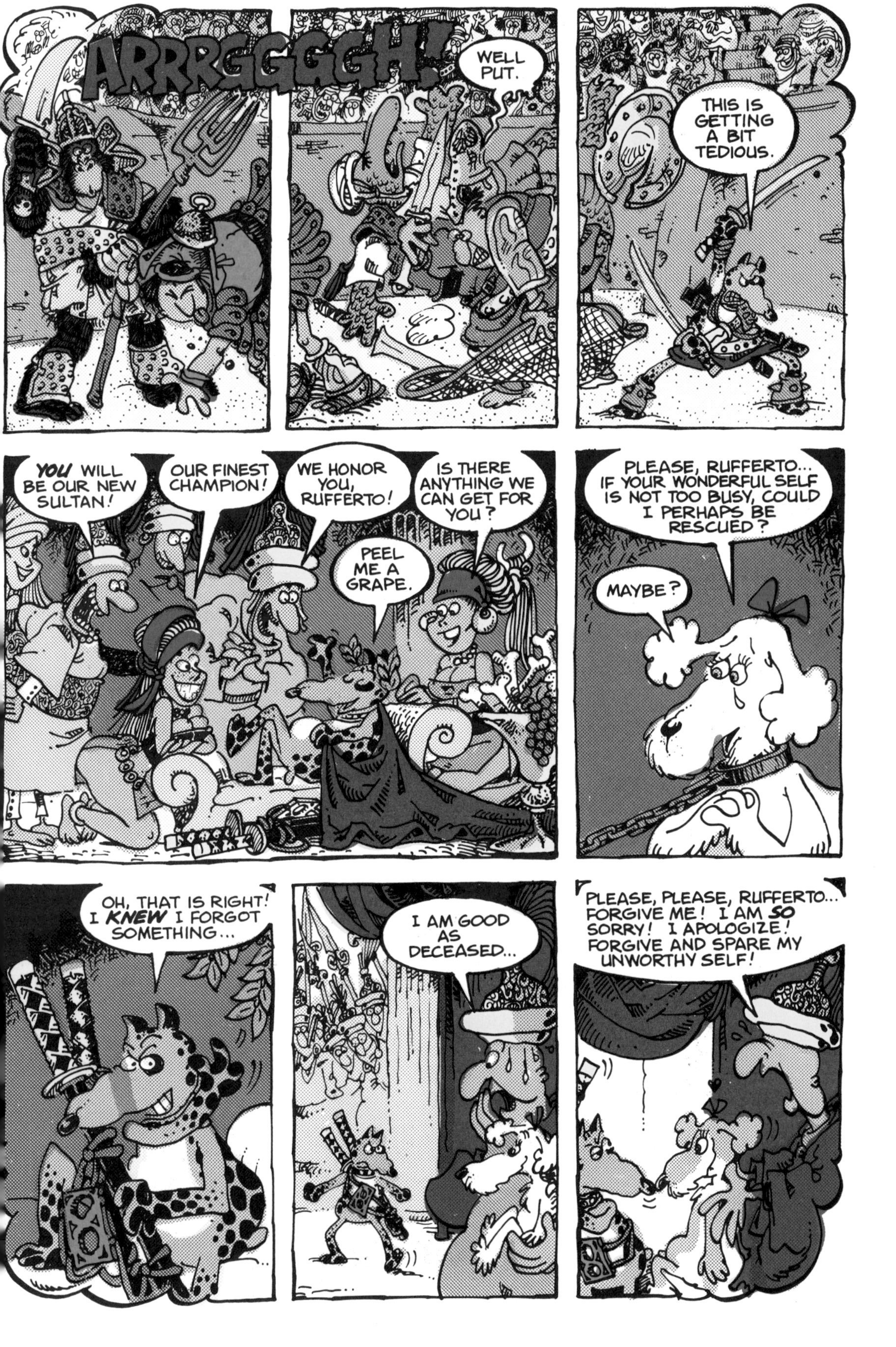
ARRRGGGGH!
WELL PUT.
THIS IS GETTING A BIT TEDIOUS.
YOU WILL BE OUR NEW SULTAN!
OUR FINEST CHAMPION!
WE HONOR YOU, RUFFERTO!
IS THERE ANYTHING WE CAN GET FOR YOU?
PEEL ME A GRAPE.
PLEASE, RUFFERTO... IF YOUR WONDERFUL SELF IS NOT TOO BUSY, COULD I PERHAPS BE RESCUED?
MAYBE?
OH, THAT IS RIGHT! I KNEW I FORGOT SOMETHING...
I AM GOOD AS DECEASED...
PLEASE, PLEASE, RUFFERTO... FORGIVE ME! I AM SO SORRY! I APOLOGIZE! FORGIVE AND SPARE MY UNWORTHY SELF!

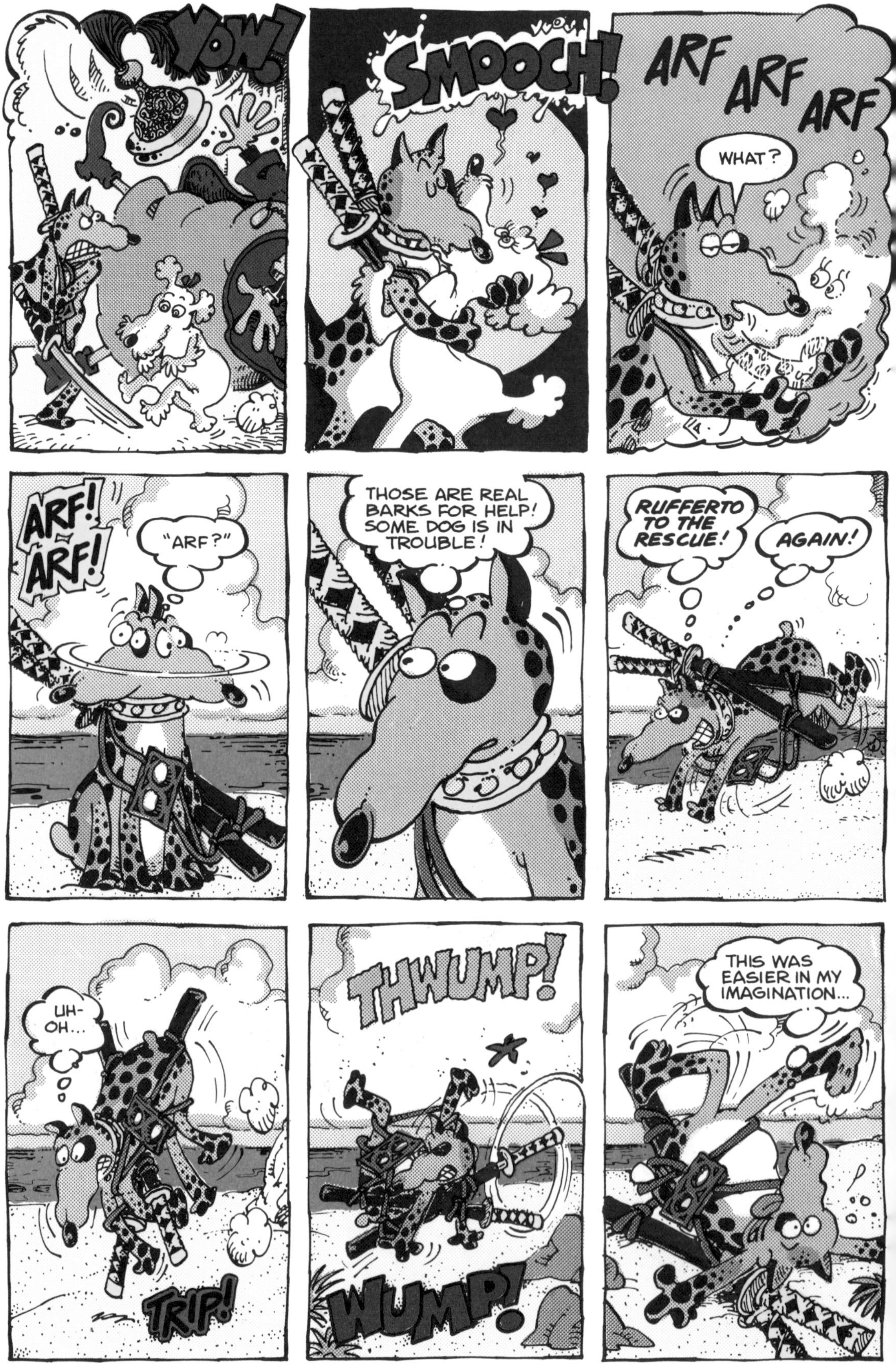

YOW!
SMOOCH!
ARF ARF ARF
WHAT?
ARF! ARF!
"ARF?"
THOSE ARE REAL BARKS FOR HELP! SOME DOG IS IN TROUBLE!
RUFFERTO TO THE RESCUE!
AGAIN!
UH-OH...
TRIP!
THWUMP!
WUMP!
THIS WAS EASIER IN MY IMAGINATION...

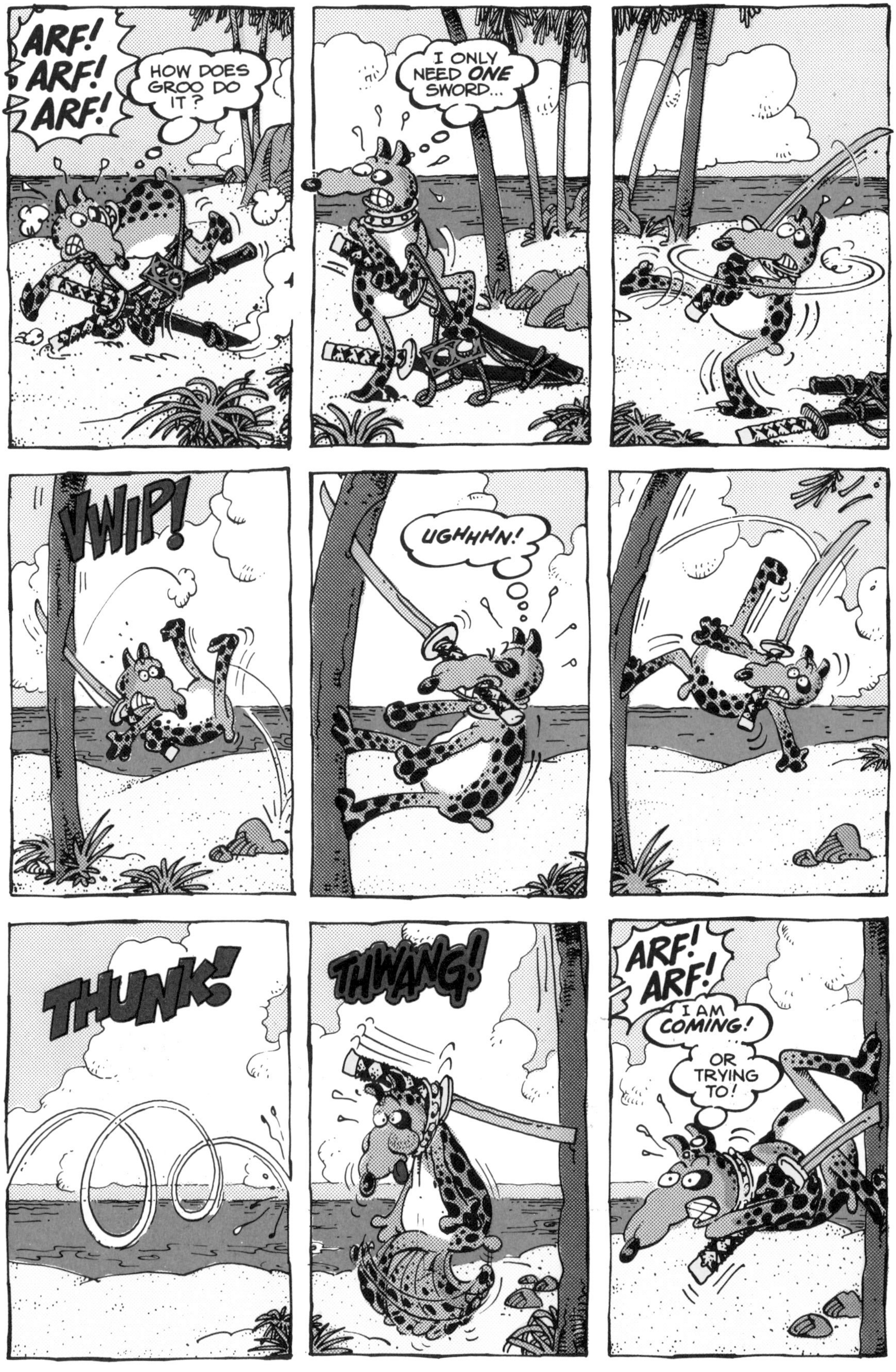
ARF! ARF! ARF!
HOW DOES GROO DO IT?
I ONLY NEED ONE SWORD...
VWIP!
UGHHHN!
THUNK!
THWANG!
ARF! ARF!
I AM COMING!
OR TRYING TO!

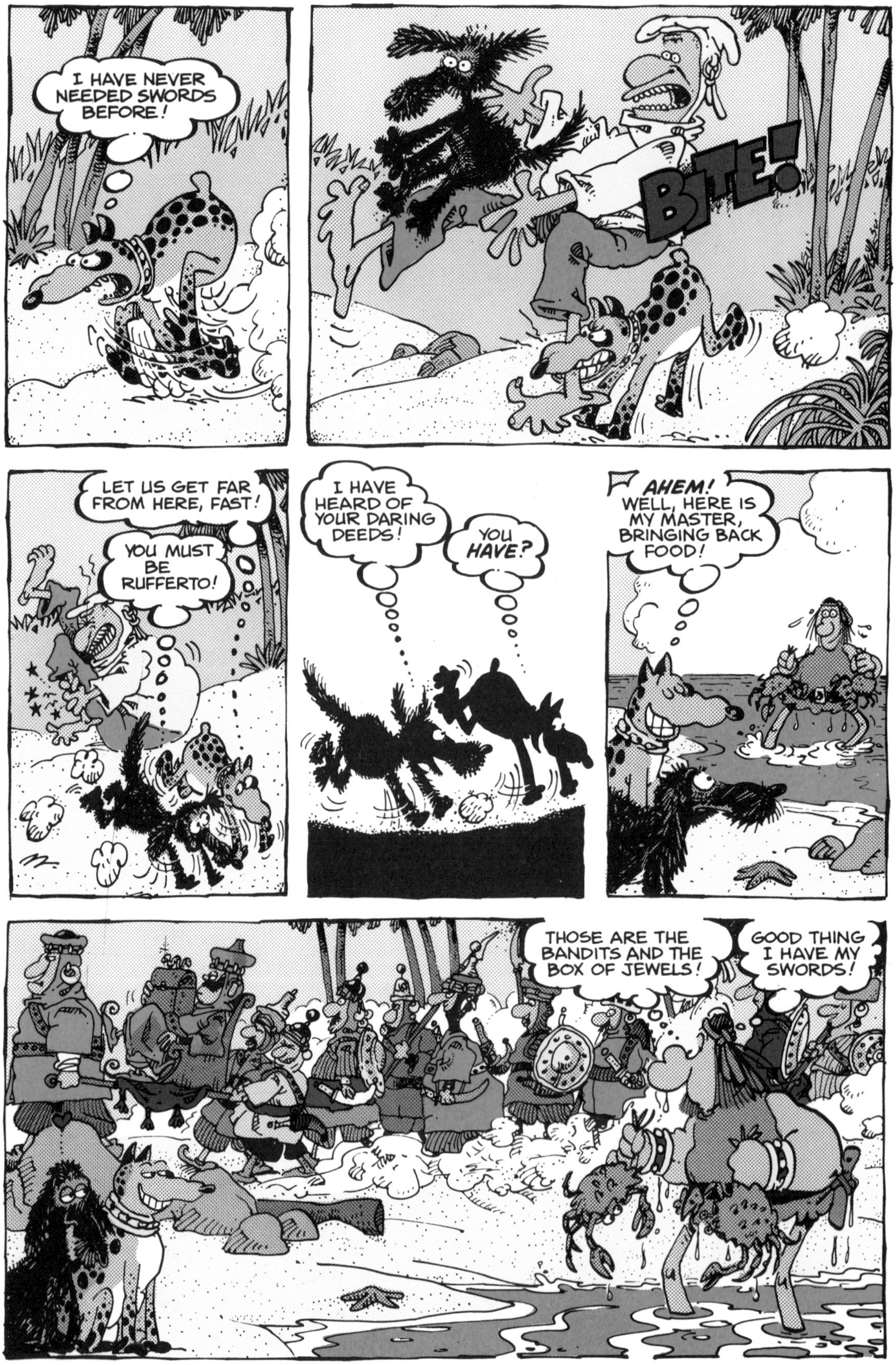
I HAVE NEVER NEEDED SWORDS BEFORE!
BITE!
LET US GET FAR FROM HERE, FAST!
YOU MUST BE RUFFERTO!
I HAVE HEARD OF YOUR DARING DEEDS!
YOU HAVE?
AHEM! WELL, HERE IS MY MASTER, BRINGING BACK FOOD!
THOSE ARE THE BANDITS AND THE BOX OF JEWELS!
GOOD THING I HAVE MY SWORDS!

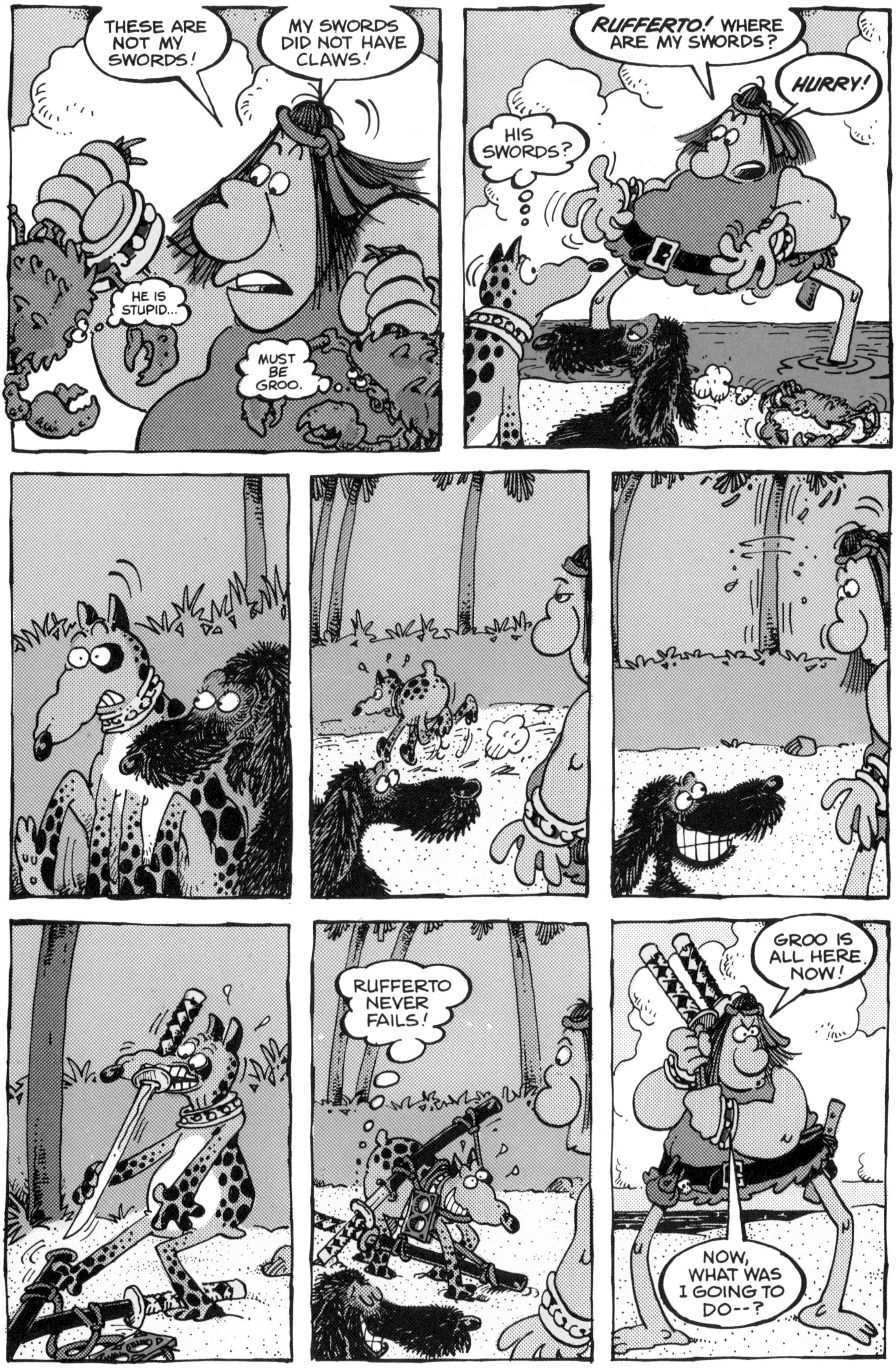
THESE ARE NOT MY SWORDS!
MY SWORDS DID NOT HAVE CLAWS!
HE IS STUPID...
MUST BE GROO.
RUFFERTO! WHERE ARE MY SWORDS?
HURRY!
HIS SWORDS?
RUFFERTO NEVER FAILS!
GROO IS ALL HERE NOW!
NOW, WHAT WAS I GOING TO DO--?

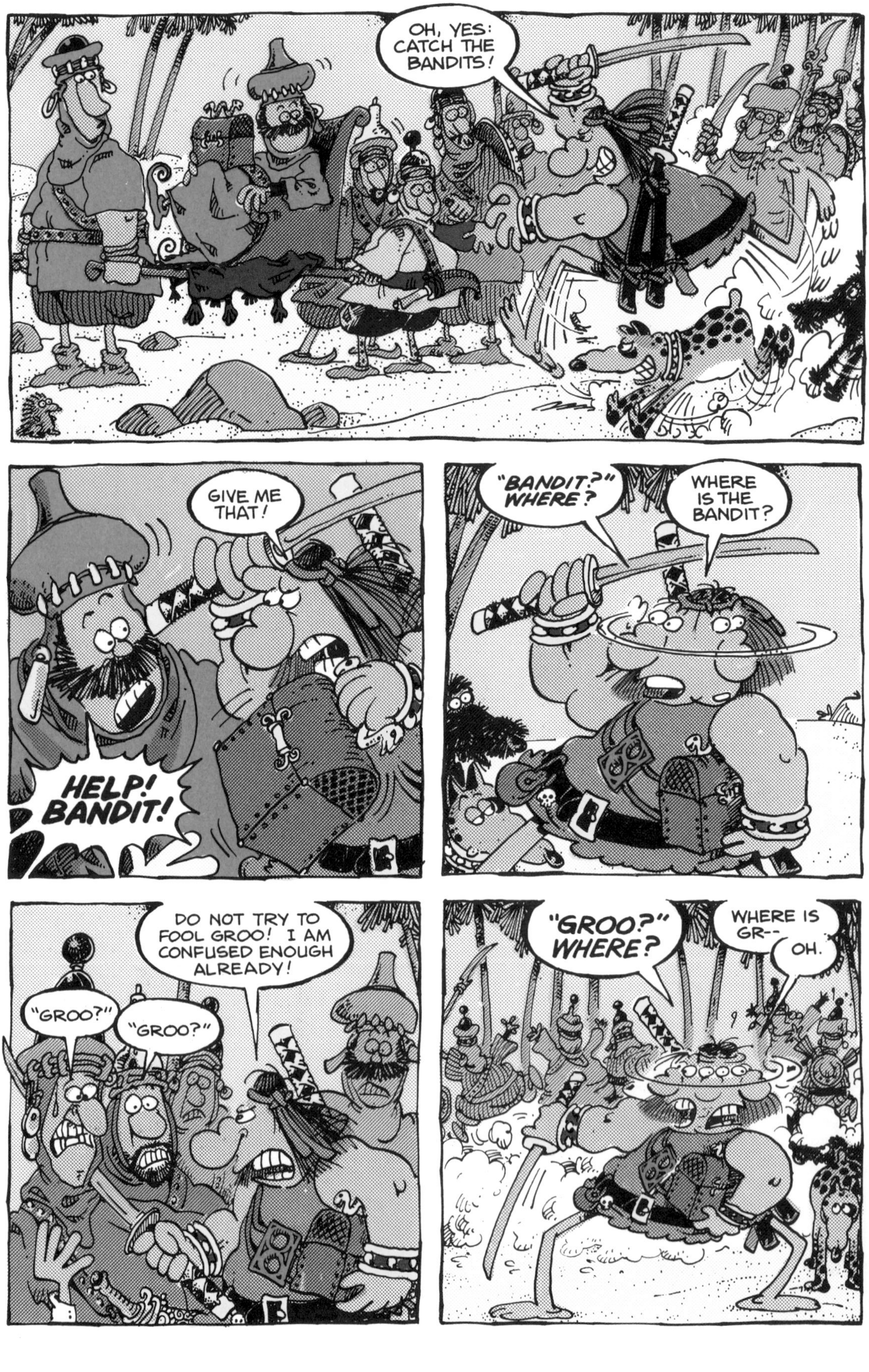
OH, YES: CATCH THE BANDITS!
GIVE ME THAT!
HELP! BANDIT!
"BANDIT?" WHERE?
WHERE IS THE BANDIT?
DO NOT TRY TO FOOL GROO! I AM CONFUSED ENOUGH ALREADY!
"GROO?"
"GROO?"
"GROO?" WHERE?
WHERE IS GR--
OH.

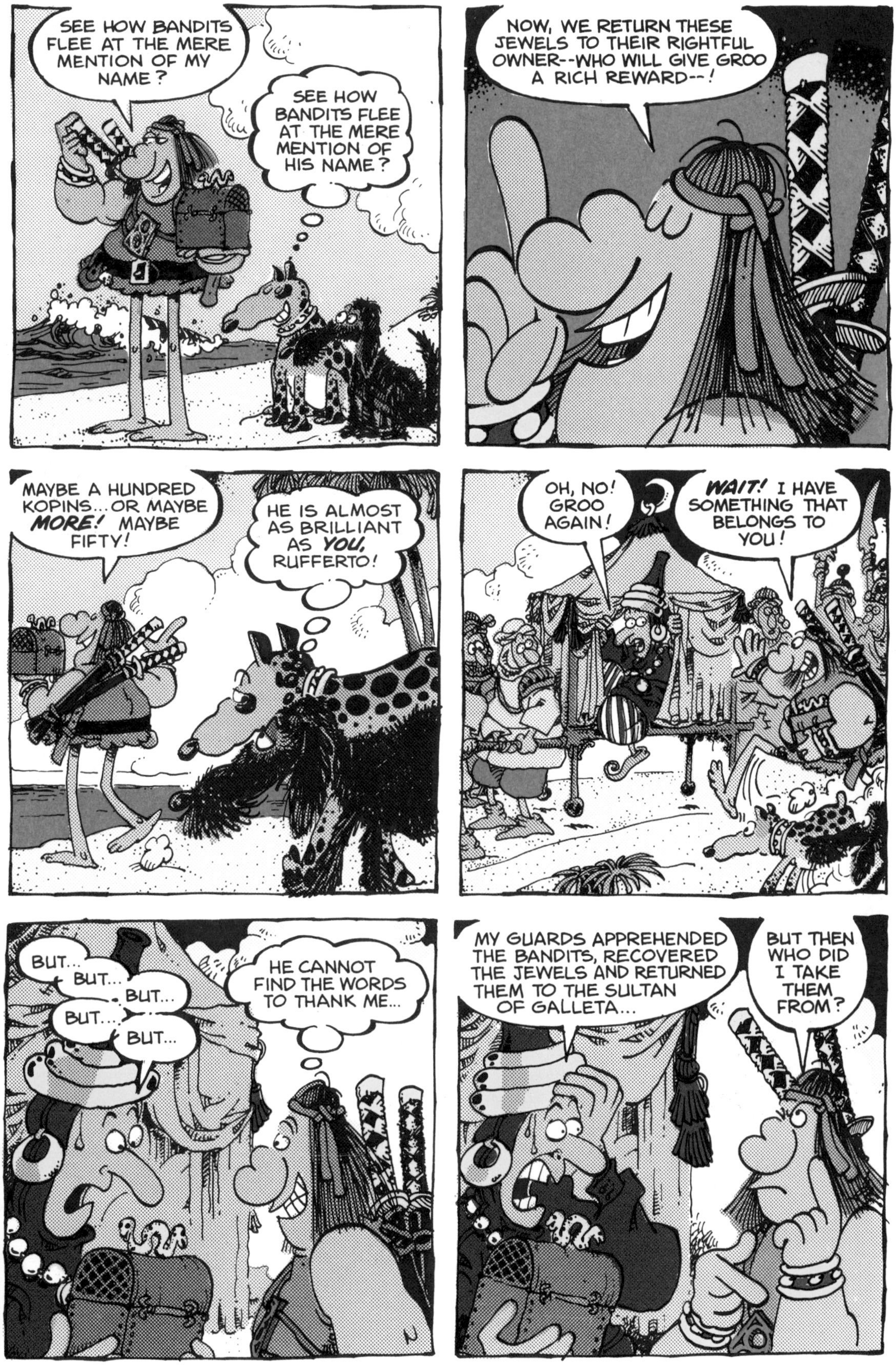
SEE HOW BANDITS FLEE AT THE MERE MENTION OF MY NAME?
SEE HOW BANDITS FLEE AT THE MERE MENTION OF HIS NAME?
NOW, WE RETURN THESE JEWELS TO THEIR RIGHTFUL OWNER--WHO WILL GIVE GROO A RICH REWARD--!
MAYBE A HUNDRED KOPINS... OR MAYBE MORE! MAYBE FIFTY!
HE IS ALMOST AS BRILLIANT AS YOU, RUFFERTO!
OH, NO! GROO AGAIN!
WAIT! I HAVE SOMETHING THAT BELONGS TO YOU!
BUT... BUT... BUT... BUT... BUT...
HE CANNOT FIND THE WORDS TO THANK ME...
MY GUARDS APPREHENDED THE BANDITS, RECOVERED THE JEWELS AND RETURNED THEM TO THE SULTAN OF GALLETA...
BUT THEN WHO DID I TAKE THEM FROM?

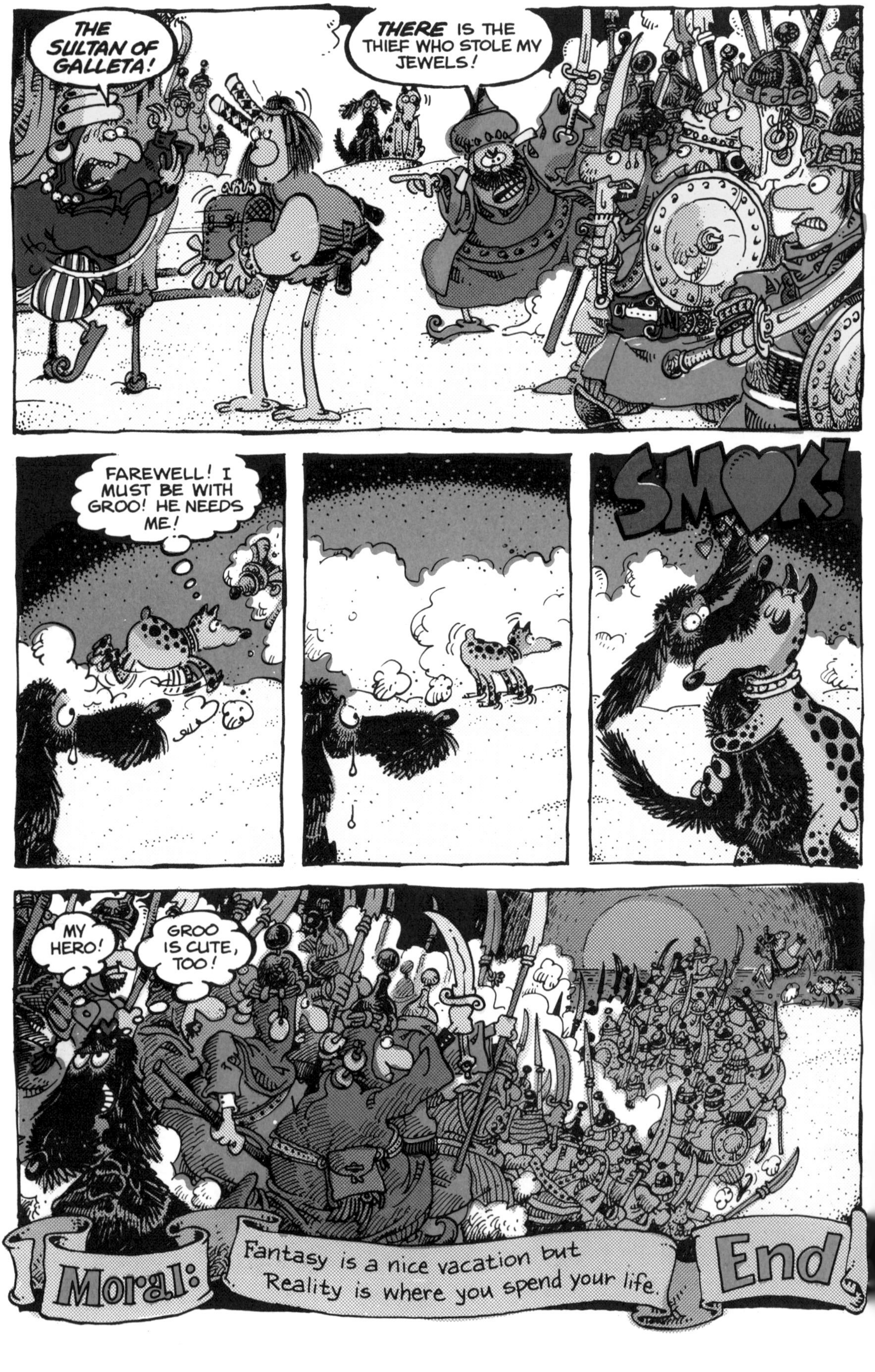
THE SULTAN OF GALLETA!
THERE IS THE THIEF WHO STOLE MY JEWELS!
FAREWELL! I MUST BE WITH GROO! HE NEEDS ME!
SMOK!
MY HERO!
GROO IS CUTE, TOO!
Moral:
Fantasy is a nice vacation but Reality is where you spend your life.
End

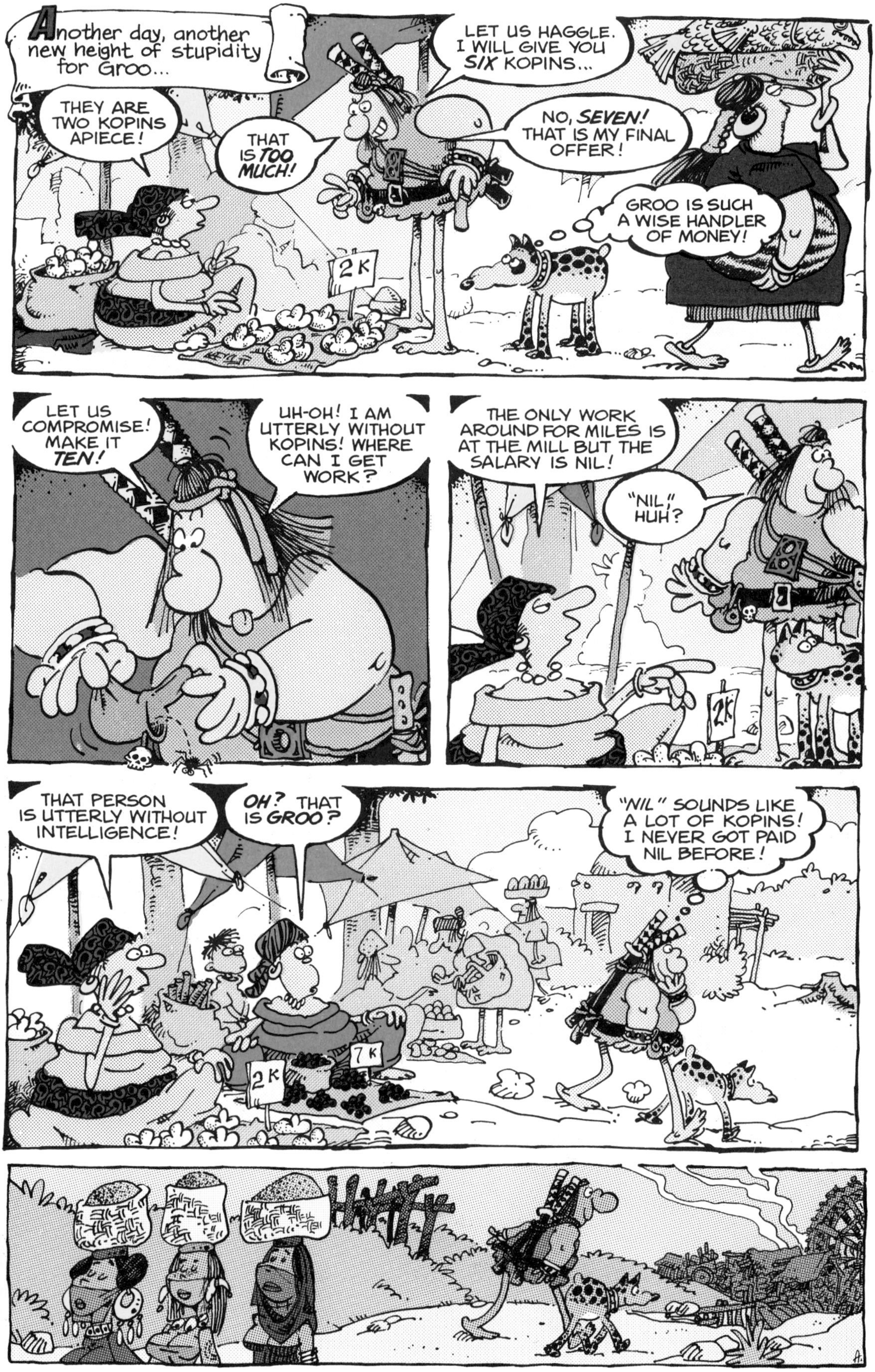
Another day, another new height of stupidity for Groo...
THEY ARE TWO KOPINS APIECE!
THAT IS TOO MUCH!
LET US HAGGLE. I WILL GIVE YOU SIX KOPINS...
NO, SEVEN! THAT IS MY FINAL OFFER!
GROO IS SUCH A WISE HANDLER OF MONEY!
2K
LET US COMPROMISE! MAKE IT TEN!
UH-OH! I AM UTTERLY WITHOUT KOPINS! WHERE CAN I GET WORK?
THE ONLY WORK AROUND FOR MILES IS AT THE MILL BUT THE SALARY IS NIL!
"NIL," HUH?
2K
THAT PERSON IS UTTERLY WITHOUT INTELLIGENCE!
OH? THAT IS GROO?
"NIL" SOUNDS LIKE A LOT OF KOPINS! I NEVER GOT PAID NIL BEFORE!
2K
7K

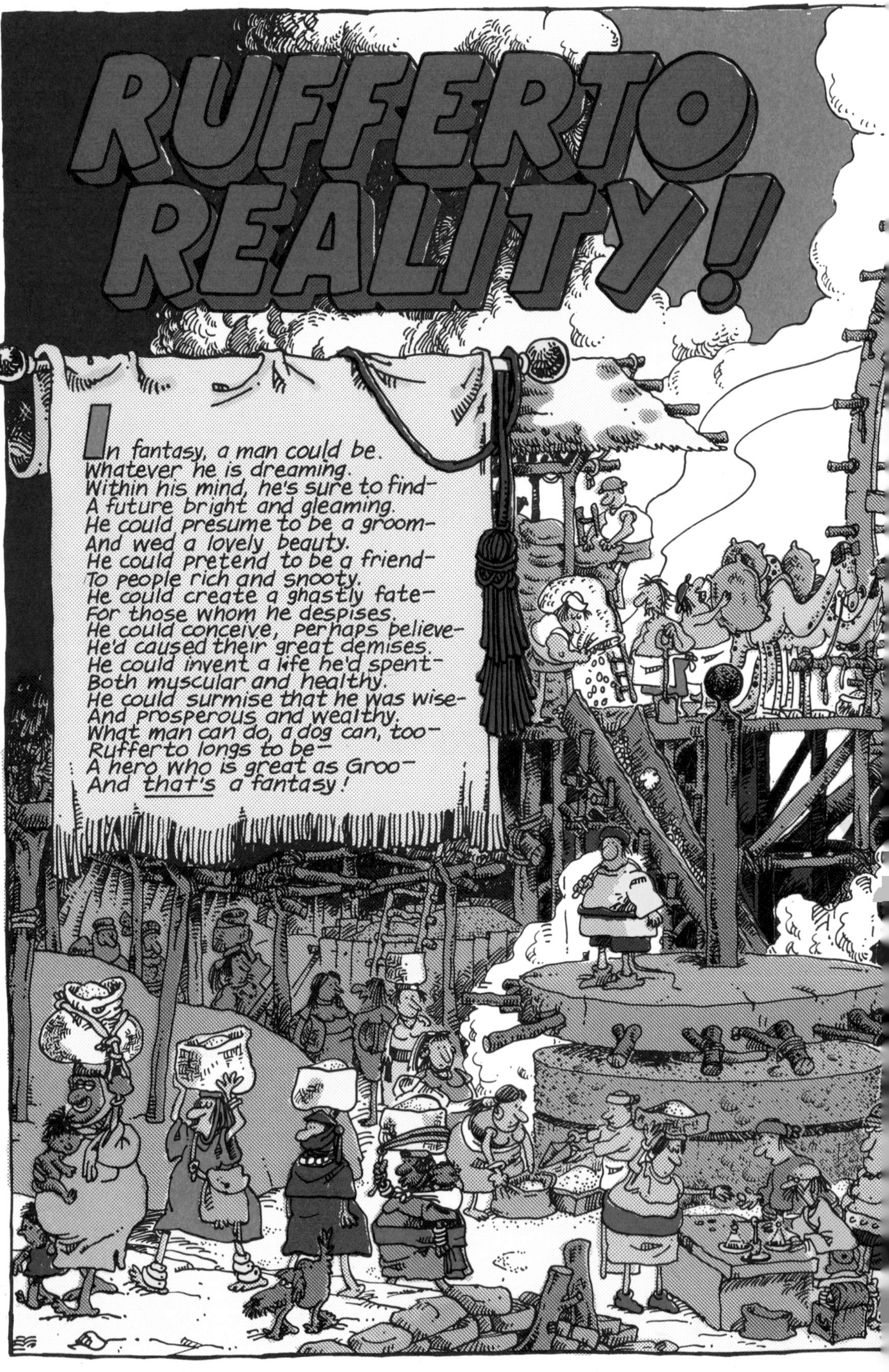
RUFFERTO REALITY!
In fantasy, a man could be
Whatever he is dreaming.
Within his mind, he's sure to find-
A future bright and gleaming.
He could presume to be a groom-
And wed a lovely beauty.
He could pretend to be a friend-
To people rich and snooty.
He could create a ghastly fate-
For those whom he despises.
He could conceive, perhaps believe-
He'd caused their great demises.
He could invent a life he'd spent-
Both muscular and healthy.
He could surmise that he was wise-
And prosperous and wealthy.
What man can do, a dog can, too-
Rufferto longs to be-
A hero who is great as Groo-
And that's a fantasy!

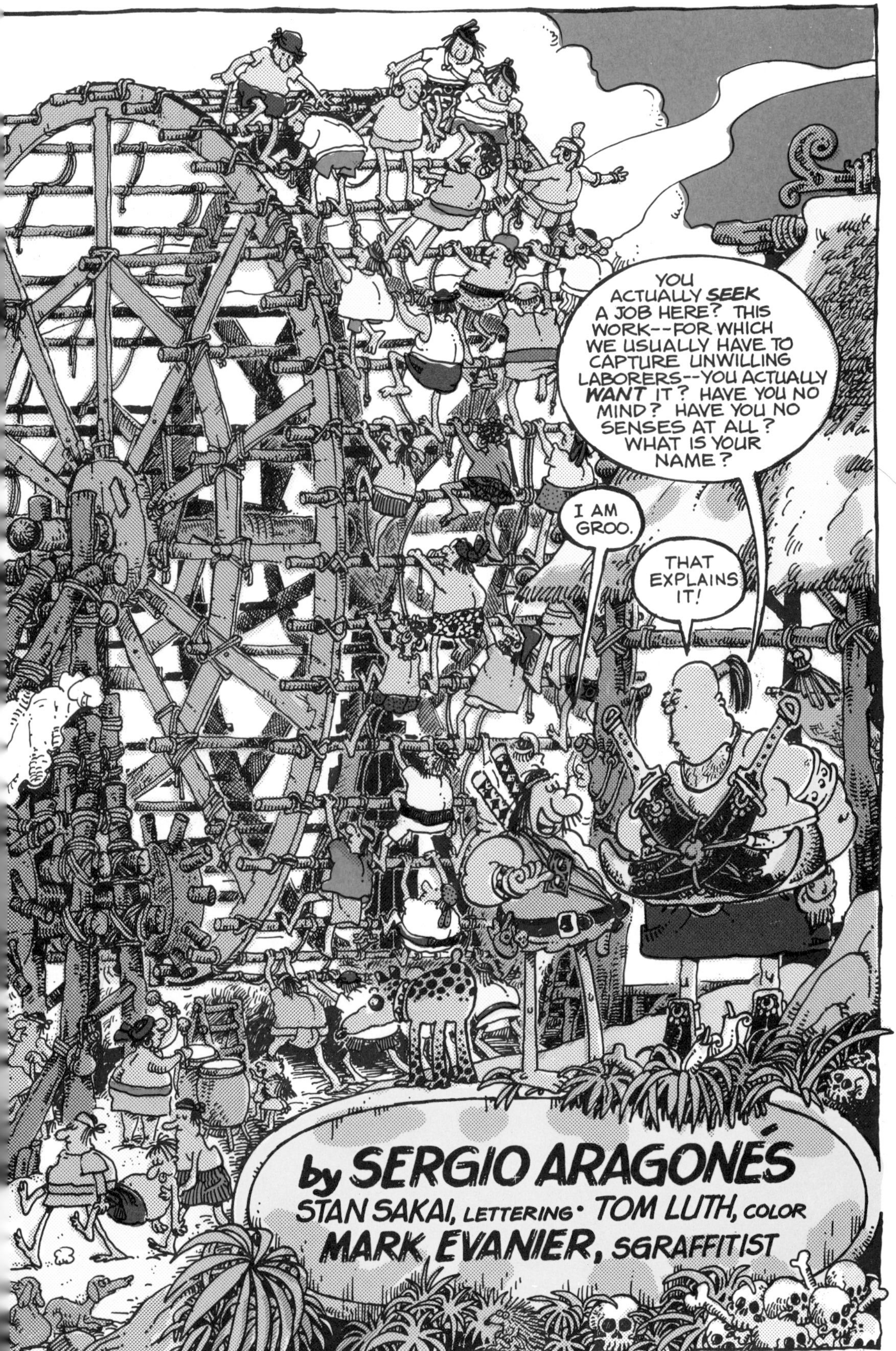
YOU ACTUALLY SEEK A JOB HERE? THIS WORK--FOR WHICH WE USUALLY HAVE TO CAPTURE UNWILLING LABORERS--YOU ACTUALLY WANT IT? HAVE YOU NO MIND? HAVE YOU NO SENSES AT ALL? WHAT IS YOUR NAME?
I AM GROO.
THAT EXPLAINS IT!
by SERGIO ARAGONÉS
STAN SAKAI, LETTERING • TOM LUTH, COLOR
MARK EVANIER, SGRAFFITIST

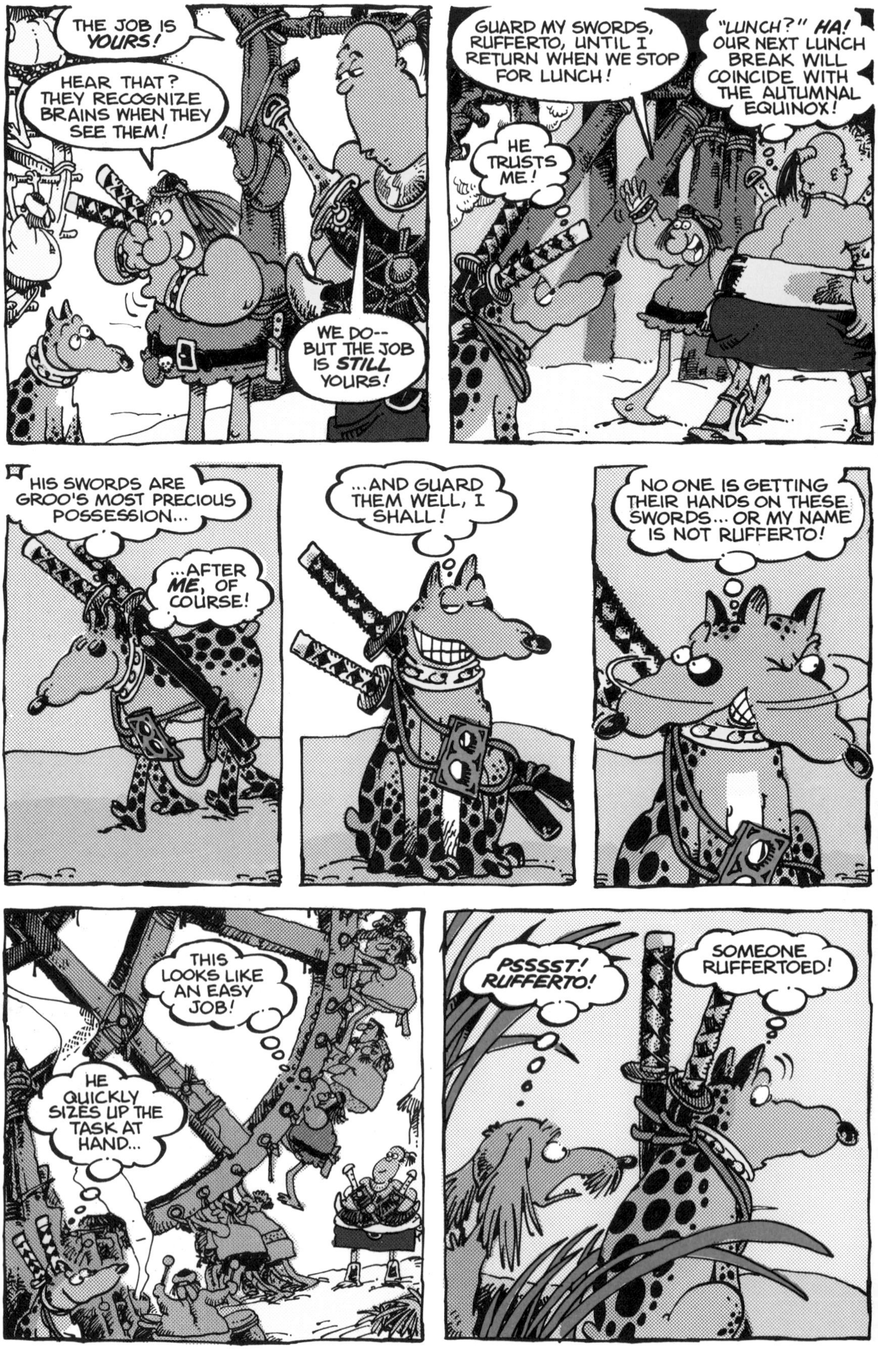
THE JOB IS YOURS!
HEAR THAT? THEY RECOGNIZE BRAINS WHEN THEY SEE THEM!
WE DO-- BUT THE JOB IS STILL YOURS!
GUARD MY SWORDS, RUFFERTO, UNTIL I RETURN WHEN WE STOP FOR LUNCH!
"LUNCH?" HA! OUR NEXT LUNCH BREAK WILL COINCIDE WITH THE AUTUMNAL EQUINOX!
HE TRUSTS ME!
HIS SWORDS ARE GROO'S MOST PRECIOUS POSSESSION...
...AFTER ME, OF COURSE!
...AND GUARD THEM WELL, I SHALL!
NO ONE IS GETTING THEIR HANDS ON THESE SWORDS... OR MY NAME IS NOT RUFFERTO!
THIS LOOKS LIKE AN EASY JOB!
HE QUICKLY SIZES UP THE TASK AT HAND...
PSSSST! RUFFERTO!
SOMEONE RUFFERTOED!

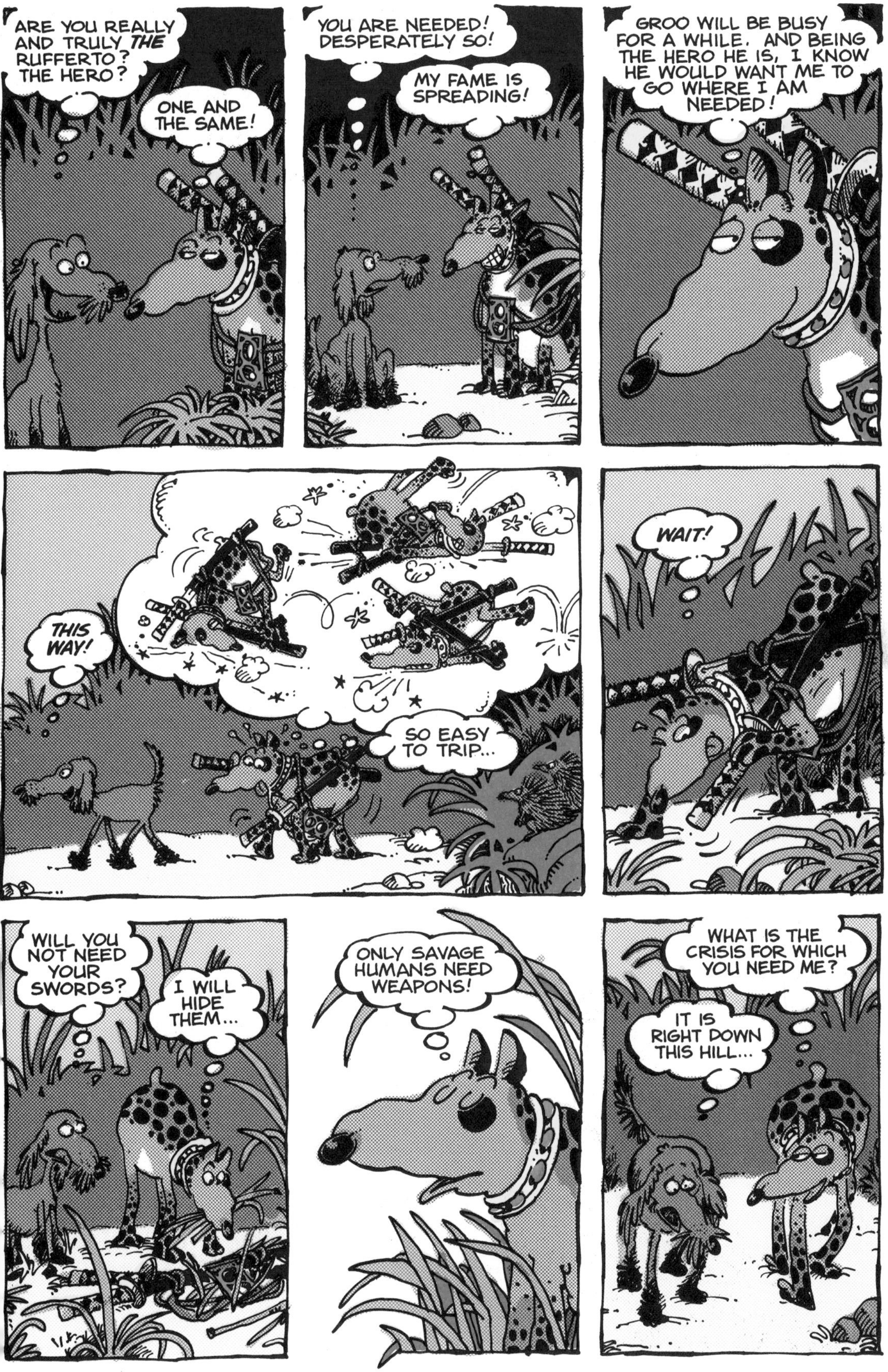
ARE YOU REALLY AND TRULY THE RUFFERTO? THE HERO?
ONE AND THE SAME!
YOU ARE NEEDED! DESPERATELY SO!
MY FAME IS SPREADING!
GROO WILL BE BUSY FOR A WHILE. AND BEING THE HERO HE IS, I KNOW HE WOULD WANT ME TO GO WHERE I AM NEEDED!
THIS WAY!
SO EASY TO TRIP...
WAIT!
WILL YOU NOT NEED YOUR SWORDS?
I WILL HIDE THEM...
ONLY SAVAGE HUMANS NEED WEAPONS!
WHAT IS THE CRISIS FOR WHICH YOU NEED ME?
IT IS RIGHT DOWN THIS HILL...

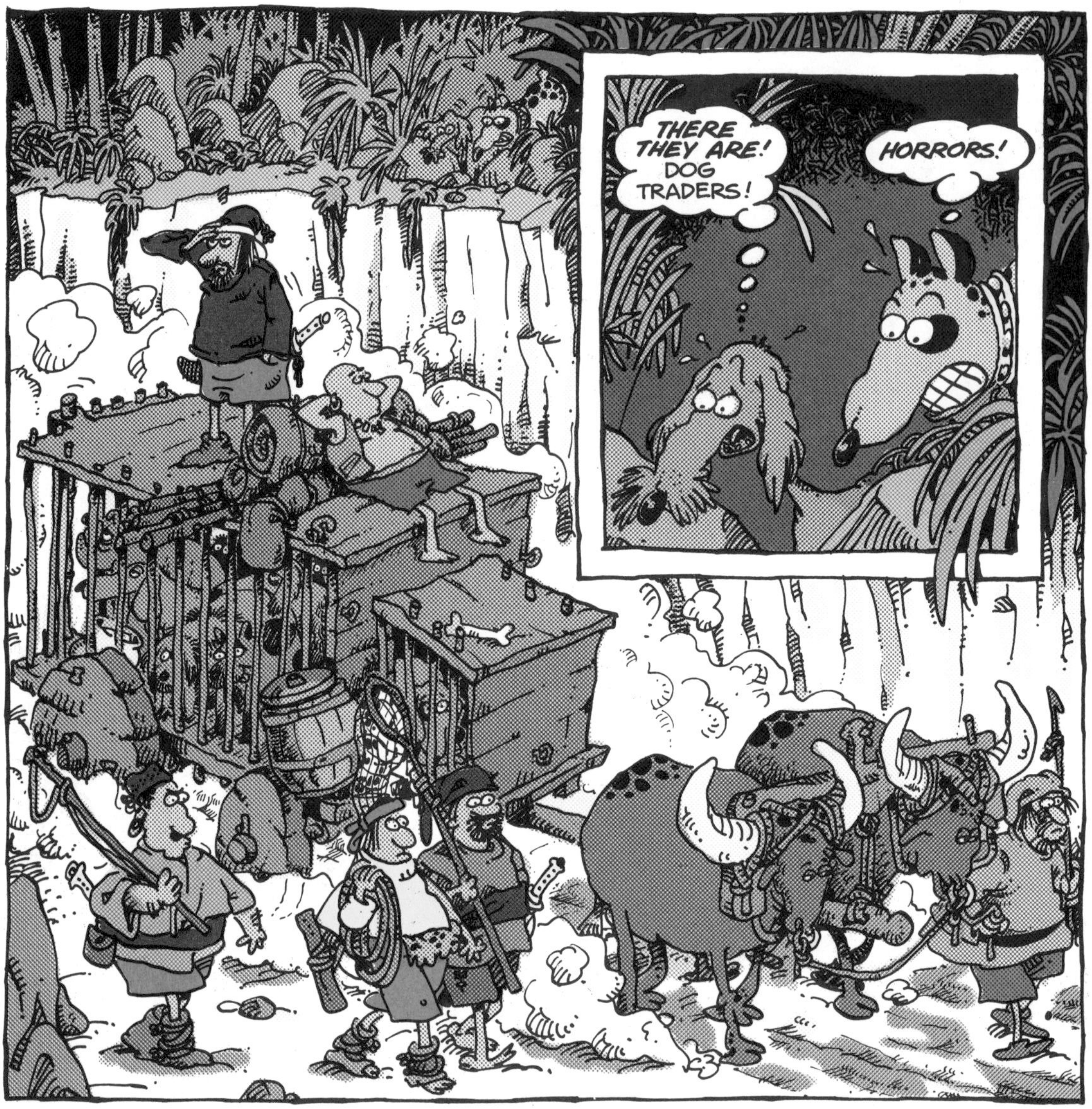
THERE THEY ARE! DOG TRADERS!
HORRORS!

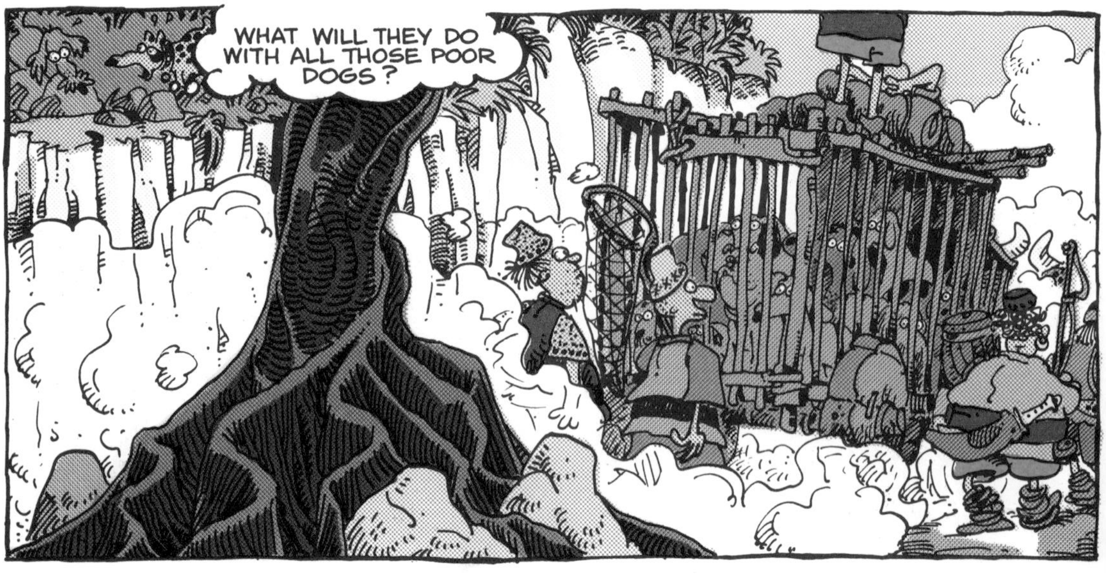
WHAT WILL THEY DO WITH ALL THOSE POOR DOGS?

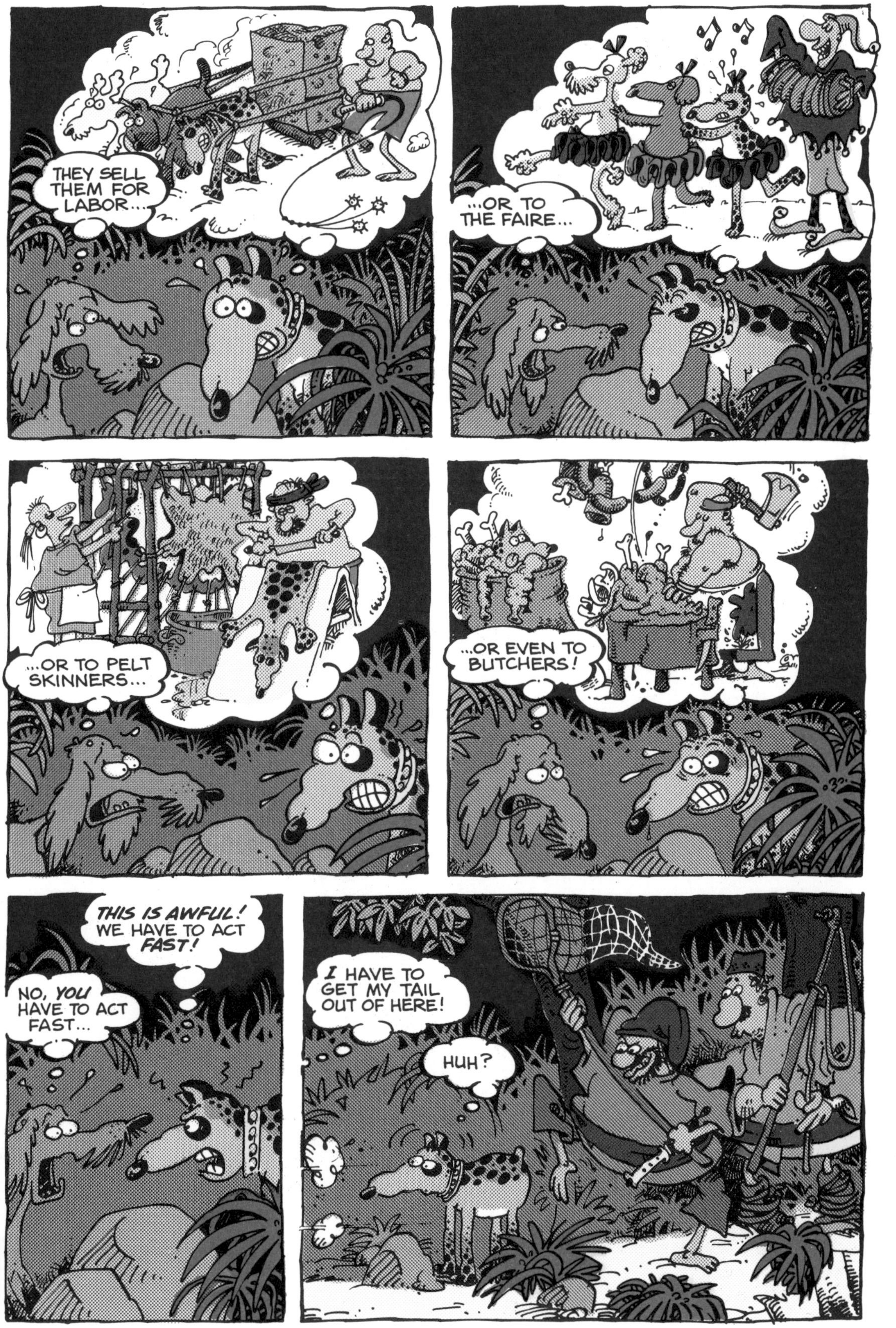
THEY SELL THEM FOR LABOR...
...OR TO THE FAIRE...
...OR TO PELT SKINNERS...
...OR EVEN TO BUTCHERS!
THIS IS AWFUL! WE HAVE TO ACT FAST!
NO, YOU HAVE TO ACT FAST...
I HAVE TO GET MY TAIL OUT OF HERE!
HUH?

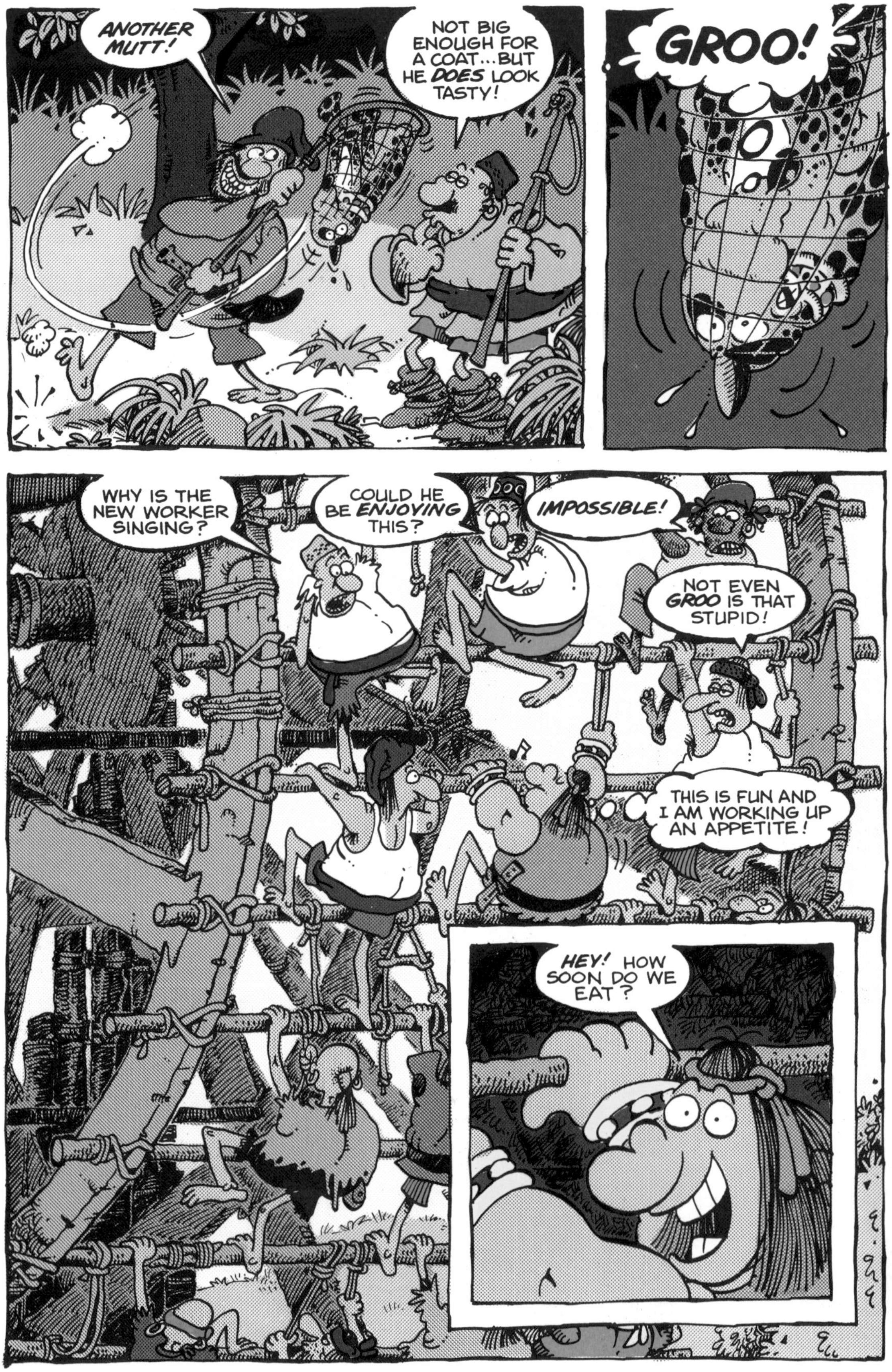
ANOTHER MUTT!
NOT BIG ENOUGH FOR A COAT...BUT HE DOES LOOK TASTY!
GROO!
WHY IS THE NEW WORKER SINGING?
COULD HE BE ENJOYING THIS?
IMPOSSIBLE!
NOT EVEN GROO IS THAT STUPID!
THIS IS FUN AND I AM WORKING UP AN APPETITE!
HEY! HOW SOON DO WE EAT?

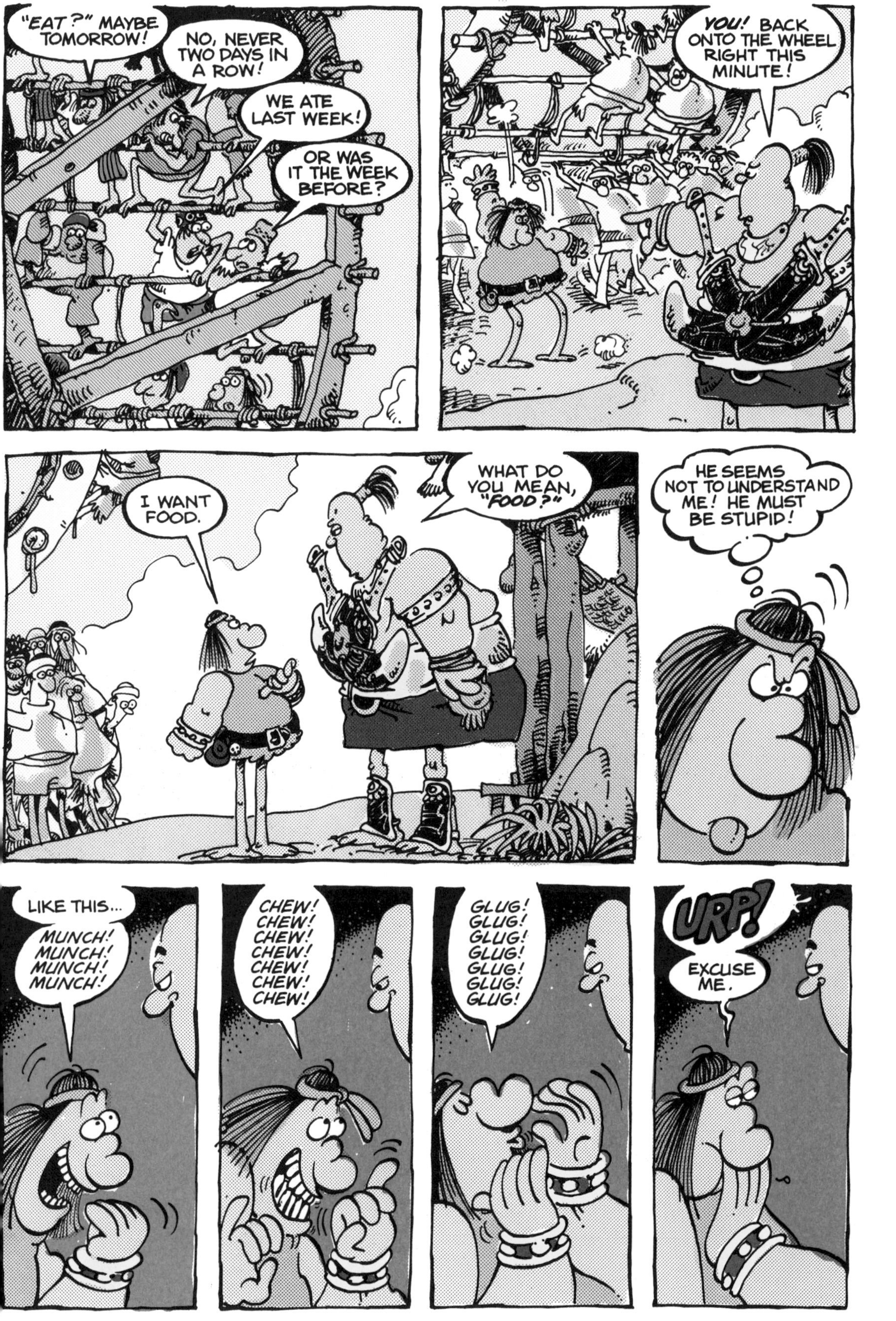
"EAT?" MAYBE TOMORROW!
NO, NEVER TWO DAYS IN A ROW!
WE ATE LAST WEEK!
OR WAS IT THE WEEK BEFORE?
YOU! BACK ONTO THE WHEEL RIGHT THIS MINUTE!
I WANT FOOD.
WHAT DO YOU MEAN, "FOOD?"
HE SEEMS NOT TO UNDERSTAND ME! HE MUST BE STUPID!
LIKE THIS...
MUNCH! MUNCH! MUNCH! MUNCH!
CHEW! CHEW! CHEW! CHEW! CHEW! CHEW! CHEW!
GLUG! GLUG! GLUG! GLUG! GLUG! GLUG! GLUG!
URP!
EXCUSE ME.

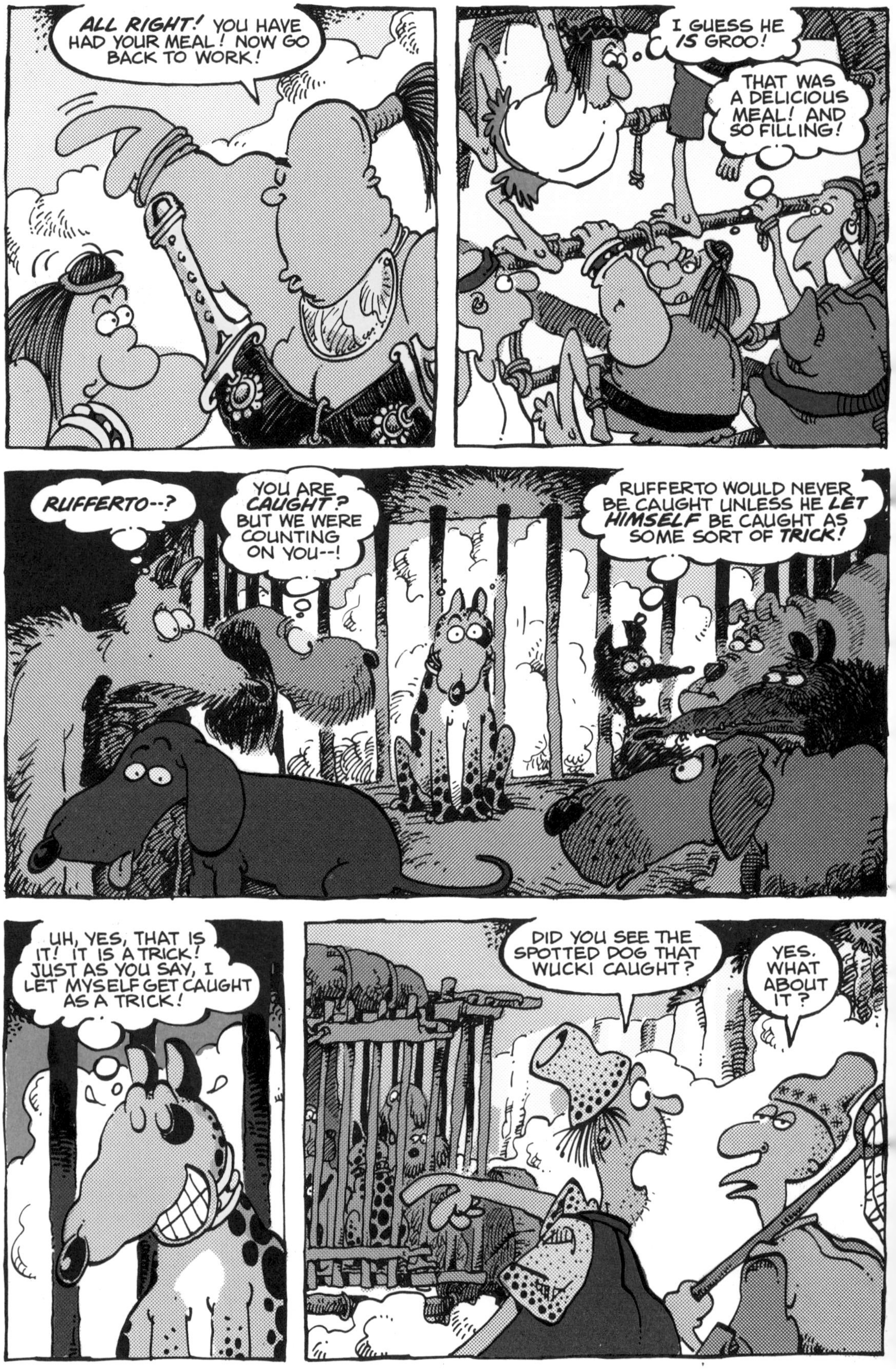
ALL RIGHT! YOU HAVE HAD YOUR MEAL! NOW GO BACK TO WORK!
I GUESS HE IS GROO!
THAT WAS A DELICIOUS MEAL! AND SO FILLING!
RUFFERTO--?
YOU ARE CAUGHT? BUT WE WERE COUNTING ON YOU--!
RUFFERTO WOULD NEVER BE CAUGHT UNLESS HE LET HIMSELF BE CAUGHT AS SOME SORT OF TRICK!
UH, YES, THAT IS IT! IT IS A TRICK! JUST AS YOU SAY, I LET MYSELF GET CAUGHT AS A TRICK!
DID YOU SEE THE SPOTTED DOG THAT WUCKI CAUGHT?
YES. WHAT ABOUT IT?

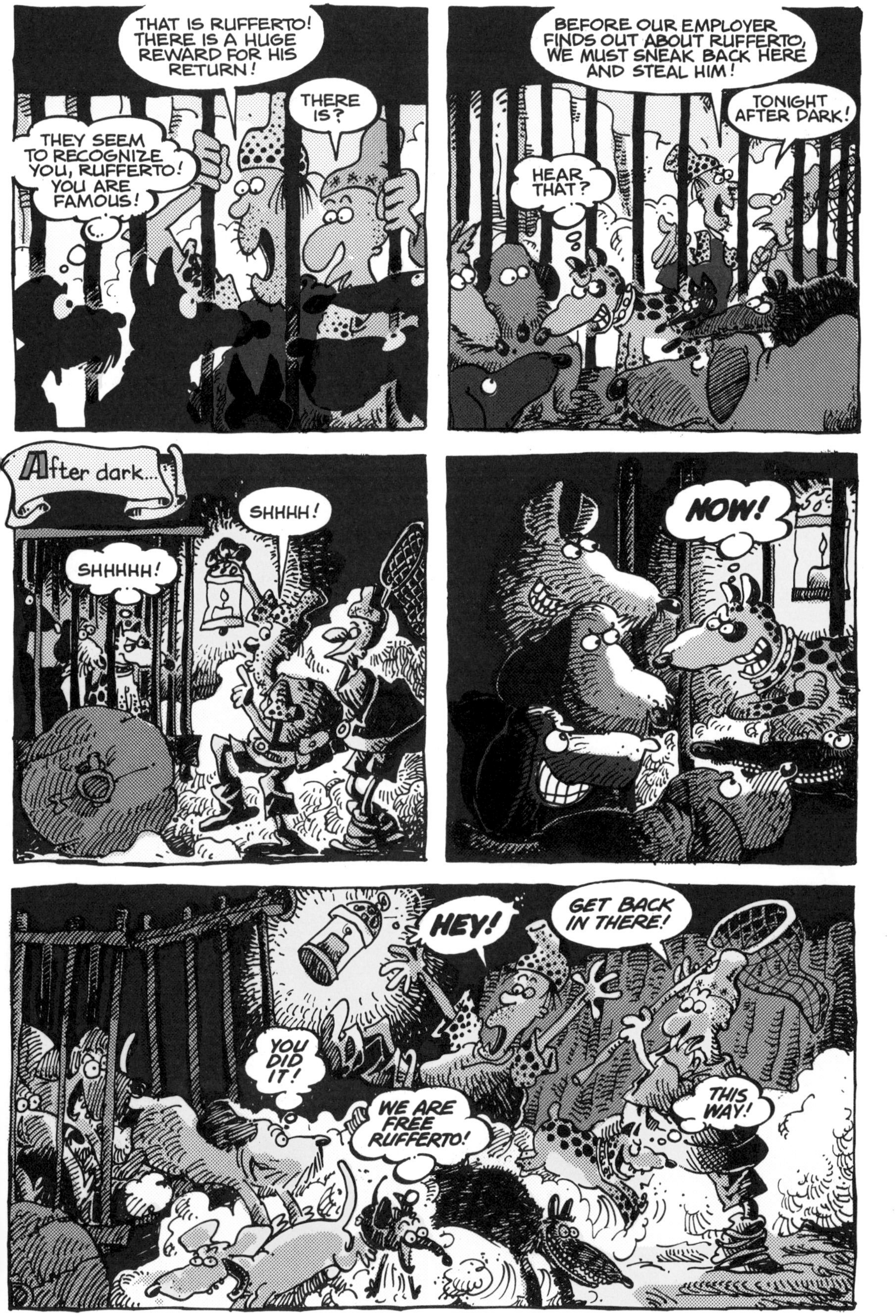
THAT IS RUFFERTO! THERE IS A HUGE REWARD FOR HIS RETURN!
THERE IS?
THEY SEEM TO RECOGNIZE YOU, RUFFERTO! YOU ARE FAMOUS!
BEFORE OUR EMPLOYER FINDS OUT ABOUT RUFFERTO, WE MUST SNEAK BACK HERE AND STEAL HIM!
TONIGHT AFTER DARK!
HEAR THAT?
After dark...
SHHHH!
SHHHHH!
NOW!
HEY!
GET BACK IN THERE!
YOU DID IT!
WE ARE FREE RUFFERTO!
THIS WAY!

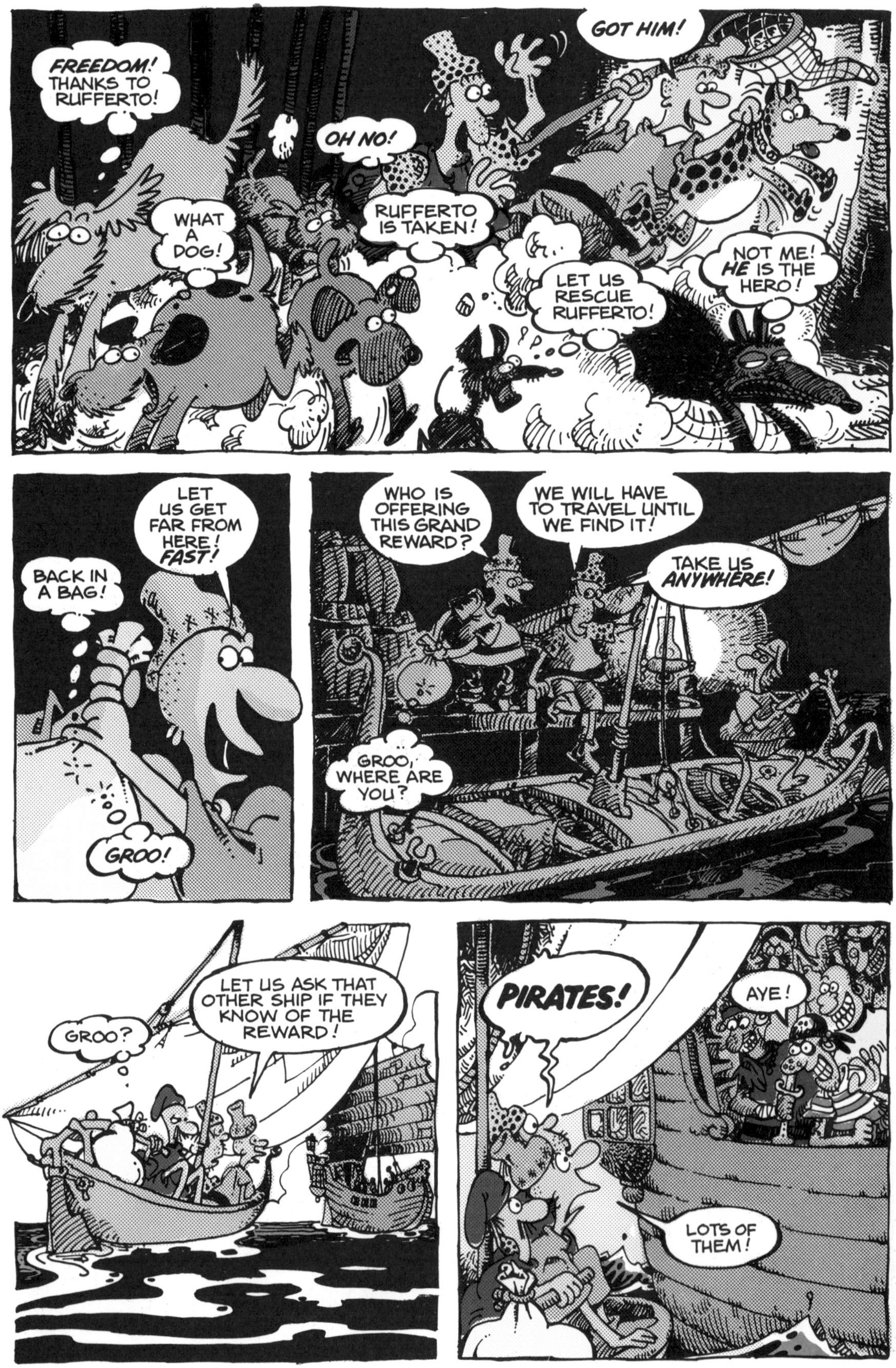
FREEDOM! THANKS TO RUFFERTO!
OH NO!
GOT HIM!
WHAT A DOG!
RUFFERTO IS TAKEN!
LET US RESCUE RUFFERTO!
NOT ME! HE IS THE HERO!
BACK IN A BAG!
LET US GET FAR FROM HERE! FAST!
GROO!
WHO IS OFFERING THIS GRAND REWARD?
WE WILL HAVE TO TRAVEL UNTIL WE FIND IT!
TAKE US ANYWHERE!
GROO, WHERE ARE YOU?
GROO?
LET US ASK THAT OTHER SHIP IF THEY KNOW OF THE REWARD!
PIRATES!
AYE!
LOTS OF THEM!

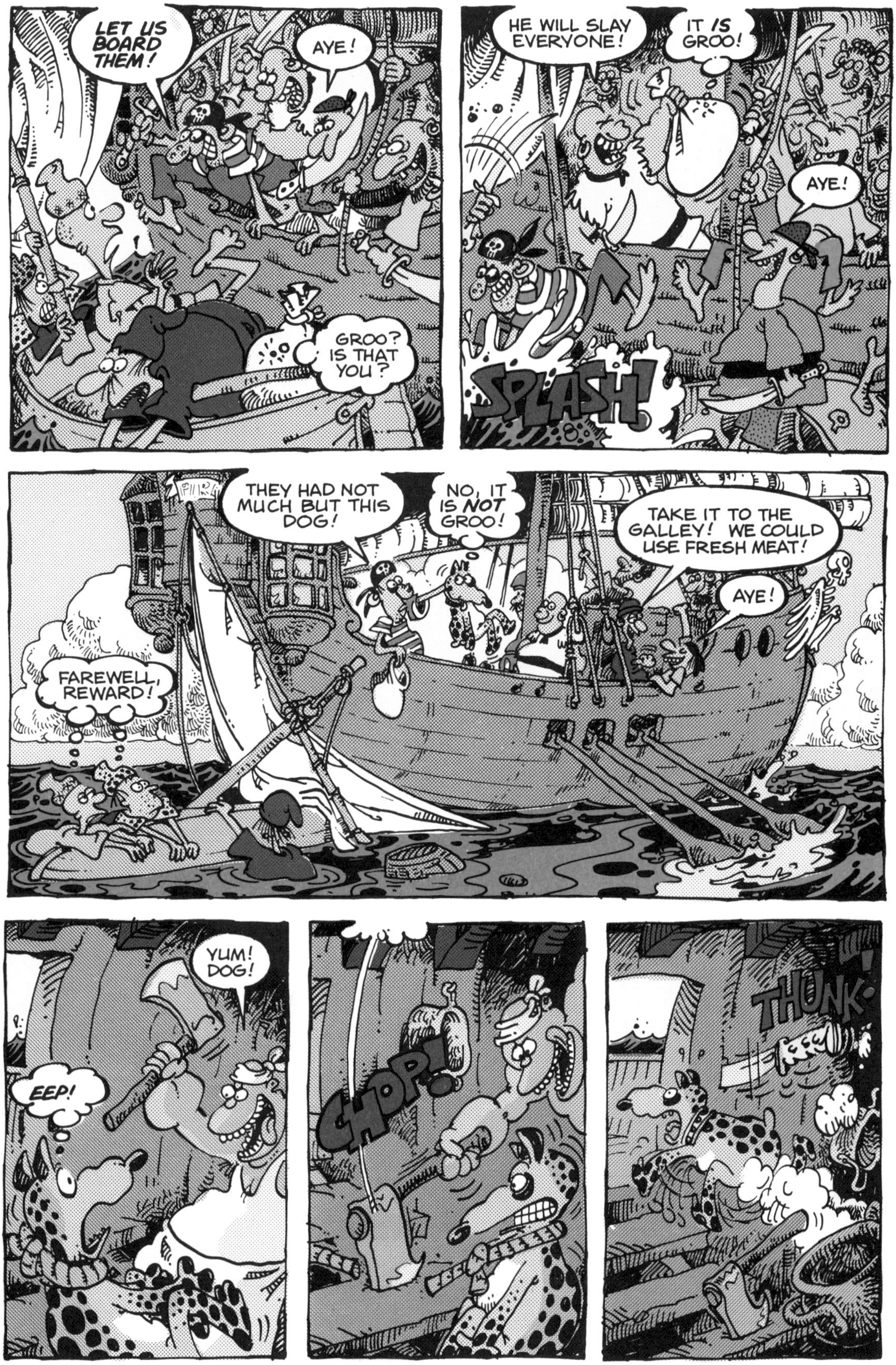
LET US BOARD THEM!
AYE!
GROO? IS THAT YOU?
HE WILL SLAY EVERYONE!
IT IS GROO!
AYE!
SPLASH!
THEY HAD NOT MUCH BUT THIS DOG!
NO, IT IS NOT GROO!
TAKE IT TO THE GALLEY! WE COULD USE FRESH MEAT!
AYE!
FAREWELL, REWARD!
YUM! DOG!
EEP!
CHOP!
THUNK!

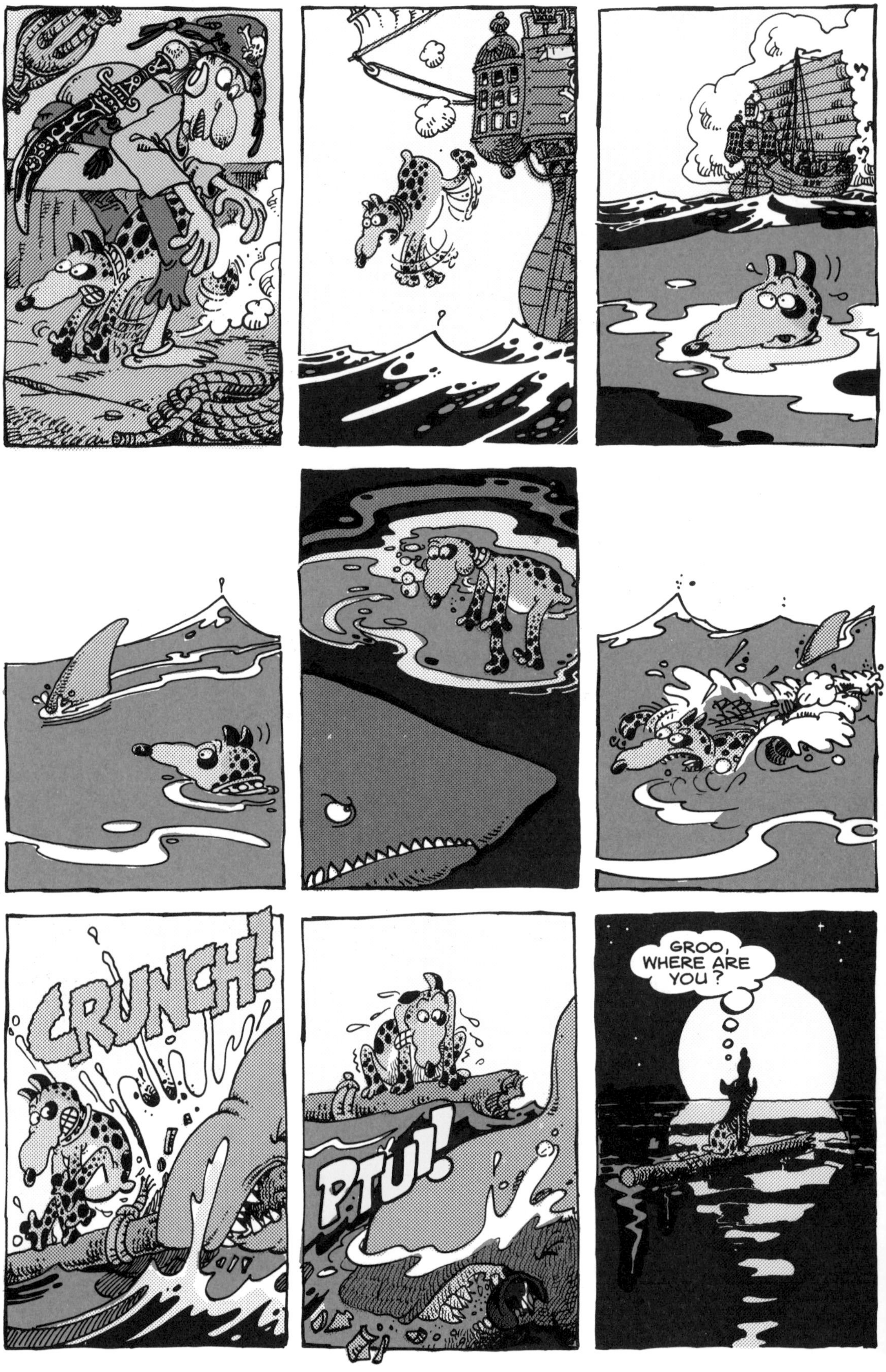
CRUNCH!
PTUI!
GROO, WHERE ARE YOU?

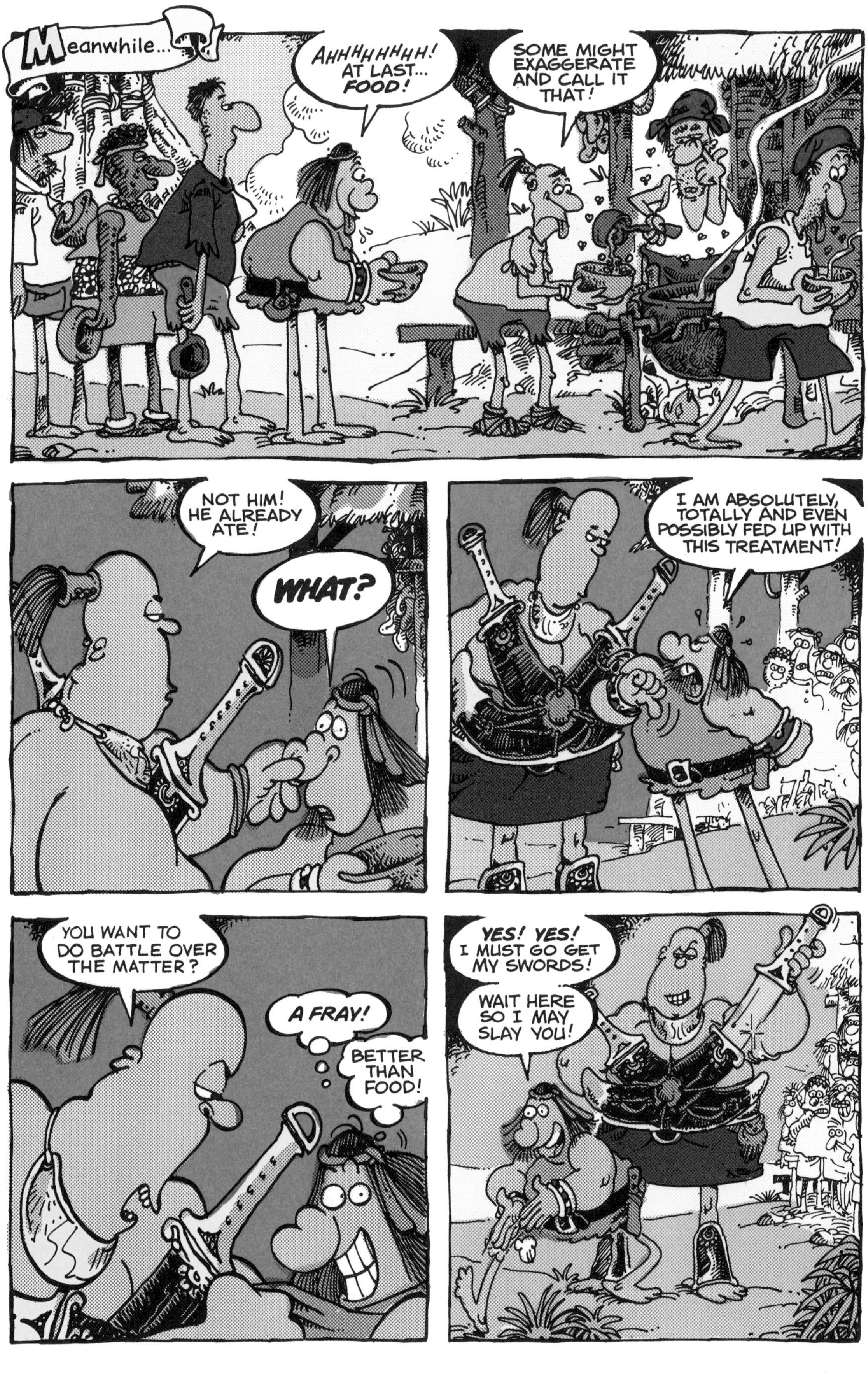
Meanwhile...
AHHHHHHHH! AT LAST... FOOD!
SOME MIGHT EXAGGERATE AND CALL IT THAT!
NOT HIM! HE ALREADY ATE!
WHAT?
I AM ABSOLUTELY, TOTALLY AND EVEN POSSIBLY FED UP WITH THIS TREATMENT!
YOU WANT TO DO BATTLE OVER THE MATTER?
A FRAY!
BETTER THAN FOOD!
YES! YES! I MUST GO GET MY SWORDS!
WAIT HERE SO I MAY SLAY YOU!

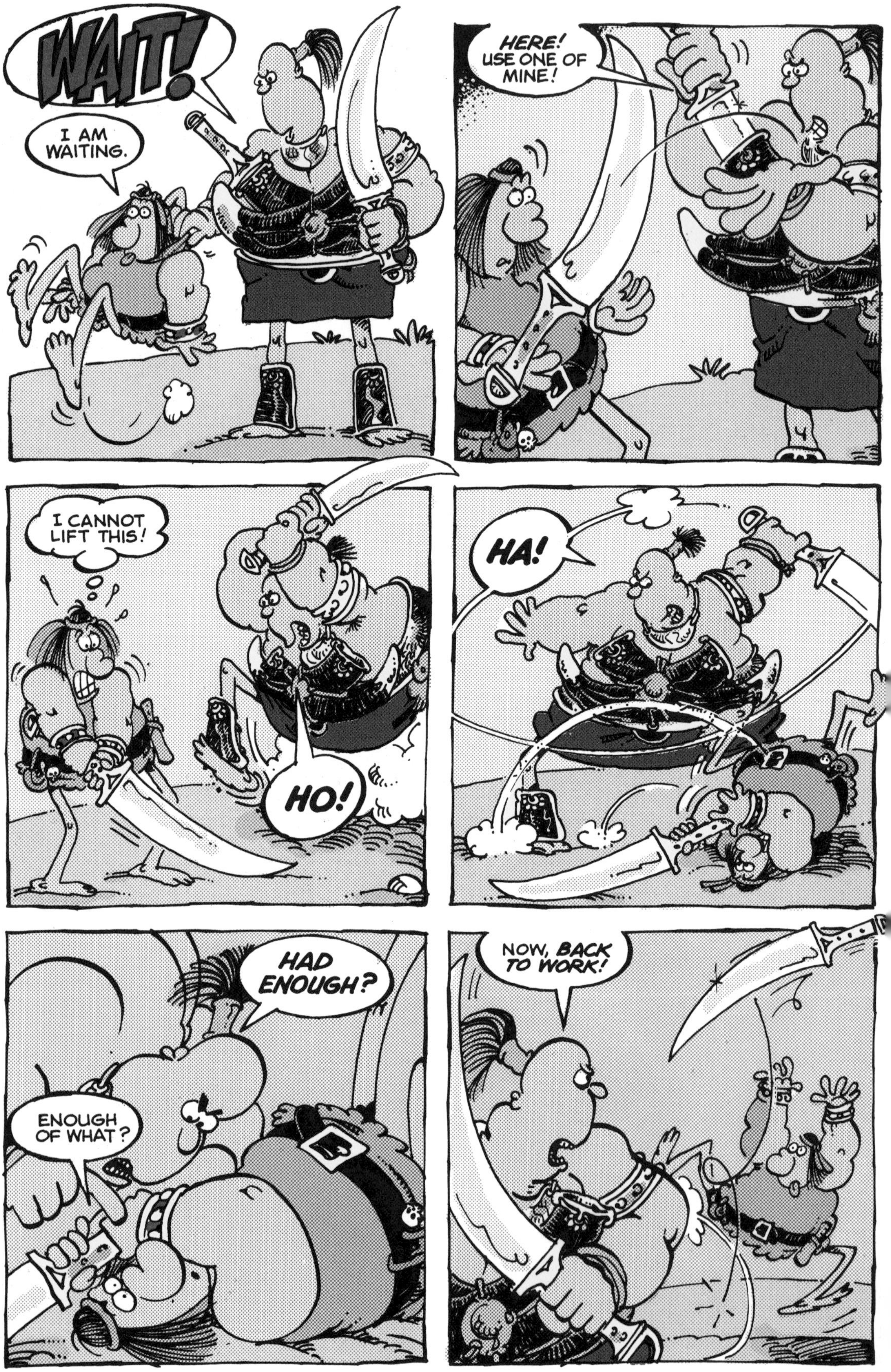
WAIT!
I AM WAITING.
HERE! USE ONE OF MINE!
I CANNOT LIFT THIS!
HO!
HA!
HAD ENOUGH?
ENOUGH OF WHAT?
NOW, BACK TO WORK!

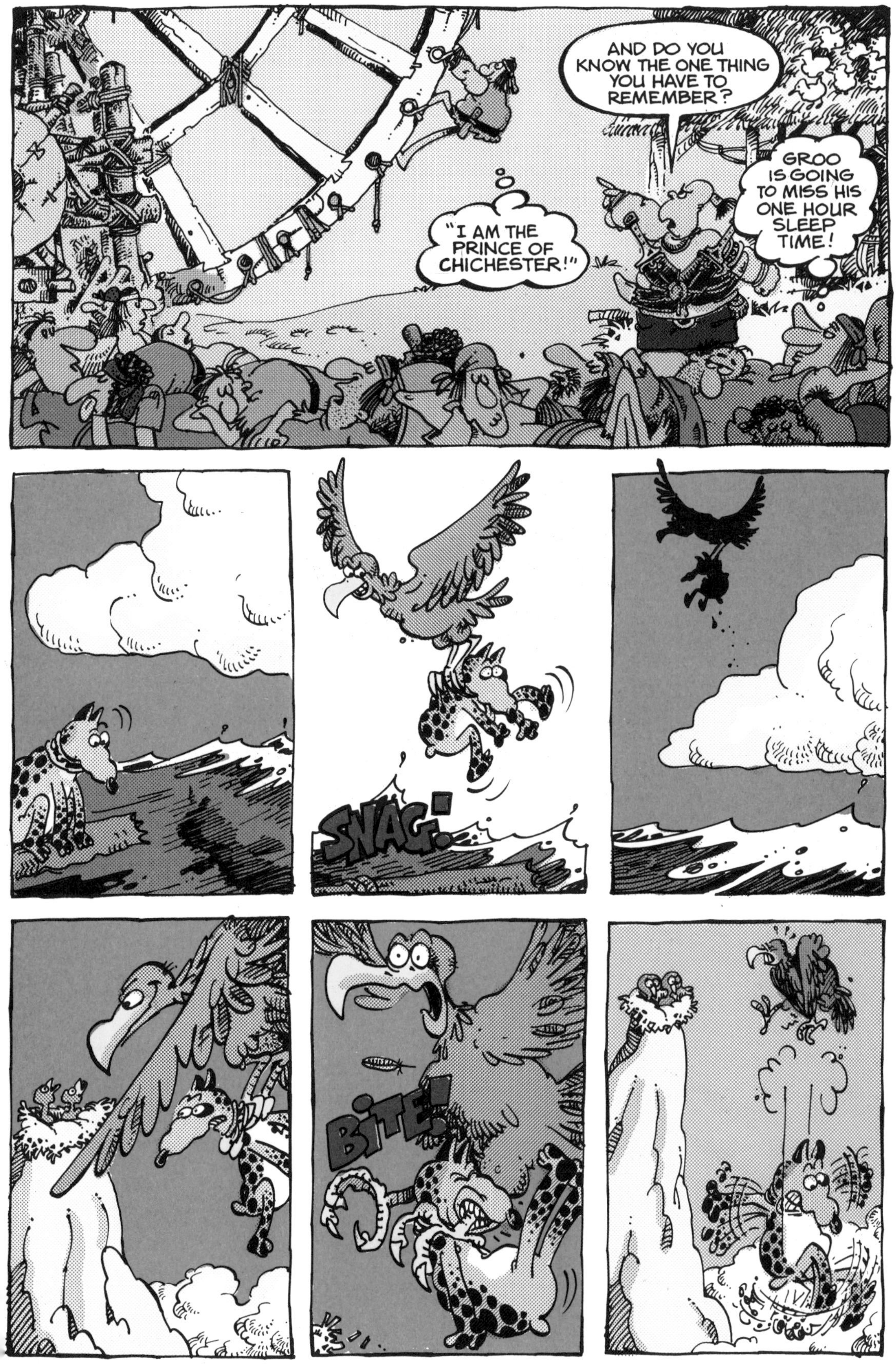
AND DO YOU KNOW THE ONE THING YOU HAVE TO REMEMBER?
"I AM THE PRINCE OF CHICHESTER!"
GROO IS GOING TO MISS HIS ONE HOUR SLEEP TIME!
SNAG!
BITE!

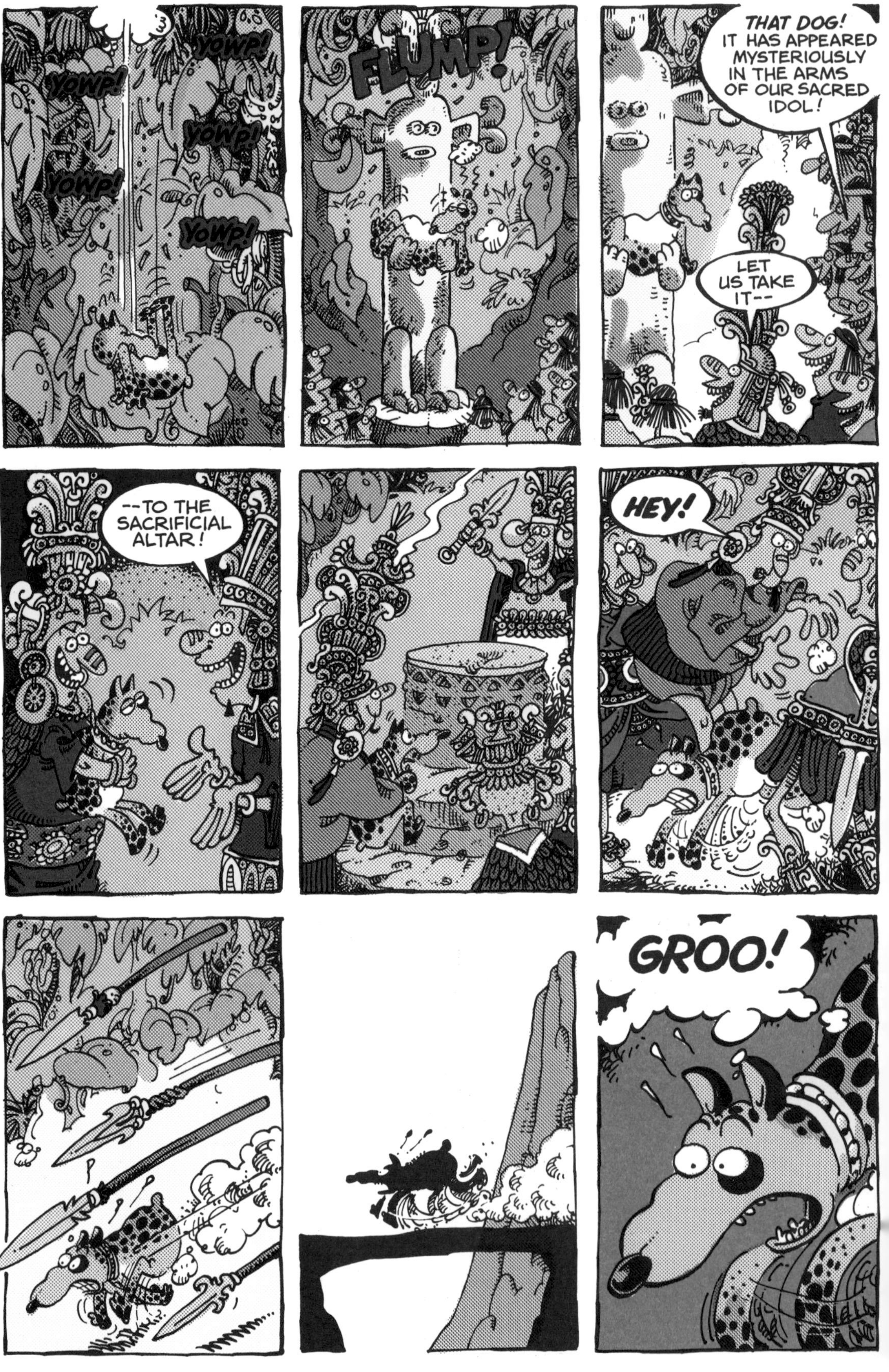
YOWP!
YOWP!
YOWP!
YOWP!
YOWP!
FLUMP!
THAT DOG! IT HAS APPEARED MYSTERIOUSLY IN THE ARMS OF OUR SACRED IDOL!
LET US TAKE IT--
--TO THE SACRIFICIAL ALTAR!
HEY!
GROO!

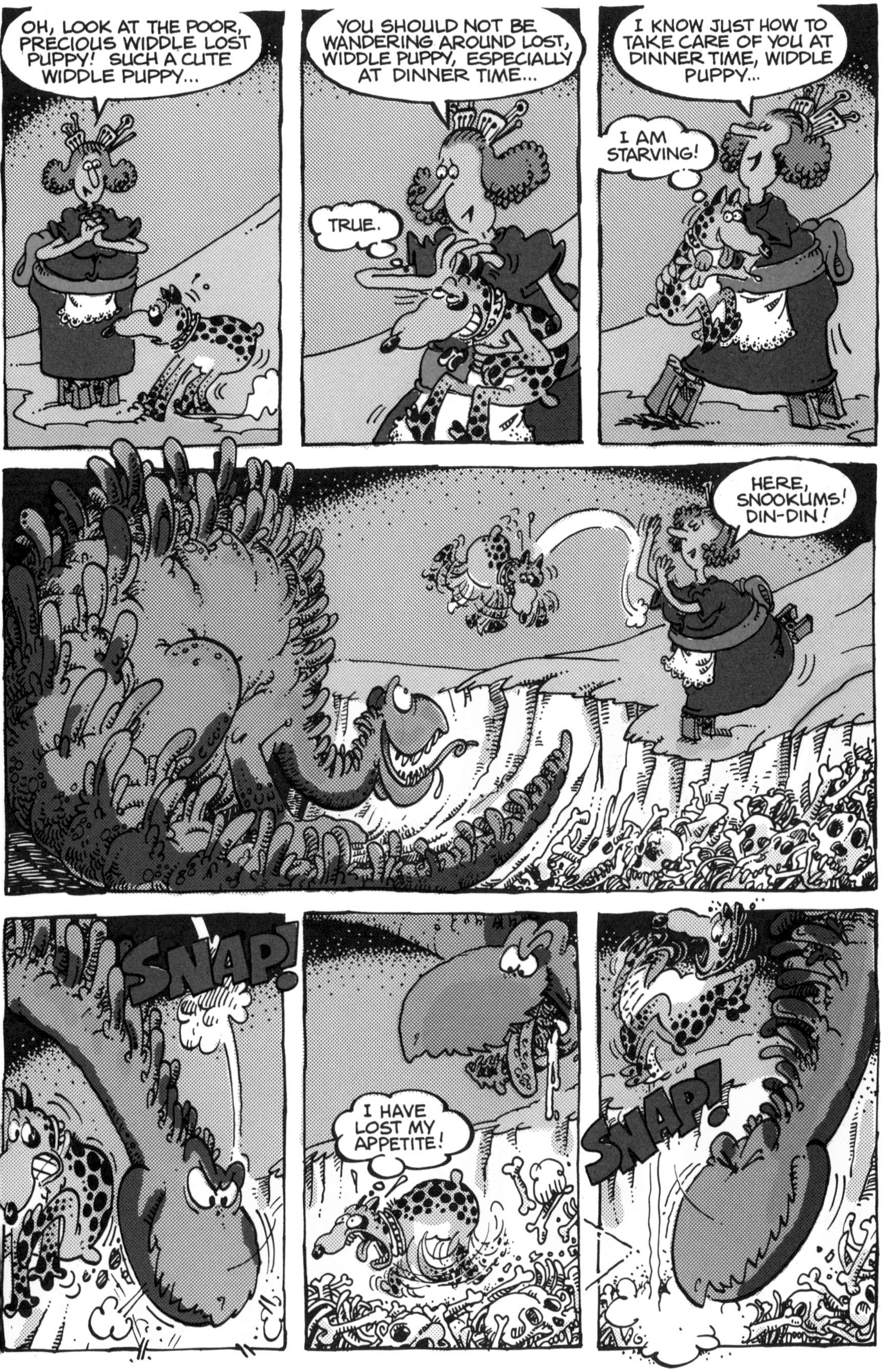
OH, LOOK AT THE POOR, PRECIOUS WIDDLE LOST PUPPY! SUCH A CUTE WIDDLE PUPPY...
YOU SHOULD NOT BE WANDERING AROUND LOST, WIDDLE PUPPY, ESPECIALLY AT DINNER TIME...
TRUE.
I KNOW JUST HOW TO TAKE CARE OF YOU AT DINNER TIME, WIDDLE PUPPY...
I AM STARVING!
HERE, SNOOKUMS! DIN-DIN!
SNAP!
I HAVE LOST MY APPETITE!
SNAP!

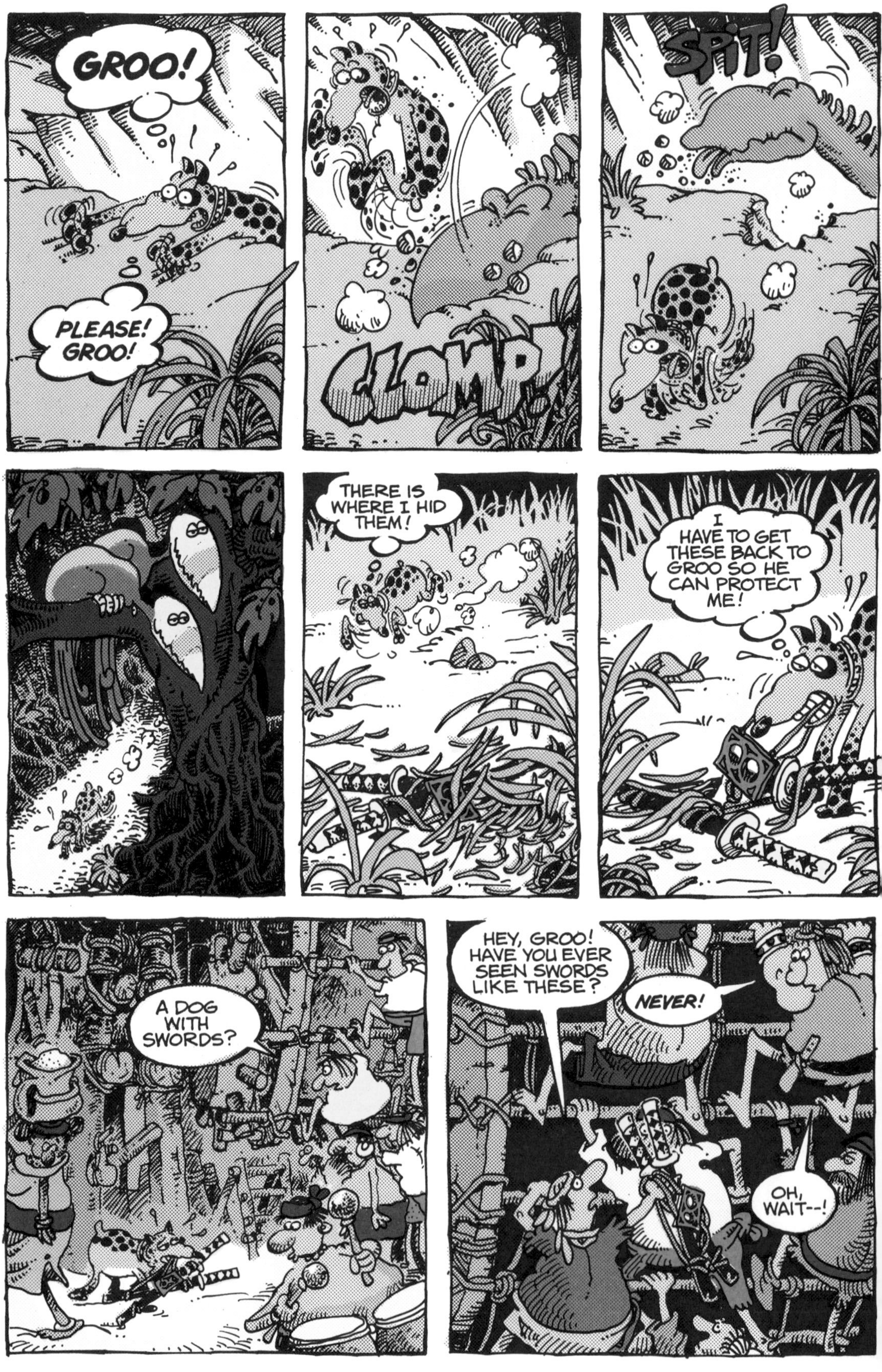
GROO!
PLEASE! GROO!
CLOMP!
SPIT!
THERE IS WHERE I HID THEM!
I HAVE TO GET THESE BACK TO GROO SO HE CAN PROTECT ME!
A DOG WITH SWORDS?
HEY, GROO! HAVE YOU EVER SEEN SWORDS LIKE THESE?
NEVER!
OH, WAIT--!

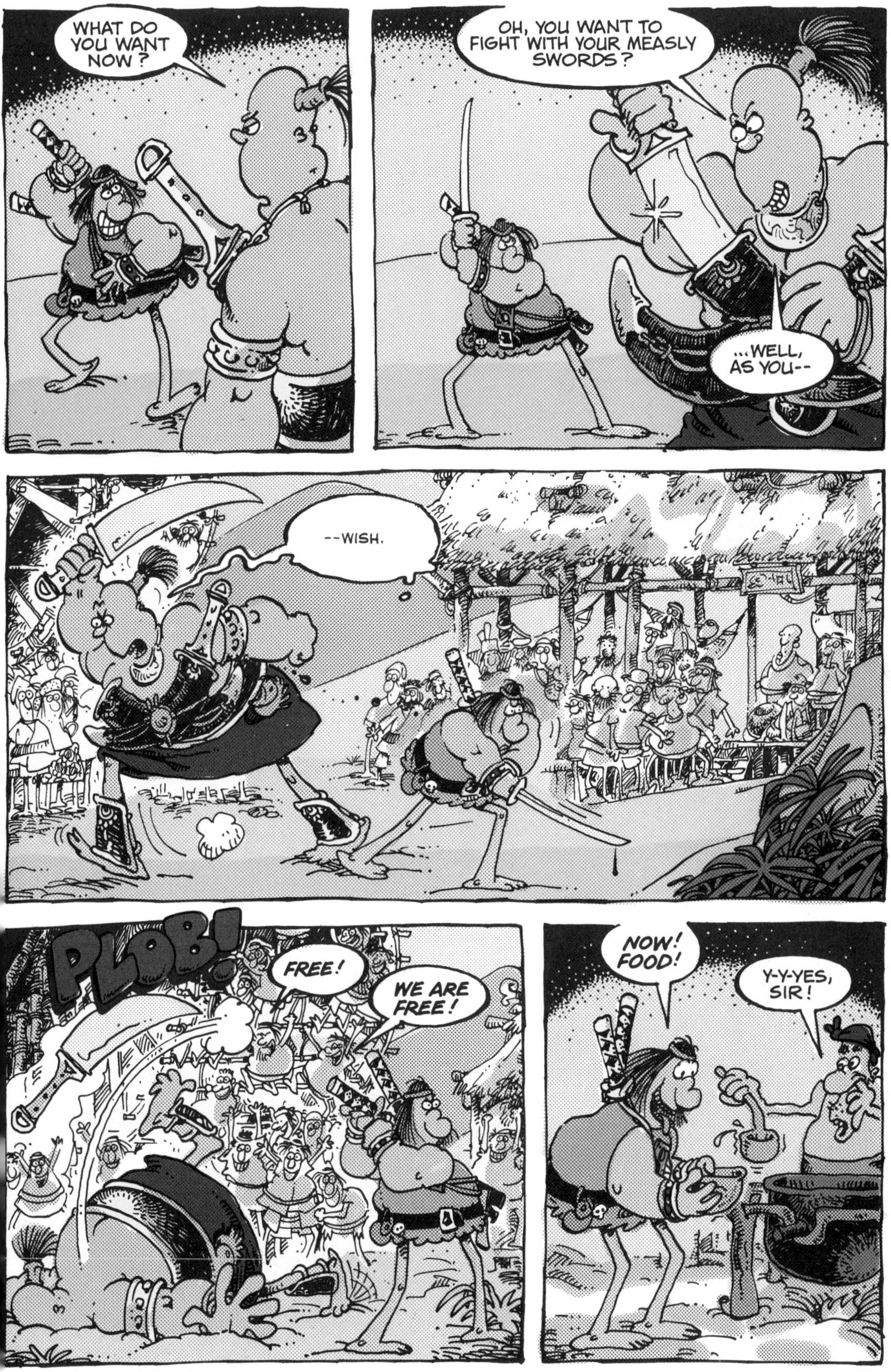
WHAT DO YOU WANT NOW?
OH, YOU WANT TO FIGHT WITH YOUR MEASLY SWORDS?
...WELL, AS YOU--
--WISH.
PLOB!
FREE!
WE ARE FREE!
NOW! FOOD!
Y-Y-YES, SIR!

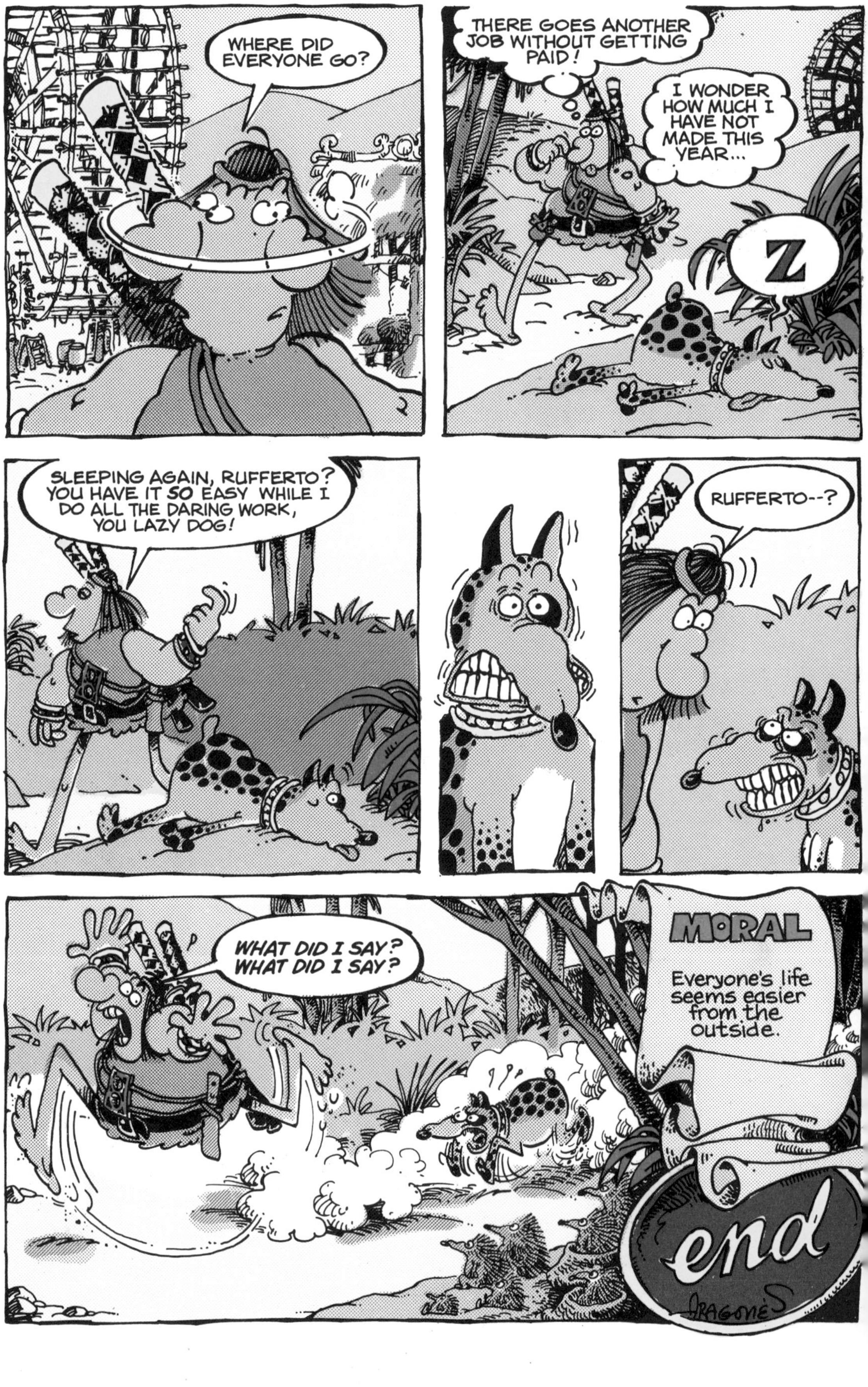
WHERE DID EVERYONE GO?
THERE GOES ANOTHER JOB WITHOUT GETTING PAID!
I WONDER HOW MUCH I HAVE NOT MADE THIS YEAR...
Z
SLEEPING AGAIN, RUFFERTO? YOU HAVE IT SO EASY WHILE I DO ALL THE DARING WORK, YOU LAZY DOG!
RUFFERTO--?
WHAT DID I SAY? WHAT DID I SAY?
MORAL
Everyone's life seems easier from the outside.
end
ARAGONÉS

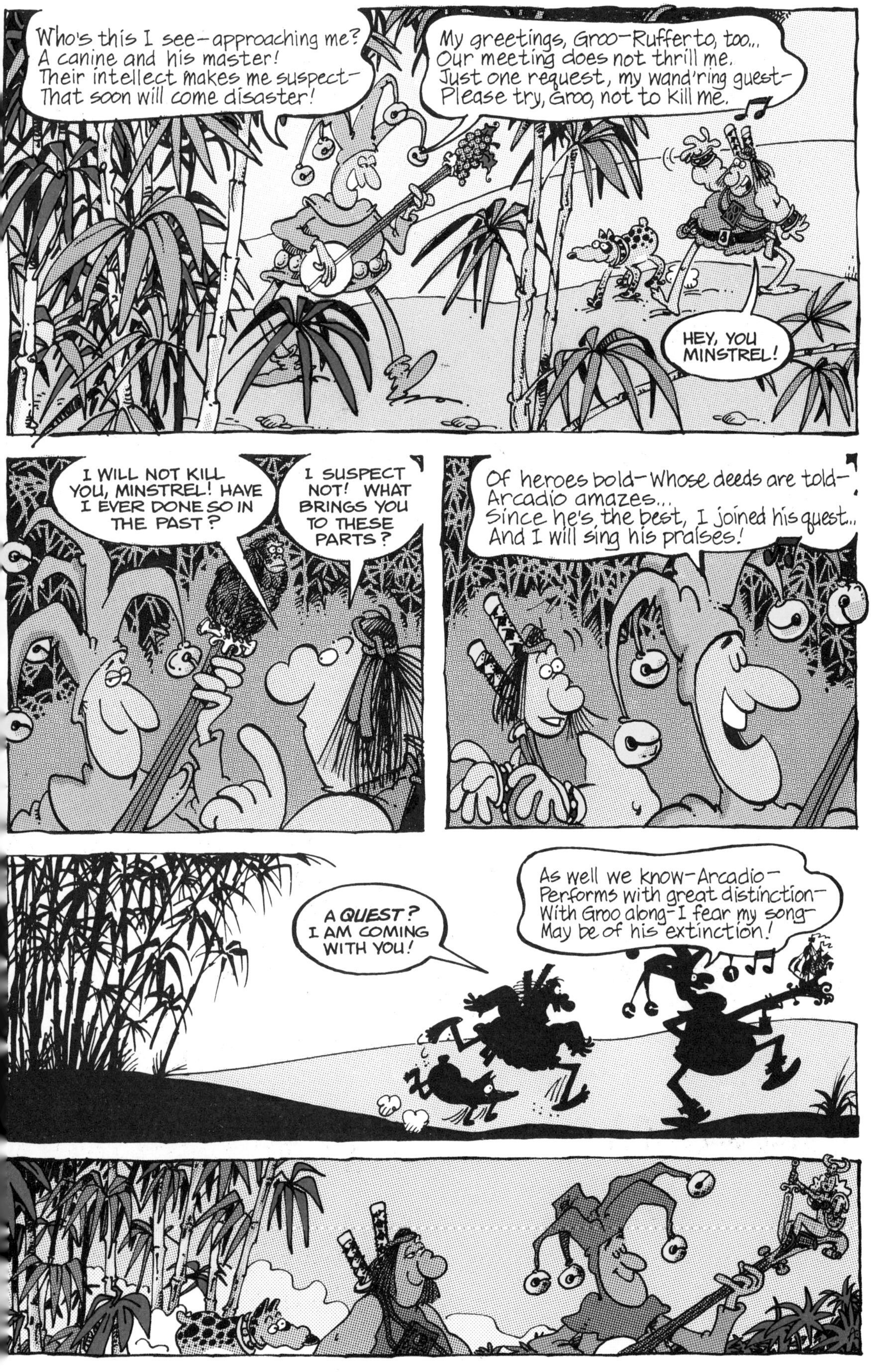
Who's this I see—approaching me? A canine and his master! Their intellect makes me suspect—That soon will come disaster!
My greetings, Groo—Rufferto, too... Our meeting does not thrill me. Just one request, my wand'ring guest—Please try, Groo, not to kill me.
HEY, YOU MINSTREL!
I WILL NOT KILL YOU, MINSTREL! HAVE I EVER DONE SO IN THE PAST?
I SUSPECT NOT! WHAT BRINGS YOU TO THESE PARTS?
Of heroes bold—Whose deeds are told—Arcadio amazes... Since he's the best, I joined his quest... And I will sing his praises!
A QUEST? I AM COMING WITH YOU!
As well we know—Arcadio—Performs with great distinction—With Groo along—I fear my song—May be of his extinction!

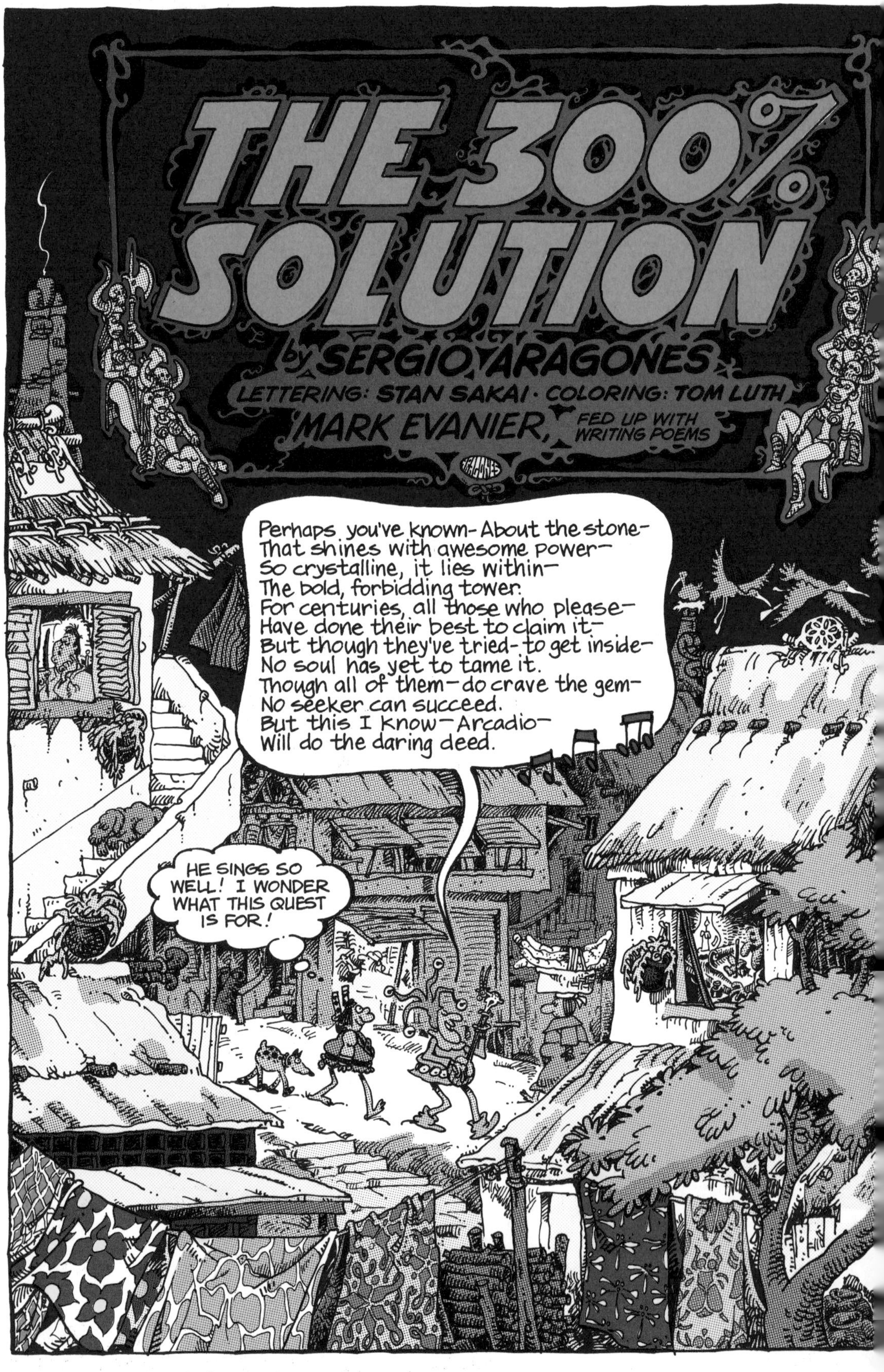
THE 300% SOLUTION
by SERGIO ARAGONES
LETTERING: STAN SAKAI · COLORING: TOM LUTH
MARK EVANIER, FED UP WITH WRITING POEMS
Perhaps you've known- About the stone- That shines with awesome power- So crystalline, it lies within- The bold, forbidding tower. For centuries, all those who please- Have done their best to claim it- But though they've tried- to get inside- No soul has yet to tame it. Though all of them- do crave the gem- No seeker can succeed. But this I know- Arcadio- Will do the daring deed.
HE SINGS SO WELL! I WONDER WHAT THIS QUEST IS FOR!

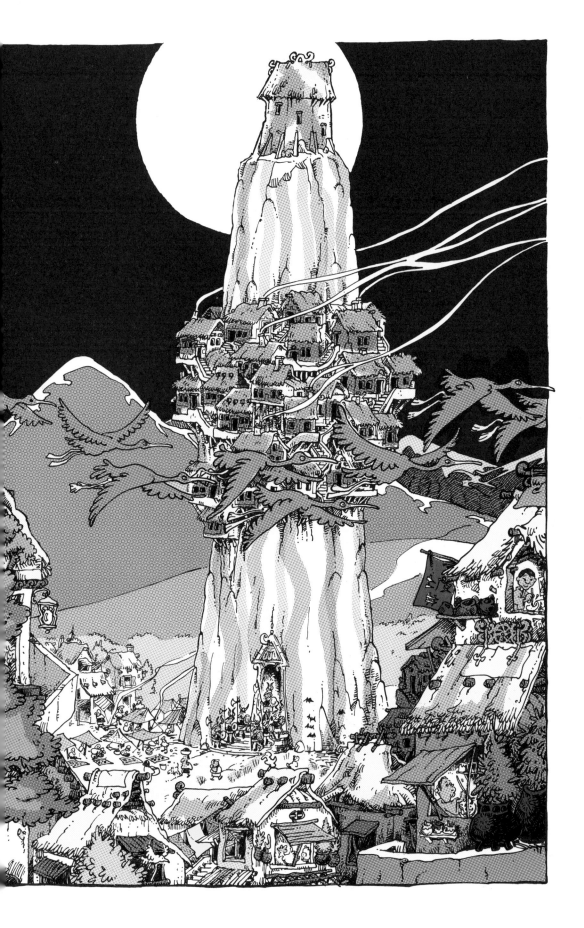

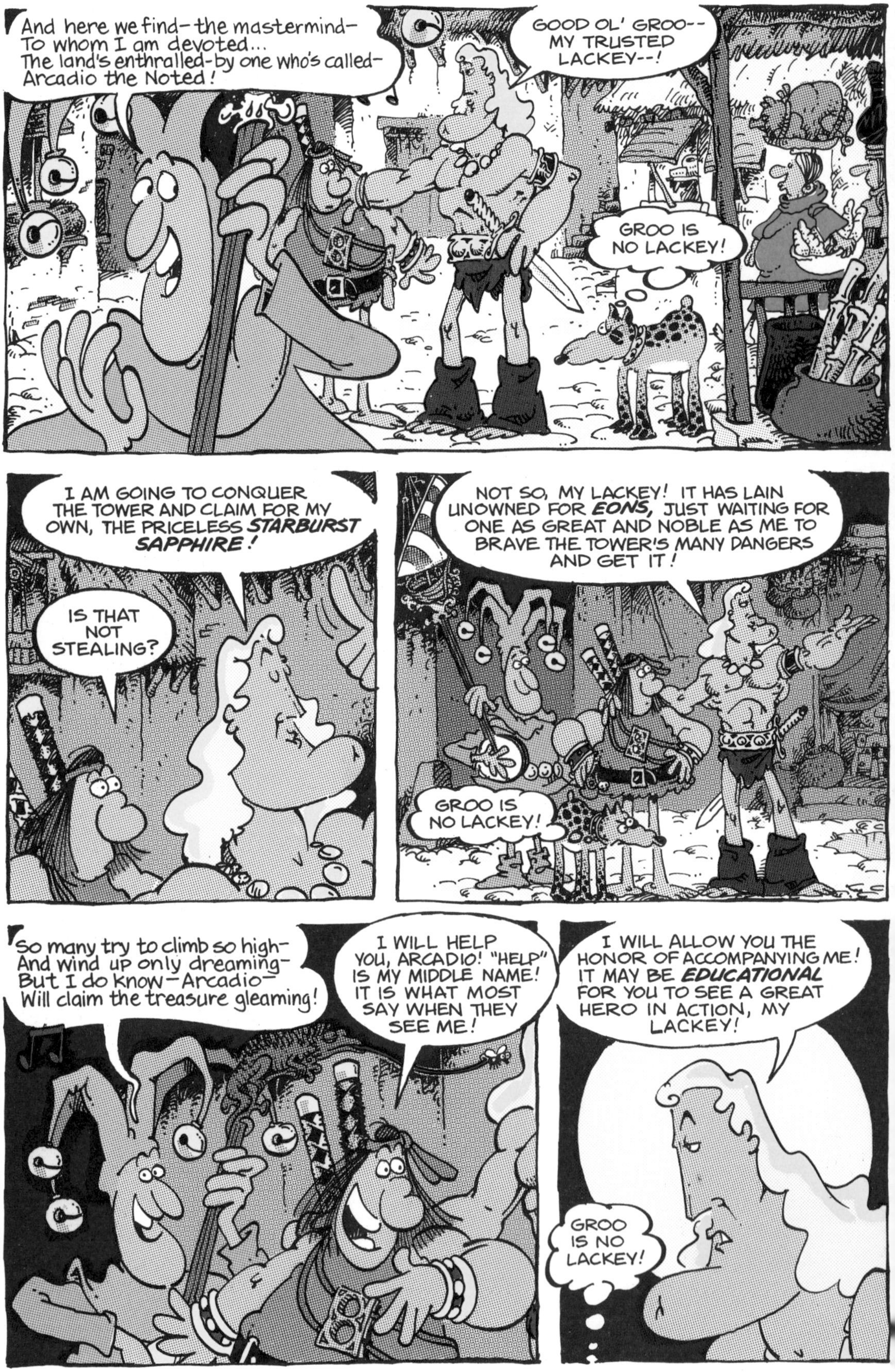
And here we find- the mastermind- To whom I am devoted... The land's enthralled-by one who's called- Arcadio the Noted!
GOOD OL' GROO-- MY TRUSTED LACKEY--!
GROO IS NO LACKEY!
I AM GOING TO CONQUER THE TOWER AND CLAIM FOR MY OWN, THE PRICELESS STARBURST SAPPHIRE!
IS THAT NOT STEALING?
NOT SO, MY LACKEY! IT HAS LAIN UNOWNED FOR EONS, JUST WAITING FOR ONE AS GREAT AND NOBLE AS ME TO BRAVE THE TOWER'S MANY DANGERS AND GET IT!
GROO IS NO LACKEY!
So many try to climb so high- And wind up only dreaming- But I do know-Arcadio- Will claim the treasure gleaming!
I WILL HELP YOU, ARCADIO! "HELP" IS MY MIDDLE NAME! IT IS WHAT MOST SAY WHEN THEY SEE ME!
I WILL ALLOW YOU THE HONOR OF ACCOMPANYING ME! IT MAY BE EDUCATIONAL FOR YOU TO SEE A GREAT HERO IN ACTION, MY LACKEY!
GROO IS NO LACKEY!

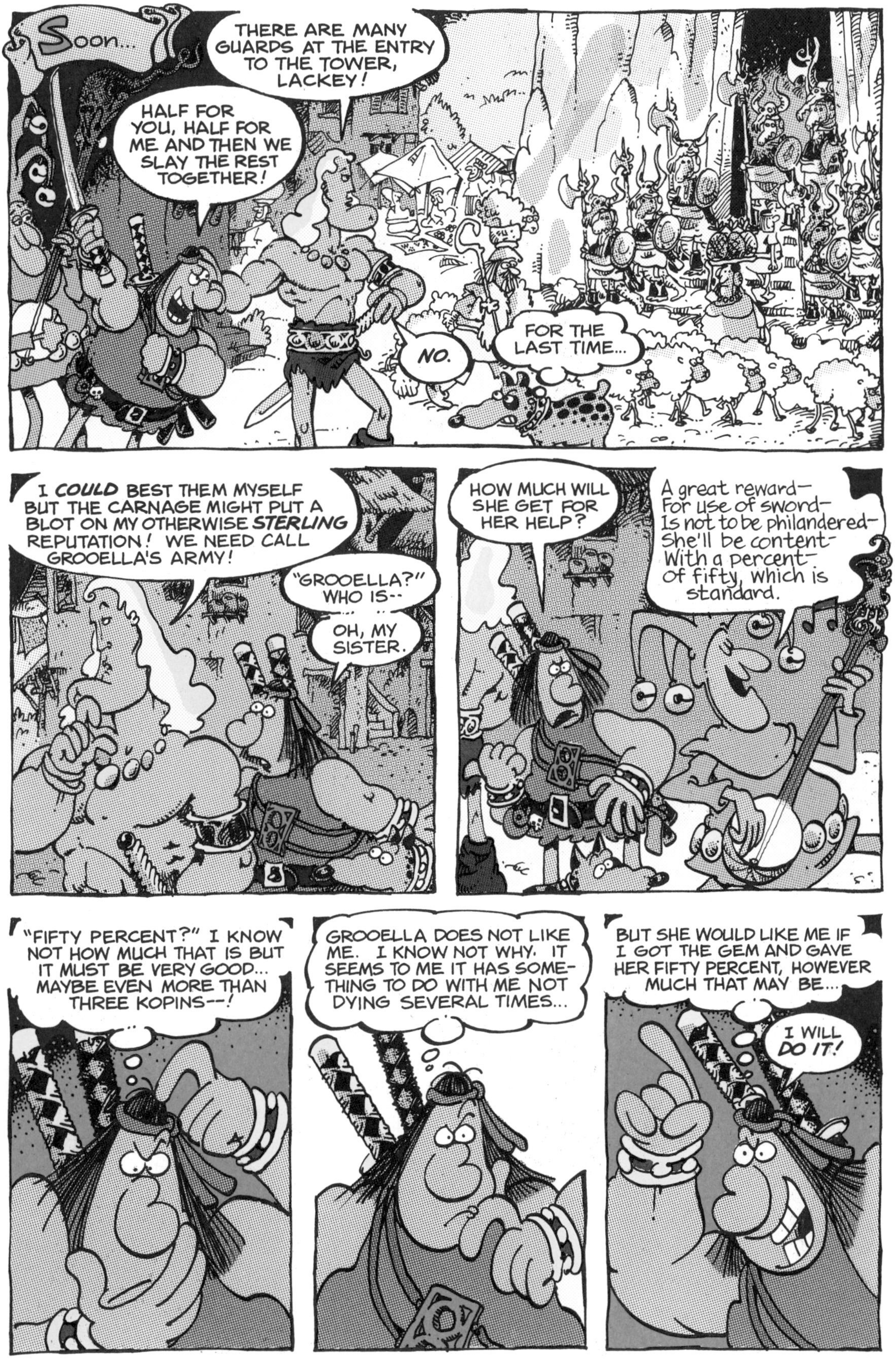
Soon...
THERE ARE MANY GUARDS AT THE ENTRY TO THE TOWER, LACKEY!
HALF FOR YOU, HALF FOR ME AND THEN WE SLAY THE REST TOGETHER!
NO.
FOR THE LAST TIME...
I COULD BEST THEM MYSELF BUT THE CARNAGE MIGHT PUT A BLOT ON MY OTHERWISE STERLING REPUTATION! WE NEED CALL GROOELLA'S ARMY!
"GROOELLA?" WHO IS--
OH, MY SISTER.
HOW MUCH WILL SHE GET FOR HER HELP?
A great reward—
For use of sword—
Is not to be philandered—
She'll be content—
With a percent—
Of fifty, which is standard.
"FIFTY PERCENT?" I KNOW NOT HOW MUCH THAT IS BUT IT MUST BE VERY GOOD... MAYBE EVEN MORE THAN THREE KOPINS--!
GROOELLA DOES NOT LIKE ME. I KNOW NOT WHY. IT SEEMS TO ME IT HAS SOMETHING TO DO WITH ME NOT DYING SEVERAL TIMES...
BUT SHE WOULD LIKE ME IF I GOT THE GEM AND GAVE HER FIFTY PERCENT, HOWEVER MUCH THAT MAY BE...
I WILL DO IT!

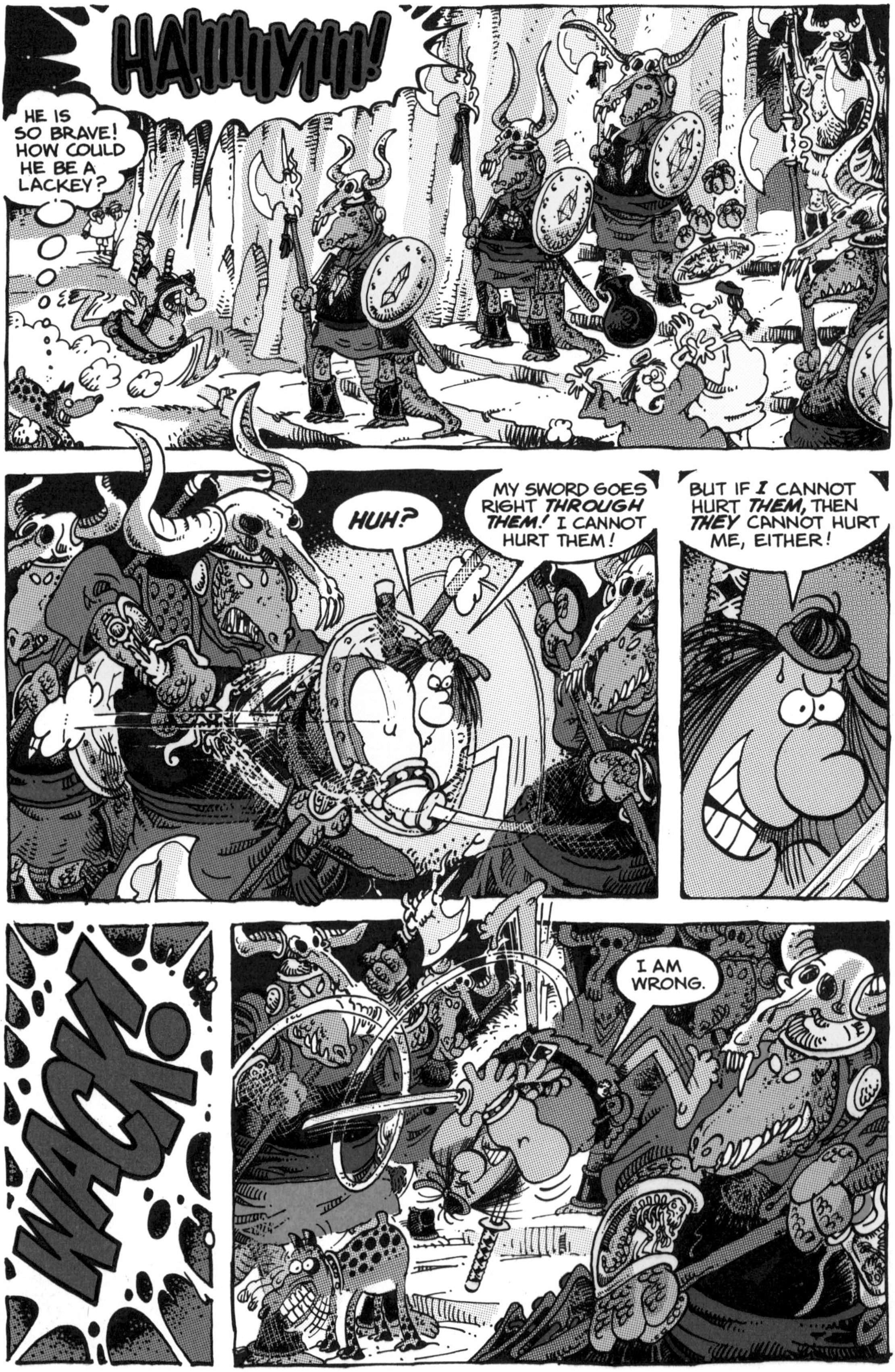
HAIIIIIYIIII!
HE IS SO BRAVE! HOW COULD HE BE A LACKEY?
HUH?
MY SWORD GOES RIGHT THROUGH THEM! I CANNOT HURT THEM!
BUT IF I CANNOT HURT THEM, THEN THEY CANNOT HURT ME, EITHER!
WACK!
I AM WRONG.

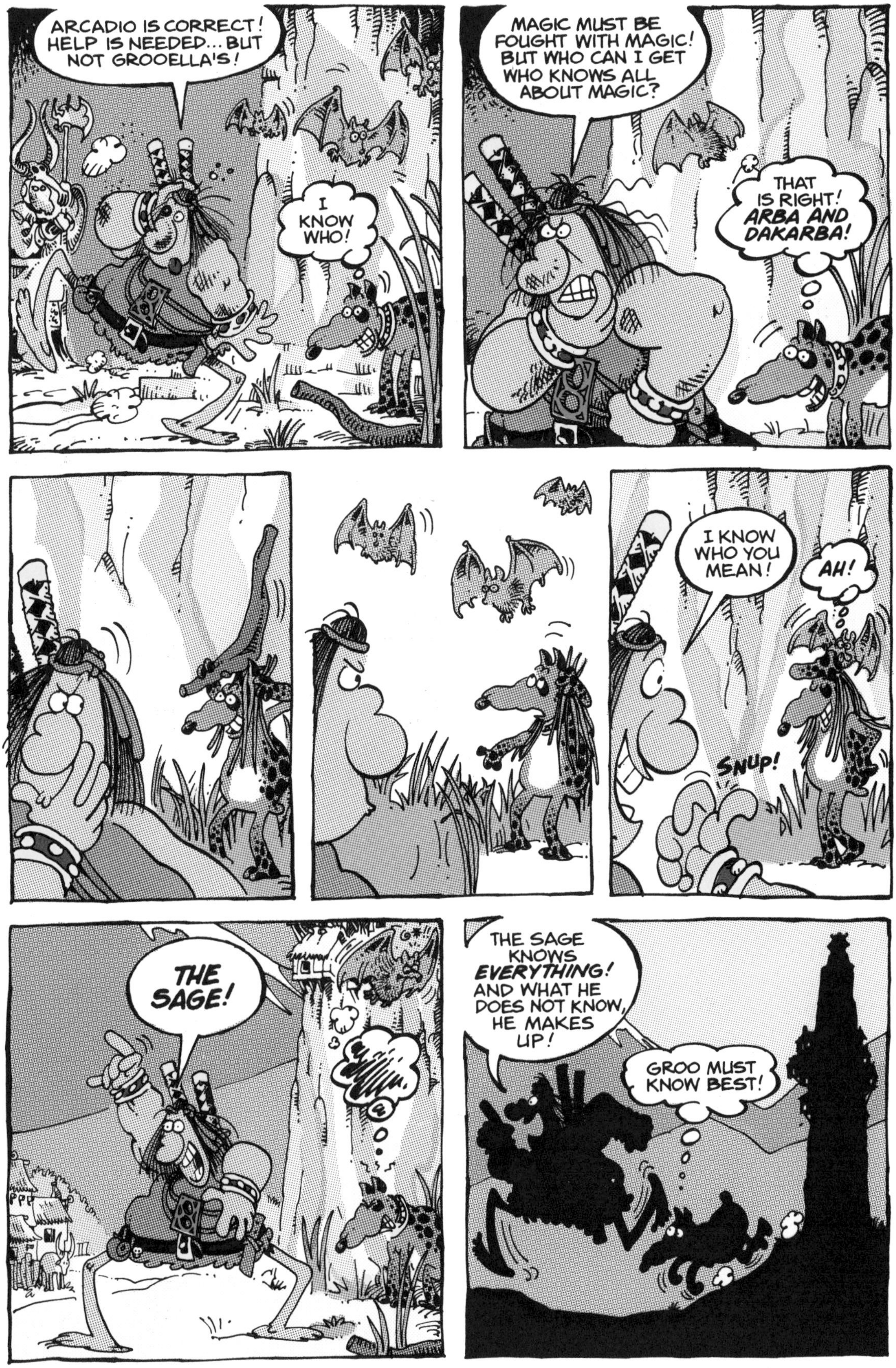
ARCADIO IS CORRECT! HELP IS NEEDED... BUT NOT GROOELLA'S!
I KNOW WHO!
MAGIC MUST BE FOUGHT WITH MAGIC! BUT WHO CAN I GET WHO KNOWS ALL ABOUT MAGIC?
THAT IS RIGHT! ARBA AND DAKARBA!
I KNOW WHO YOU MEAN!
AH!
SNUP!
THE SAGE!
THE SAGE KNOWS EVERYTHING! AND WHAT HE DOES NOT KNOW, HE MAKES UP!
GROO MUST KNOW BEST!

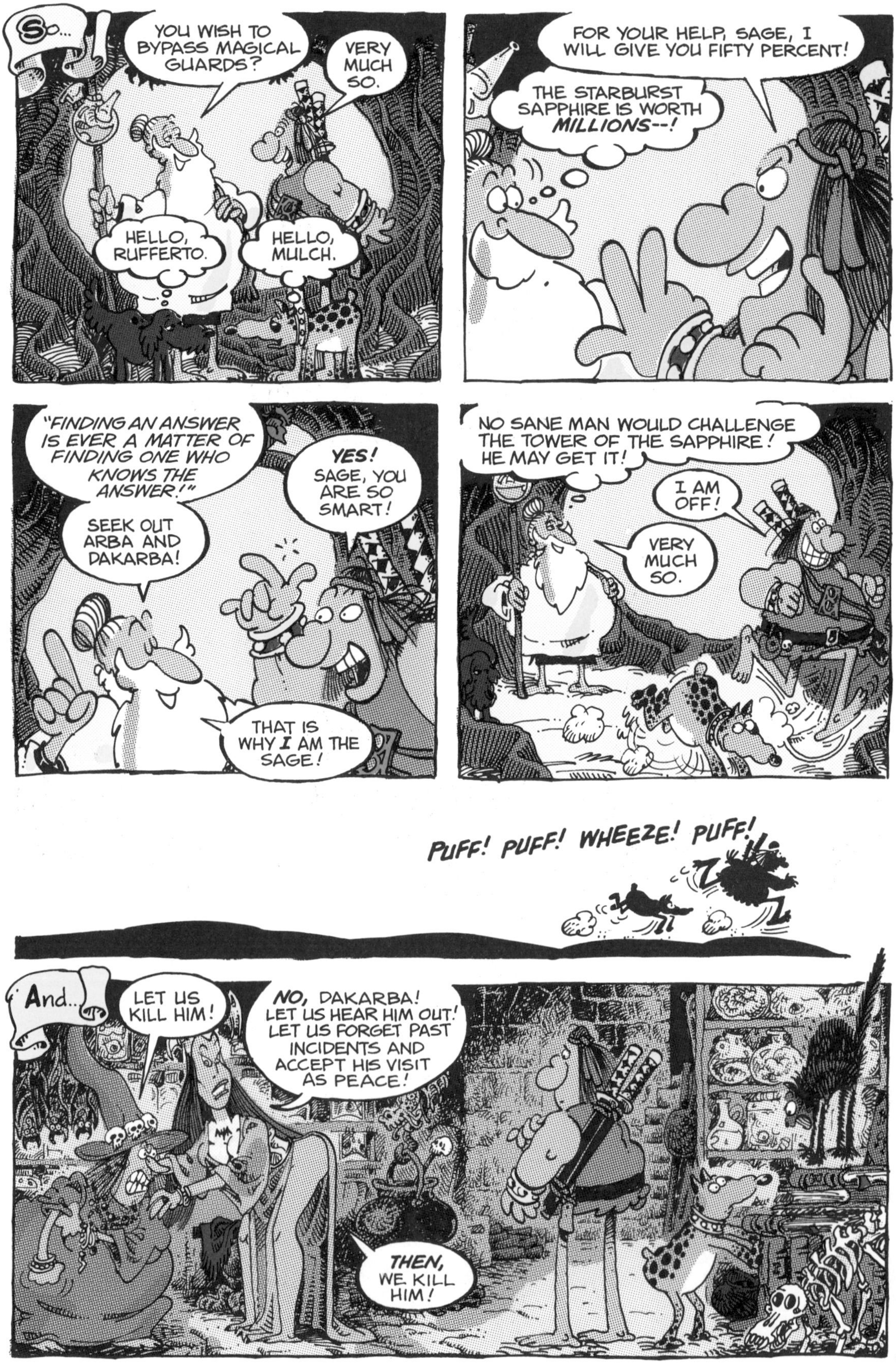
So...
YOU WISH TO BYPASS MAGICAL GUARDS?
VERY MUCH SO.
HELLO, RUFFERTO.
HELLO, MULCH.
FOR YOUR HELP, SAGE, I WILL GIVE YOU FIFTY PERCENT!
THE STARBURST SAPPHIRE IS WORTH MILLIONS--!
"FINDING AN ANSWER IS EVER A MATTER OF FINDING ONE WHO KNOWS THE ANSWER!"
SEEK OUT ARBA AND DAKARBA!
YES! SAGE, YOU ARE SO SMART!
THAT IS WHY I AM THE SAGE!
NO SANE MAN WOULD CHALLENGE THE TOWER OF THE SAPPHIRE! HE MAY GET IT!
I AM OFF!
VERY MUCH SO.
PUFF! PUFF! WHEEZE! PUFF!
And...
LET US KILL HIM!
NO, DAKARBA! LET US HEAR HIM OUT! LET US FORGET PAST INCIDENTS AND ACCEPT HIS VISIT AS PEACE!
THEN, WE KILL HIM!

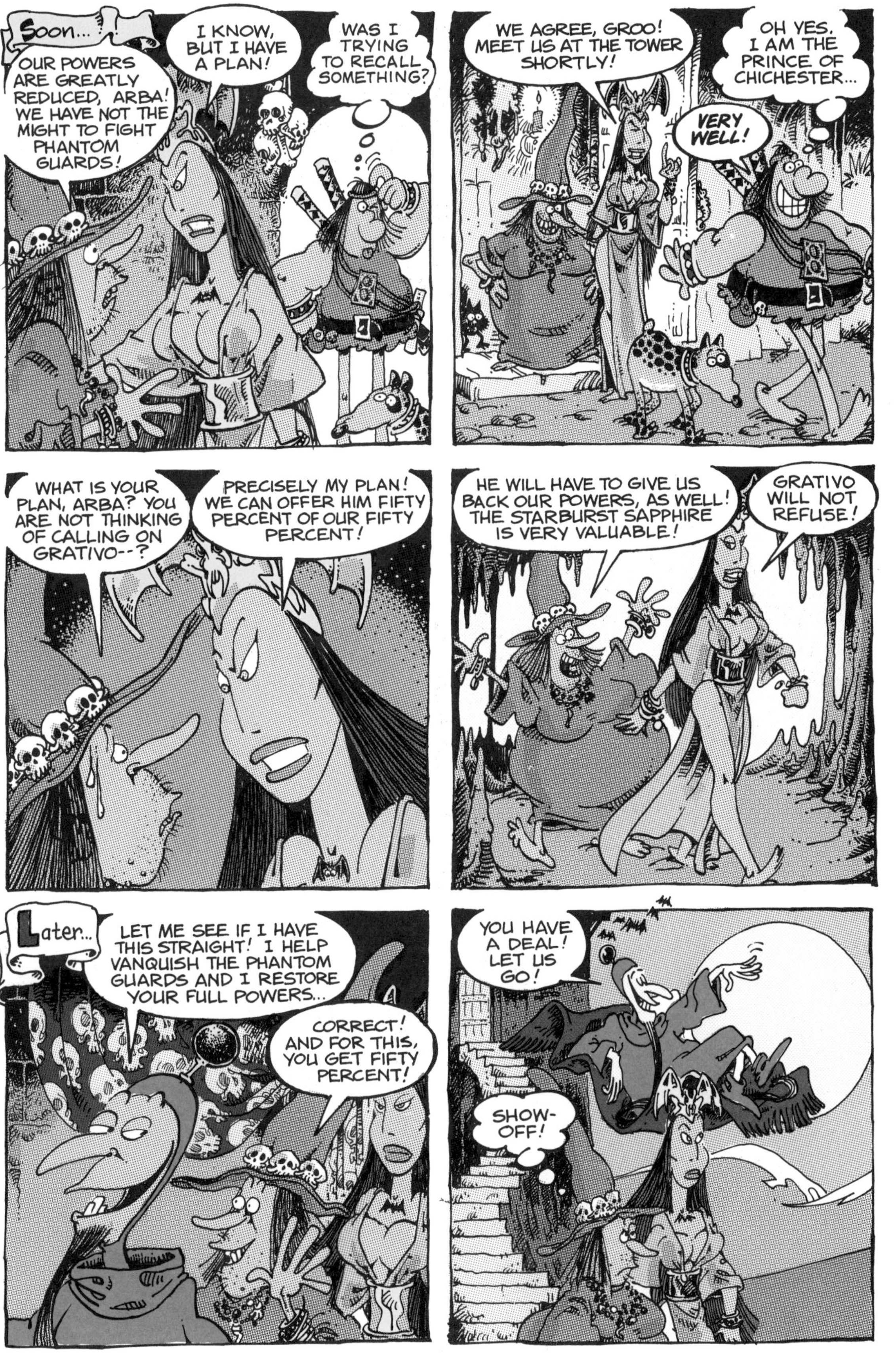
Soon...
OUR POWERS ARE GREATLY REDUCED, ARBA! WE HAVE NOT THE MIGHT TO FIGHT PHANTOM GUARDS!
I KNOW, BUT I HAVE A PLAN!
WAS I TRYING TO RECALL SOMETHING?
WE AGREE, GROO! MEET US AT THE TOWER SHORTLY!
OH YES. I AM THE PRINCE OF CHICHESTER...
VERY WELL!
WHAT IS YOUR PLAN, ARBA? YOU ARE NOT THINKING OF CALLING ON GRATIVO--?
PRECISELY MY PLAN! WE CAN OFFER HIM FIFTY PERCENT OF OUR FIFTY PERCENT!
HE WILL HAVE TO GIVE US BACK OUR POWERS, AS WELL! THE STARBURST SAPPHIRE IS VERY VALUABLE!
GRATIVO WILL NOT REFUSE!
Later...
LET ME SEE IF I HAVE THIS STRAIGHT! I HELP VANQUISH THE PHANTOM GUARDS AND I RESTORE YOUR FULL POWERS...
CORRECT! AND FOR THIS, YOU GET FIFTY PERCENT!
YOU HAVE A DEAL! LET US GO!
SHOW-OFF!

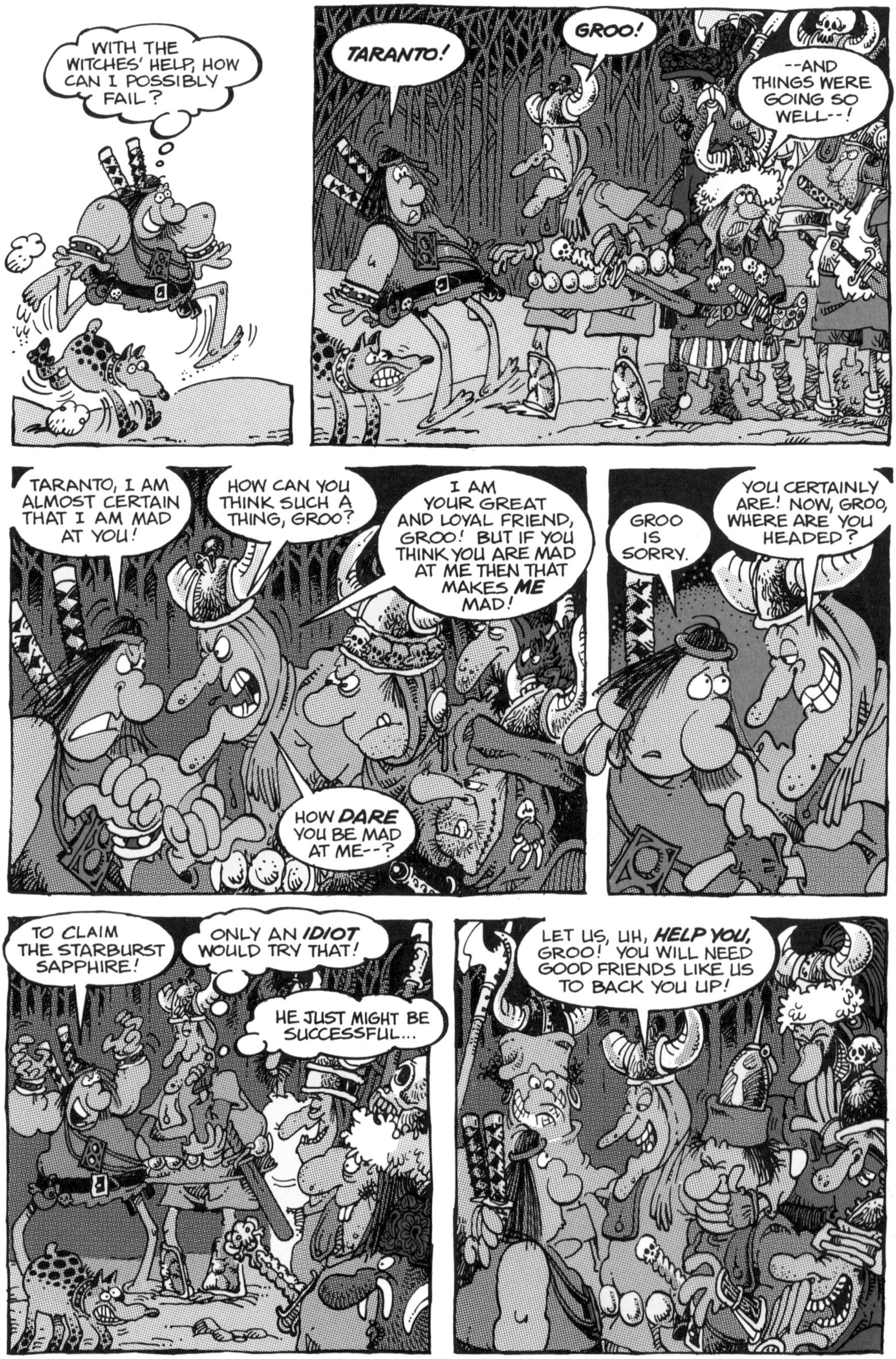
WITH THE WITCHES' HELP, HOW CAN I POSSIBLY FAIL?
TARANTO!
GROO!
--AND THINGS WERE GOING SO WELL--!
TARANTO, I AM ALMOST CERTAIN THAT I AM MAD AT YOU!
HOW CAN YOU THINK SUCH A THING, GROO?
HOW DARE YOU BE MAD AT ME--?
I AM YOUR GREAT AND LOYAL FRIEND, GROO! BUT IF YOU THINK YOU ARE MAD AT ME THEN THAT MAKES ME MAD!
GROO IS SORRY.
YOU CERTAINLY ARE! NOW, GROO, WHERE ARE YOU HEADED?
TO CLAIM THE STARBURST SAPPHIRE!
ONLY AN IDIOT WOULD TRY THAT!
HE JUST MIGHT BE SUCCESSFUL...
LET US, UH, HELP YOU, GROO! YOU WILL NEED GOOD FRIENDS LIKE US TO BACK YOU UP!

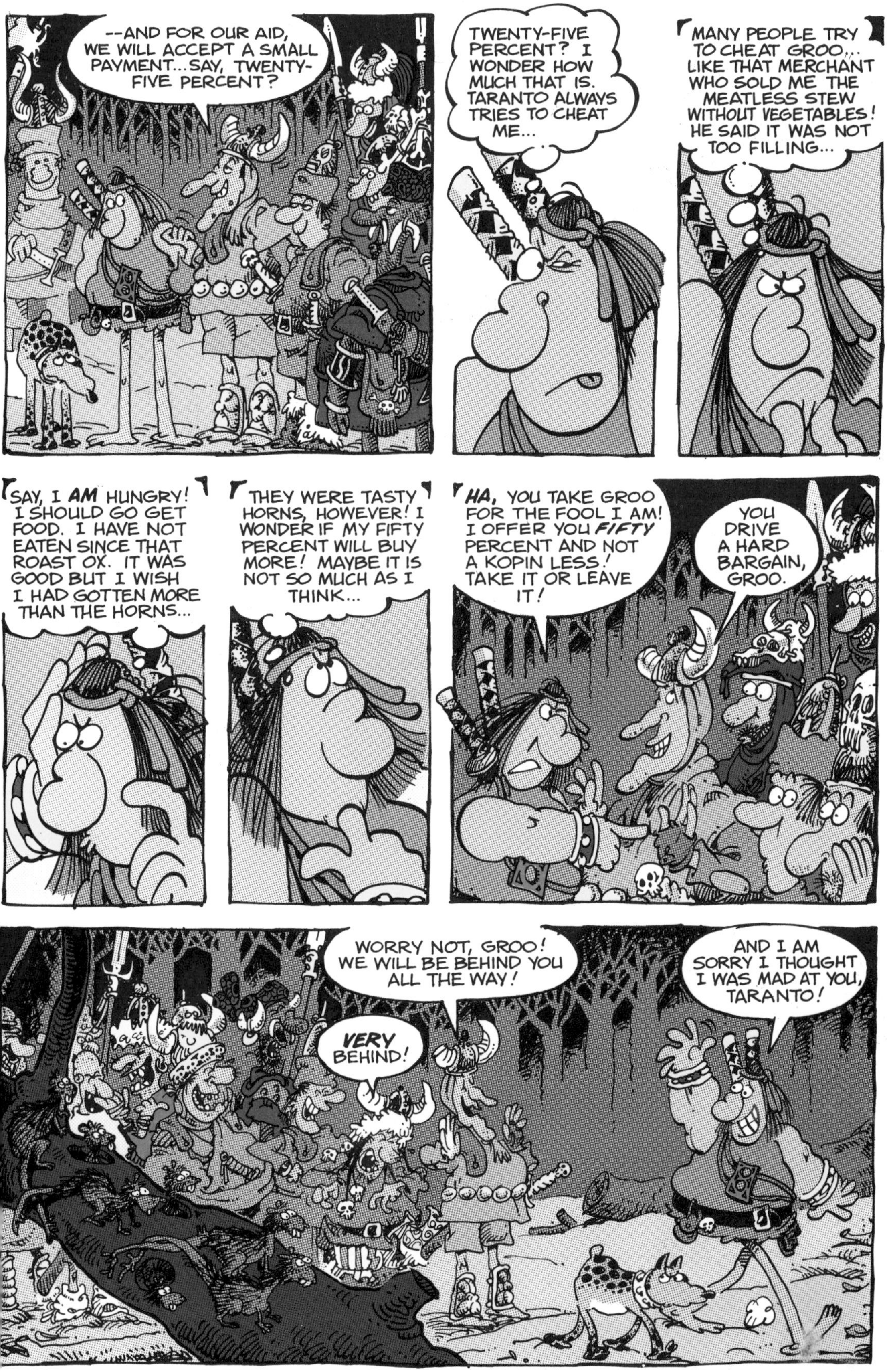
--AND FOR OUR AID, WE WILL ACCEPT A SMALL PAYMENT...SAY, TWENTY-FIVE PERCENT?
TWENTY-FIVE PERCENT? I WONDER HOW MUCH THAT IS. TARANTO ALWAYS TRIES TO CHEAT ME...
MANY PEOPLE TRY TO CHEAT GROO... LIKE THAT MERCHANT WHO SOLD ME THE MEATLESS STEW WITHOUT VEGETABLES! HE SAID IT WAS NOT TOO FILLING...
SAY, I AM HUNGRY! I SHOULD GO GET FOOD. I HAVE NOT EATEN SINCE THAT ROAST OX. IT WAS GOOD BUT I WISH I HAD GOTTEN MORE THAN THE HORNS...
THEY WERE TASTY HORNS, HOWEVER! I WONDER IF MY FIFTY PERCENT WILL BUY MORE! MAYBE IT IS NOT SO MUCH AS I THINK...
HA, YOU TAKE GROO FOR THE FOOL I AM! I OFFER YOU FIFTY PERCENT AND NOT A KOPIN LESS! TAKE IT OR LEAVE IT!
YOU DRIVE A HARD BARGAIN, GROO.
WORRY NOT, GROO! WE WILL BE BEHIND YOU ALL THE WAY!
VERY BEHIND!
AND I AM SORRY I THOUGHT I WAS MAD AT YOU, TARANTO!

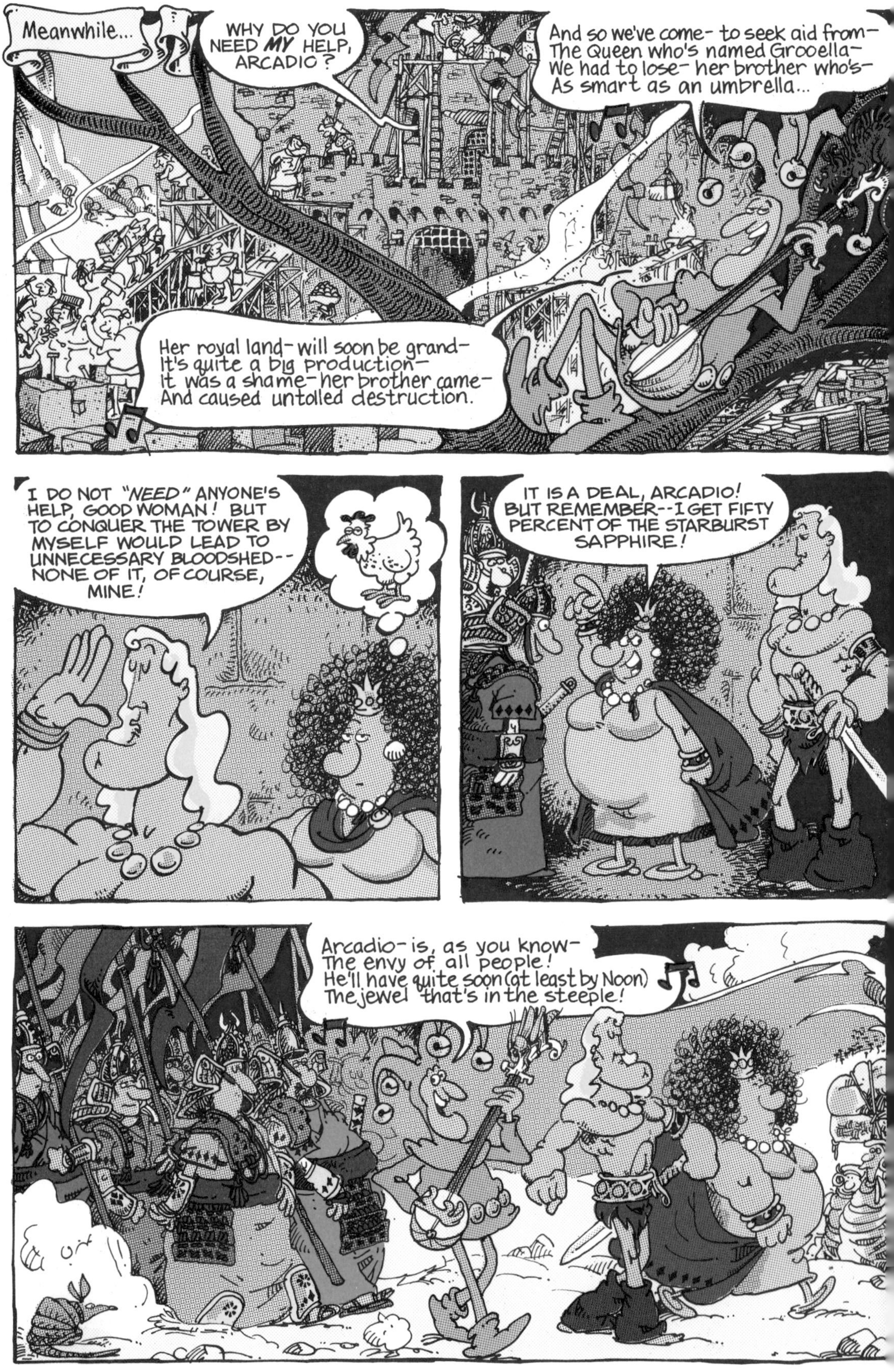
Meanwhile...
WHY DO YOU NEED MY HELP, ARCADIO?
And so we've come- to seek aid from- The Queen who's named Grooella- We had to lose- her brother who's- As smart as an umbrella...
Her royal land- will soon be grand- It's quite a big production- It was a shame- her brother came- And caused untolled destruction.
I DO NOT "NEED" ANYONE'S HELP, GOOD WOMAN! BUT TO CONQUER THE TOWER BY MYSELF WOULD LEAD TO UNNECESSARY BLOODSHED-- NONE OF IT, OF COURSE, MINE!
IT IS A DEAL, ARCADIO! BUT REMEMBER--I GET FIFTY PERCENT OF THE STARBURST SAPPHIRE!
Arcadio- is, as you know- The envy of all people! He'll have quite soon (at least by Noon) The jewel that's in the steeple!

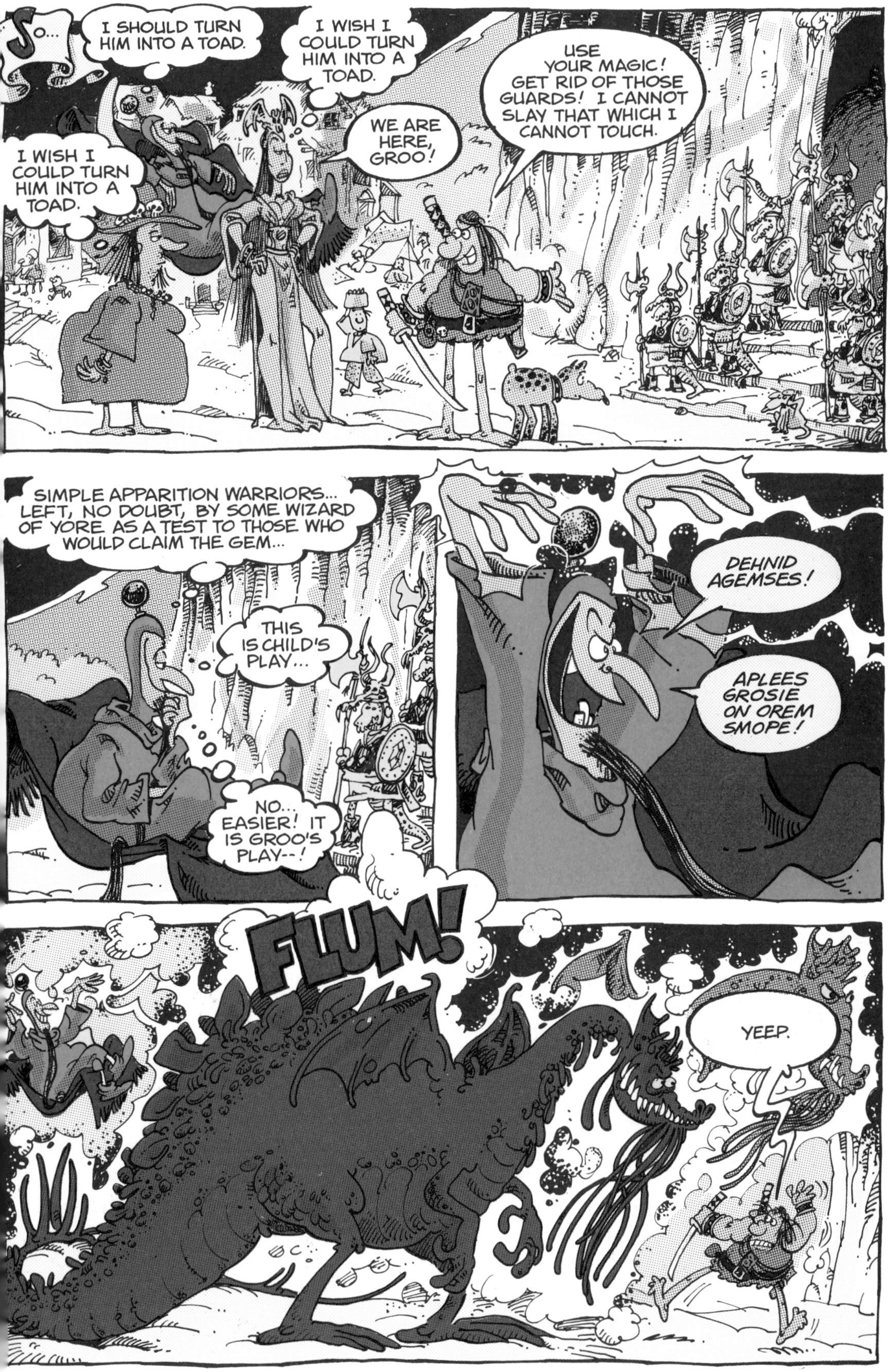

SO...
I SHOULD TURN HIM INTO A TOAD.
I WISH I COULD TURN HIM INTO A TOAD.
I WISH I COULD TURN HIM INTO A TOAD.
WE ARE HERE, GROO!
USE YOUR MAGIC! GET RID OF THOSE GUARDS! I CANNOT SLAY THAT WHICH I CANNOT TOUCH.
SIMPLE APPARITION WARRIORS... LEFT, NO DOUBT, BY SOME WIZARD OF YORE AS A TEST TO THOSE WHO WOULD CLAIM THE GEM...
THIS IS CHILD'S PLAY...
NO... EASIER! IT IS GROO'S PLAY--!
DEHNID AGEMSES!
APLEES GROSIE ON OREM SMOPE!
FLUM!
YEEP.

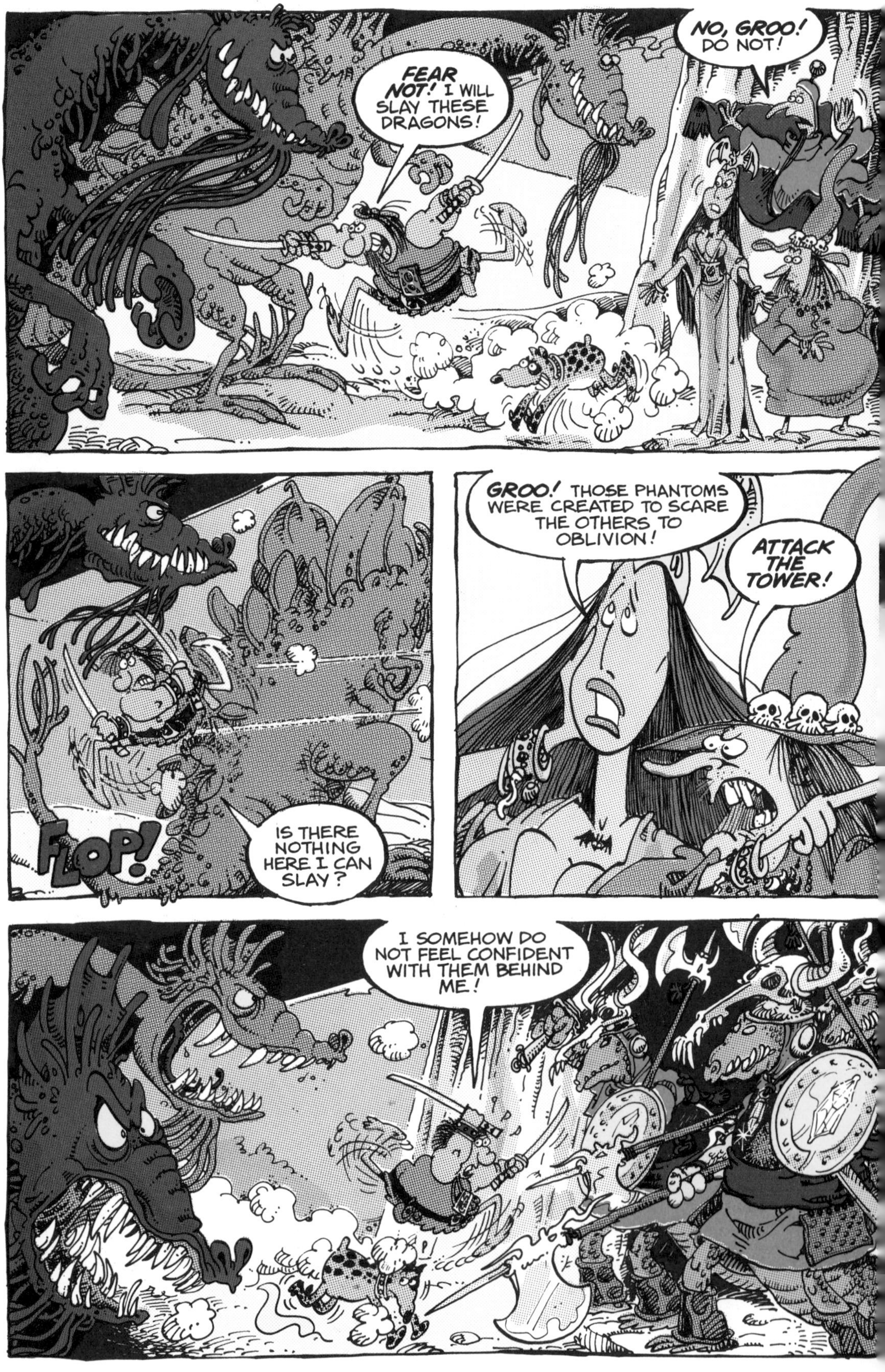
FEAR NOT! I WILL SLAY THESE DRAGONS!
NO, GROO! DO NOT!
IS THERE NOTHING HERE I CAN SLAY?
FLOP!
GROO! THOSE PHANTOMS WERE CREATED TO SCARE THE OTHERS TO OBLIVION!
ATTACK THE TOWER!
I SOMEHOW DO NOT FEEL CONFIDENT WITH THEM BEHIND ME!

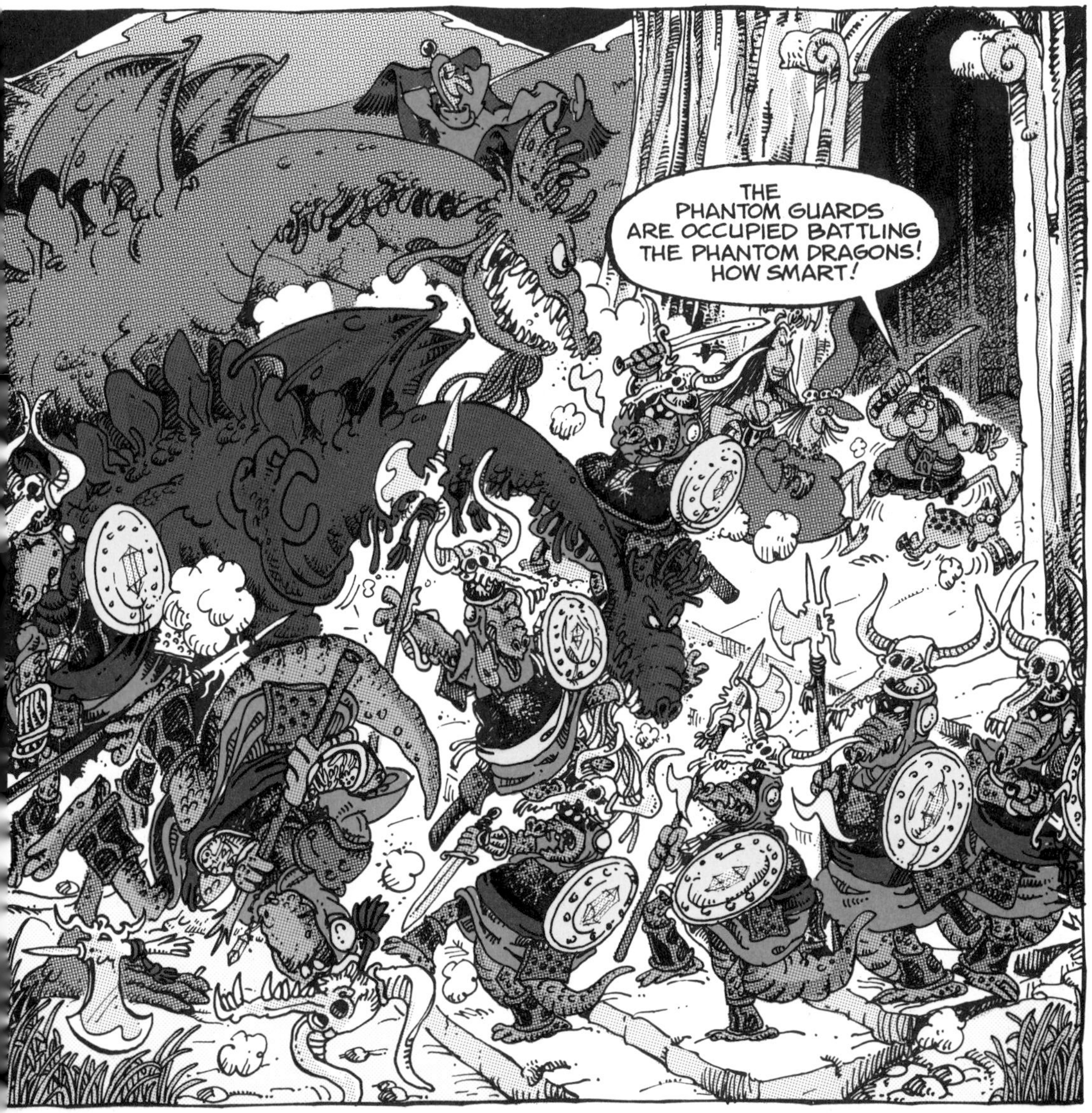
THE PHANTOM GUARDS ARE OCCUPIED BATTLING THE PHANTOM DRAGONS! HOW SMART!

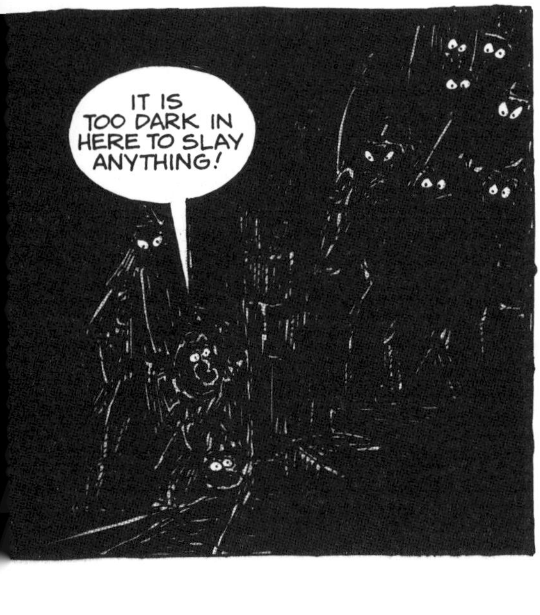
IT IS TOO DARK IN HERE TO SLAY ANYTHING!

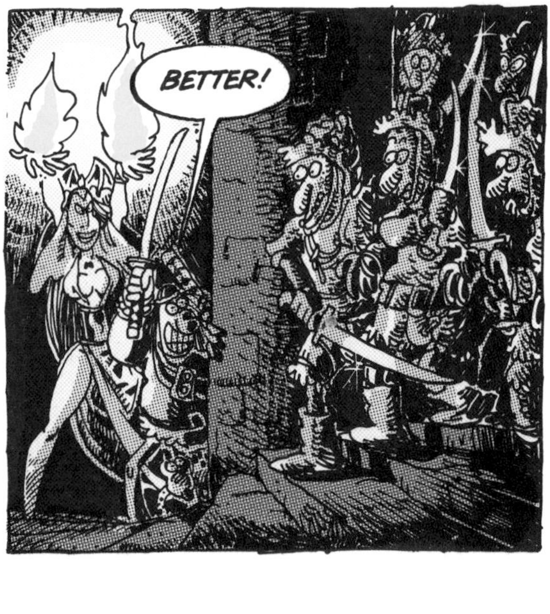
BETTER!

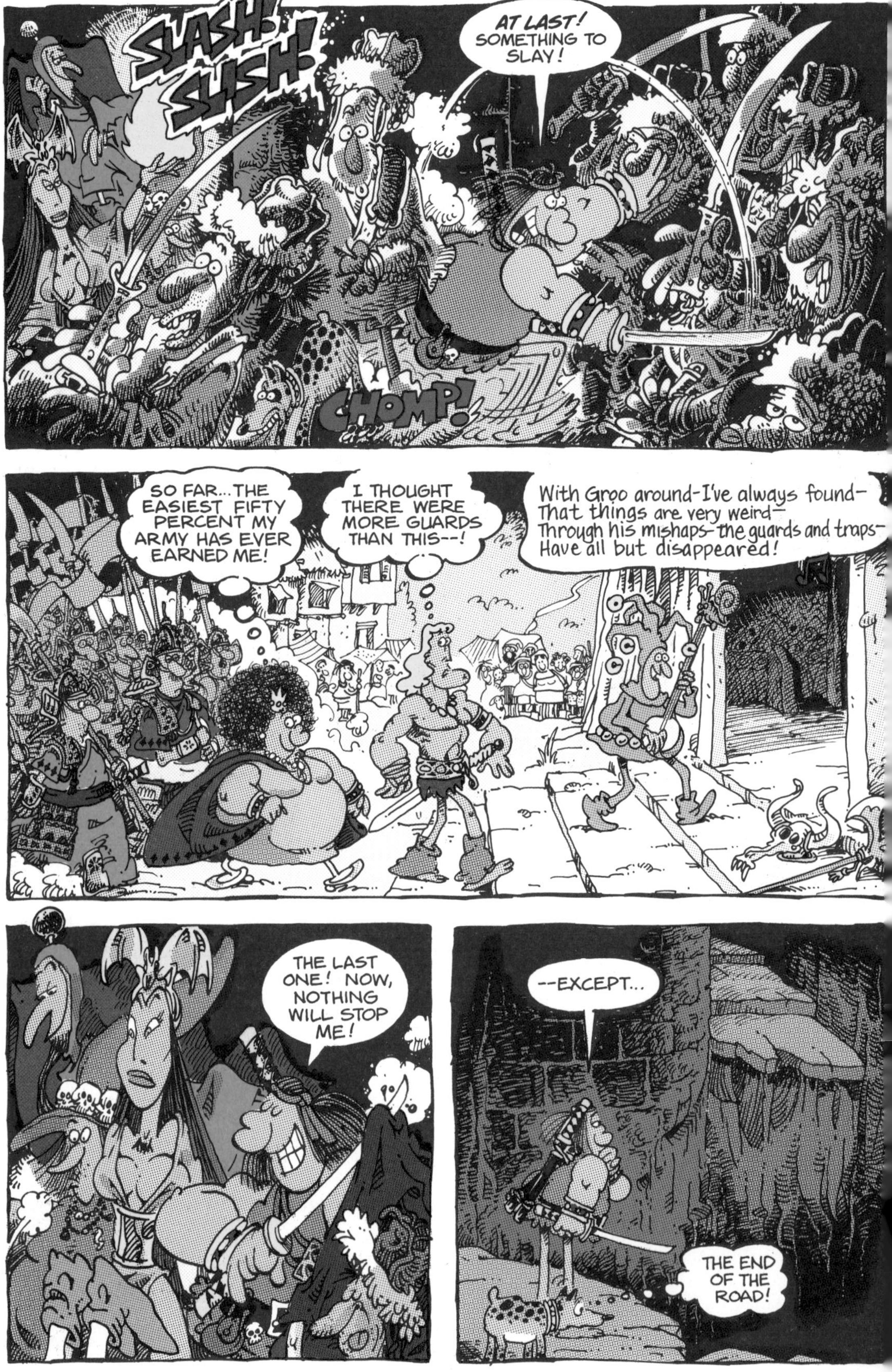
SLASH! SLISH!
AT LAST! SOMETHING TO SLAY!
CHOMP!
SO FAR... THE EASIEST FIFTY PERCENT MY ARMY HAS EVER EARNED ME!
I THOUGHT THERE WERE MORE GUARDS THAN THIS--!
With Groo around-I've always found-
That things are very weird-
Through his mishaps-the guards and traps-
Have all but disappeared!
THE LAST ONE! NOW, NOTHING WILL STOP ME!
--EXCEPT...
THE END OF THE ROAD!

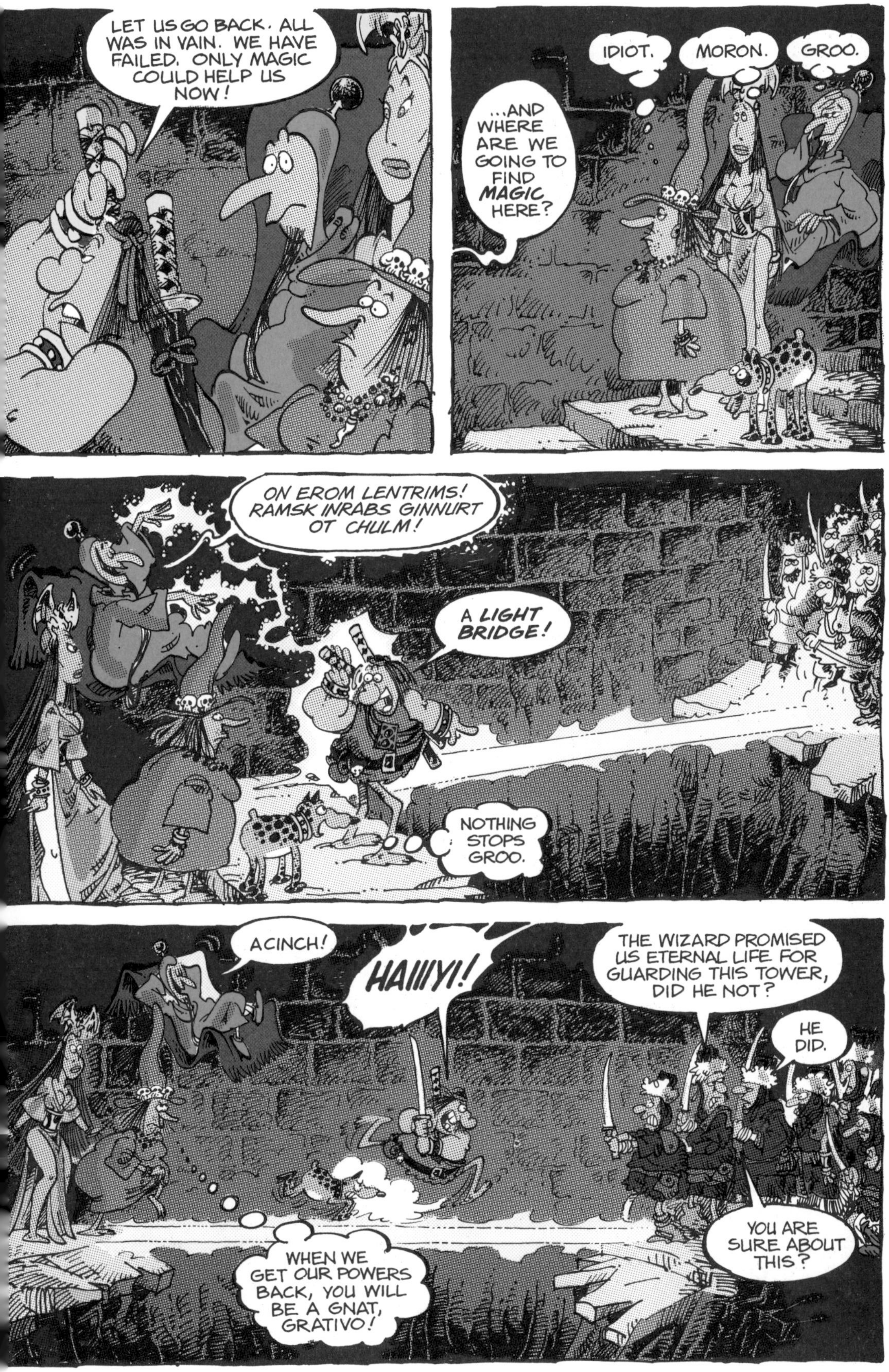
LET US GO BACK. ALL WAS IN VAIN. WE HAVE FAILED. ONLY MAGIC COULD HELP US NOW!
IDIOT.
MORON.
GROO.
...AND WHERE ARE WE GOING TO FIND MAGIC HERE?
ON EROM LENTRIMS! RAMSK INRABS GINNURT OT CHULM!
A LIGHT BRIDGE!
NOTHING STOPS GROO.
ACINCH!
HAIIIYI!
THE WIZARD PROMISED US ETERNAL LIFE FOR GUARDING THIS TOWER, DID HE NOT?
HE DID.
YOU ARE SURE ABOUT THIS?
WHEN WE GET OUR POWERS BACK, YOU WILL BE A GNAT, GRATIVO!

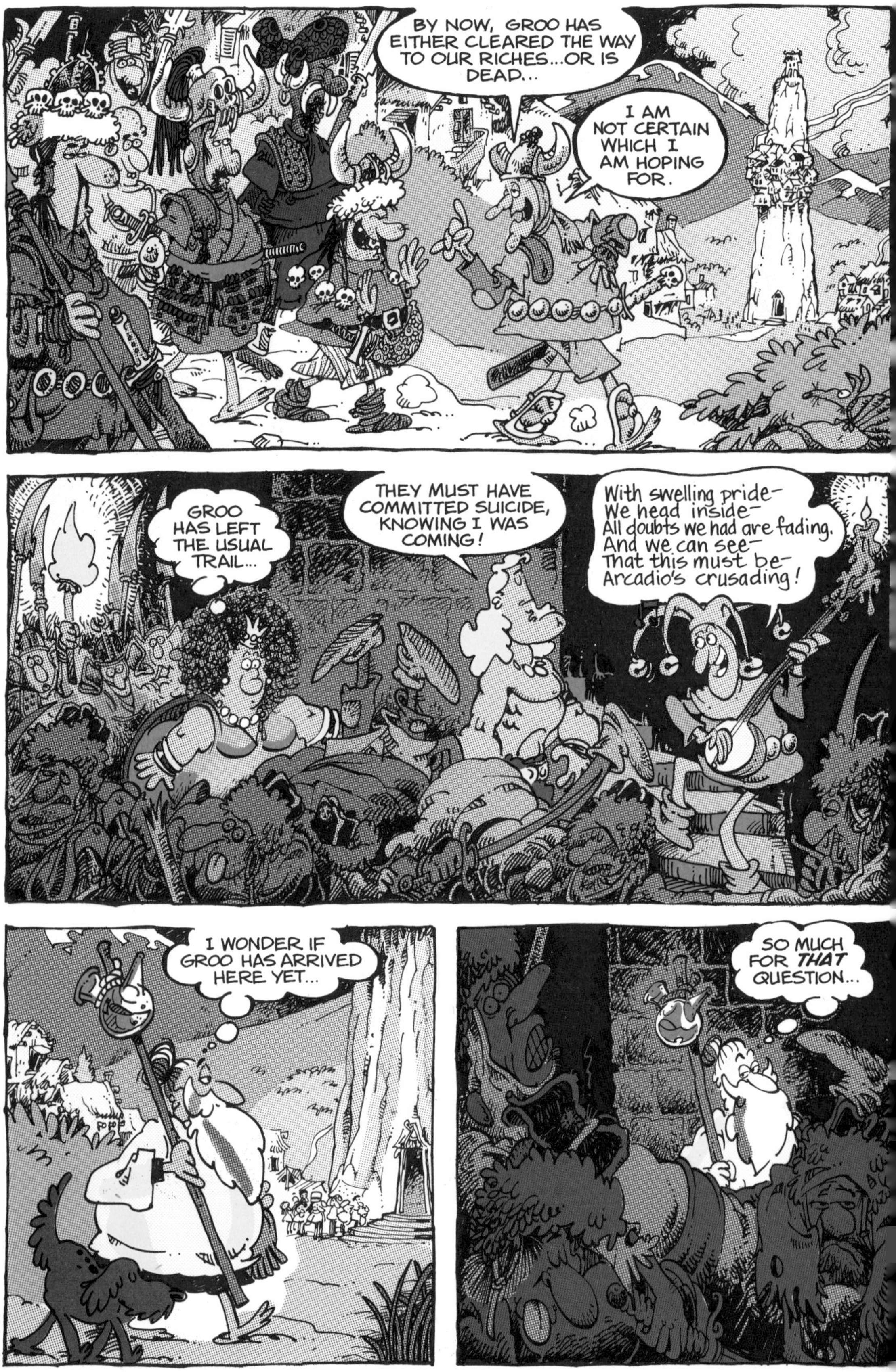
BY NOW, GROO HAS EITHER CLEARED THE WAY TO OUR RICHES...OR IS DEAD...
I AM NOT CERTAIN WHICH I AM HOPING FOR.
GROO HAS LEFT THE USUAL TRAIL...
THEY MUST HAVE COMMITTED SUICIDE, KNOWING I WAS COMING!
With swelling pride- We head inside- All doubts we had are fading. And we can see- That this must be- Arcadio's crusading!
I WONDER IF GROO HAS ARRIVED HERE YET...
SO MUCH FOR THAT QUESTION...

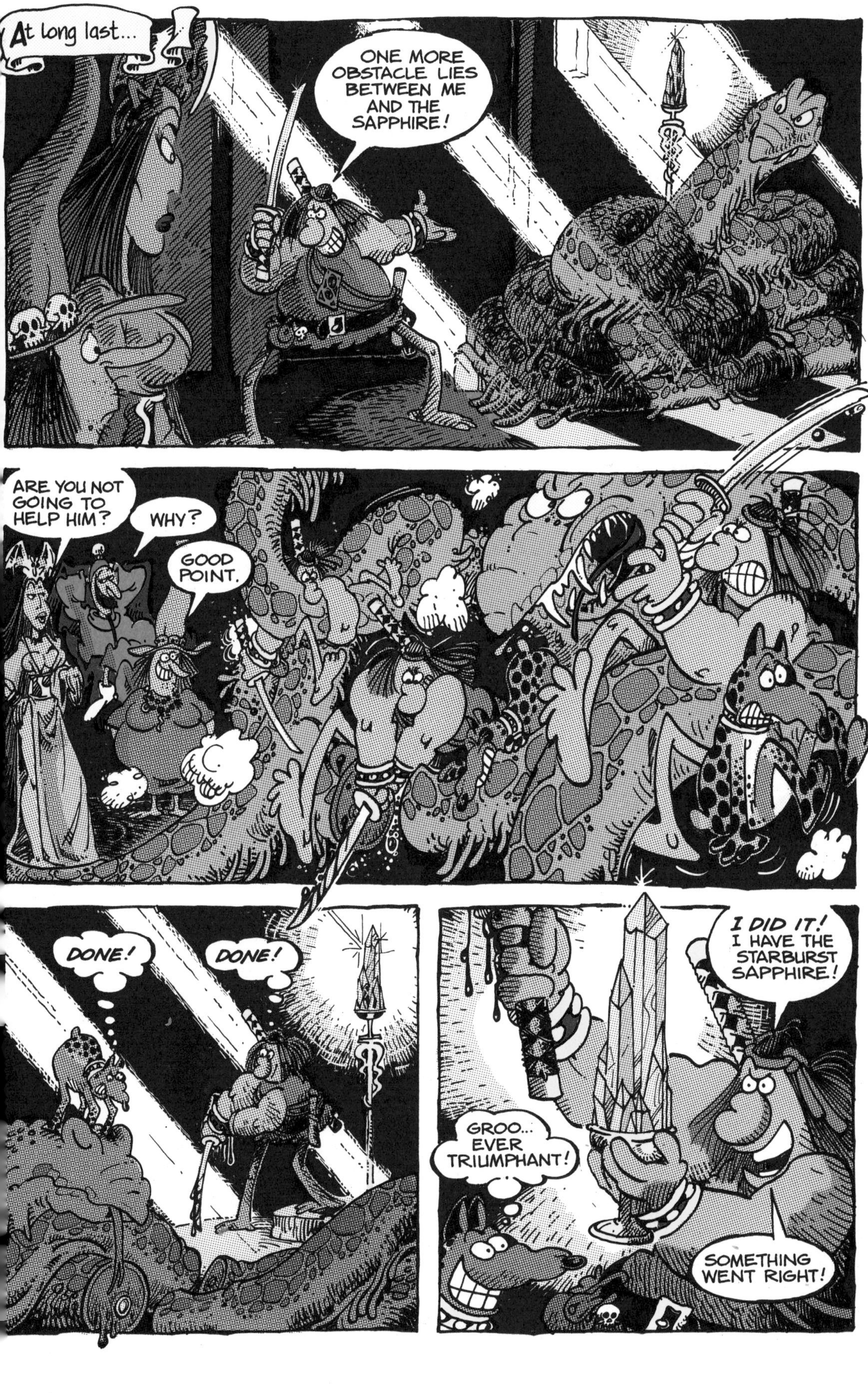
At long last...
ONE MORE OBSTACLE LIES BETWEEN ME AND THE SAPPHIRE!
ARE YOU NOT GOING TO HELP HIM?
WHY?
GOOD POINT.
DONE!
DONE!
I DID IT! I HAVE THE STARBURST SAPPHIRE!
GROO... EVER TRIUMPHANT!
SOMETHING WENT RIGHT!

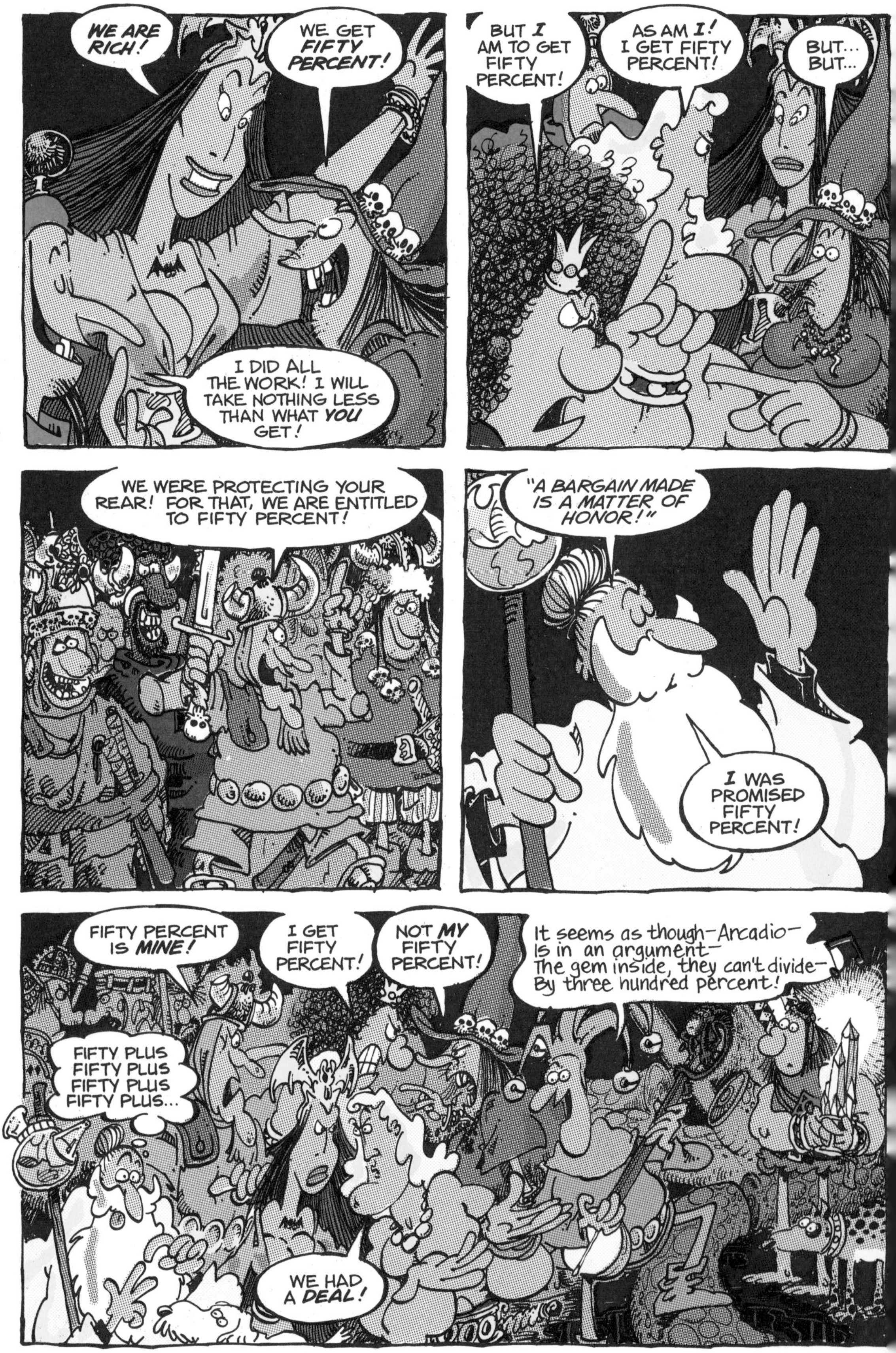
WE ARE RICH!
WE GET FIFTY PERCENT!
I DID ALL THE WORK! I WILL TAKE NOTHING LESS THAN WHAT YOU GET!
BUT I AM TO GET FIFTY PERCENT!
AS AM I! I GET FIFTY PERCENT!
BUT... BUT...
WE WERE PROTECTING YOUR REAR! FOR THAT, WE ARE ENTITLED TO FIFTY PERCENT!
"A BARGAIN MADE IS A MATTER OF HONOR!"
I WAS PROMISED FIFTY PERCENT!
FIFTY PERCENT IS MINE!
I GET FIFTY PERCENT!
NOT MY FIFTY PERCENT!
It seems as though-Arcadio-
Is in an argument-
The gem inside, they can't divide-
By three hundred percent!
FIFTY PLUS FIFTY PLUS FIFTY PLUS FIFTY PLUS...
WE HAD A DEAL!

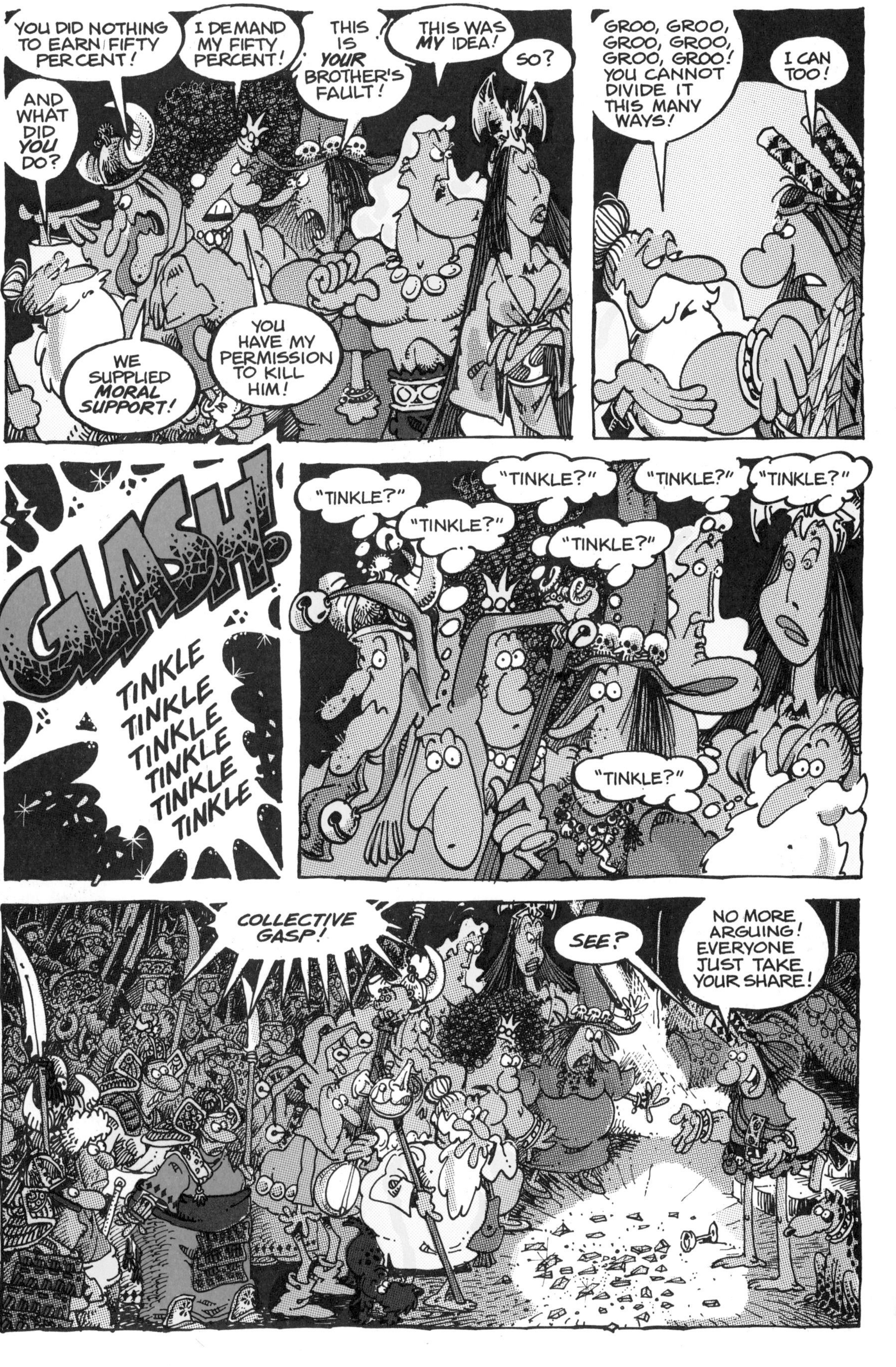

YOU DID NOTHING TO EARN FIFTY PERCENT!
I DEMAND MY FIFTY PERCENT!
THIS IS *YOUR* BROTHER'S FAULT!
THIS WAS *MY* IDEA!
SO?
AND WHAT DID *YOU* DO?
WE SUPPLIED *MORAL SUPPORT*!
YOU HAVE MY PERMISSION TO KILL HIM!
GROO, GROO, GROO, GROO, GROO, GROO! YOU CANNOT DIVIDE IT THIS MANY WAYS!
I CAN TOO!
CLASH!
TINKLE TINKLE TINKLE TINKLE TINKLE TINKLE
"TINKLE?"
"TINKLE?"
"TINKLE?"
"TINKLE?"
"TINKLE?"
"TINKLE?"
"TINKLE?"
COLLECTIVE GASP!
SEE?
NO MORE ARGUING! EVERYONE JUST TAKE YOUR SHARE!

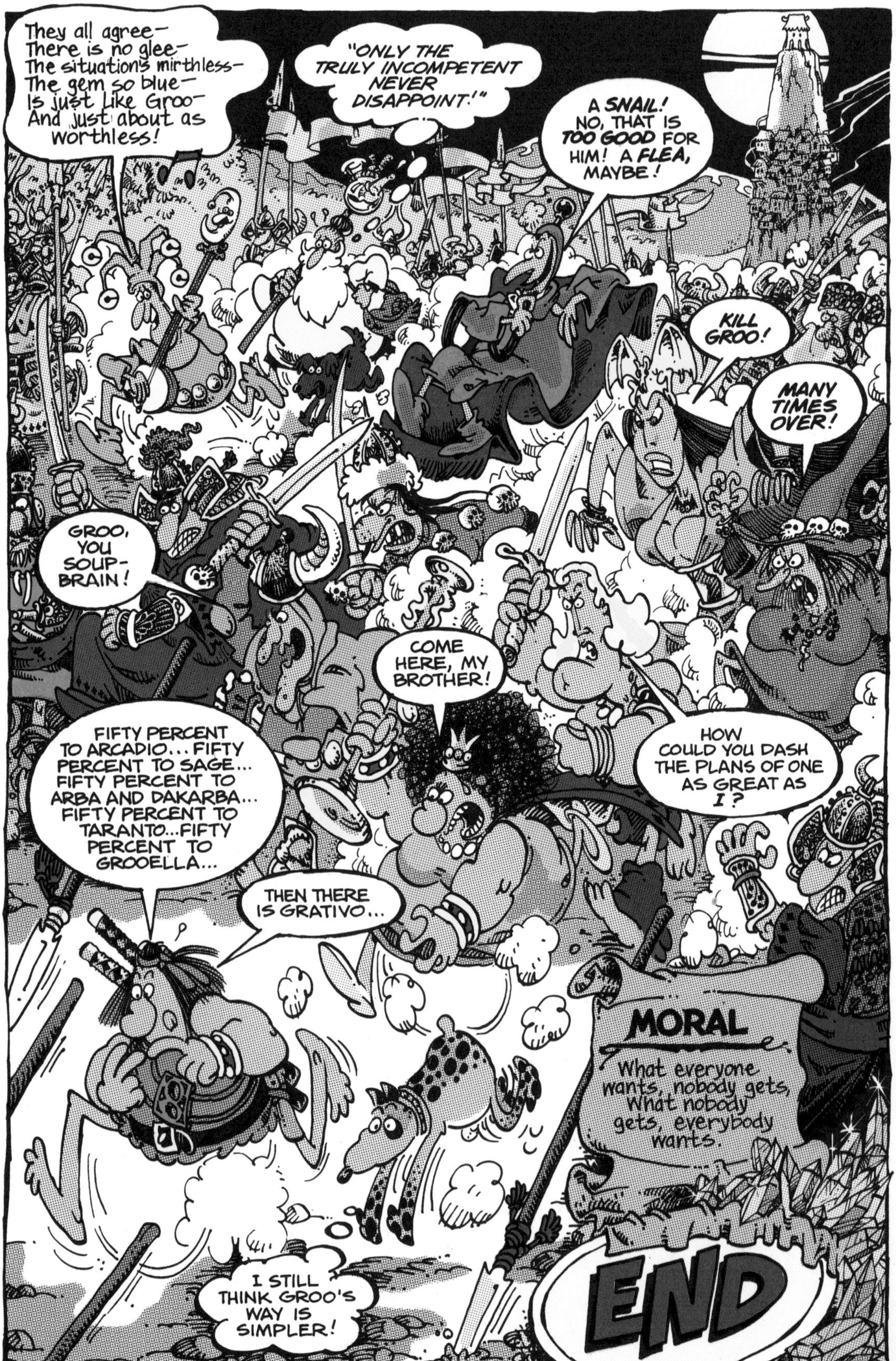
They all agree—
There is no glee—
The situation's mirthless—
The gem so blue—
Is just like Groo—
And just about as
worthless!
"ONLY THE
TRULY INCOMPETENT
NEVER
DISAPPOINT!"
A SNAIL!
NO, THAT IS
TOO GOOD FOR
HIM! A FLEA,
MAYBE!
KILL
GROO!
MANY
TIMES
OVER!
GROO,
YOU
SOUP-
BRAIN!
COME
HERE, MY
BROTHER!
FIFTY PERCENT
TO ARCADIO... FIFTY
PERCENT TO SAGE...
FIFTY PERCENT TO
ARBA AND DAKARBA...
FIFTY PERCENT TO
TARANTO... FIFTY
PERCENT TO
GROOELLA...
HOW
COULD YOU DASH
THE PLANS OF ONE
AS GREAT AS
I?
THEN THERE
IS GRATIVO...
MORAL
What everyone
wants, nobody gets,
What nobody
gets, everybody
wants.
I STILL
THINK GROO'S
WAY IS
SIMPLER!
END

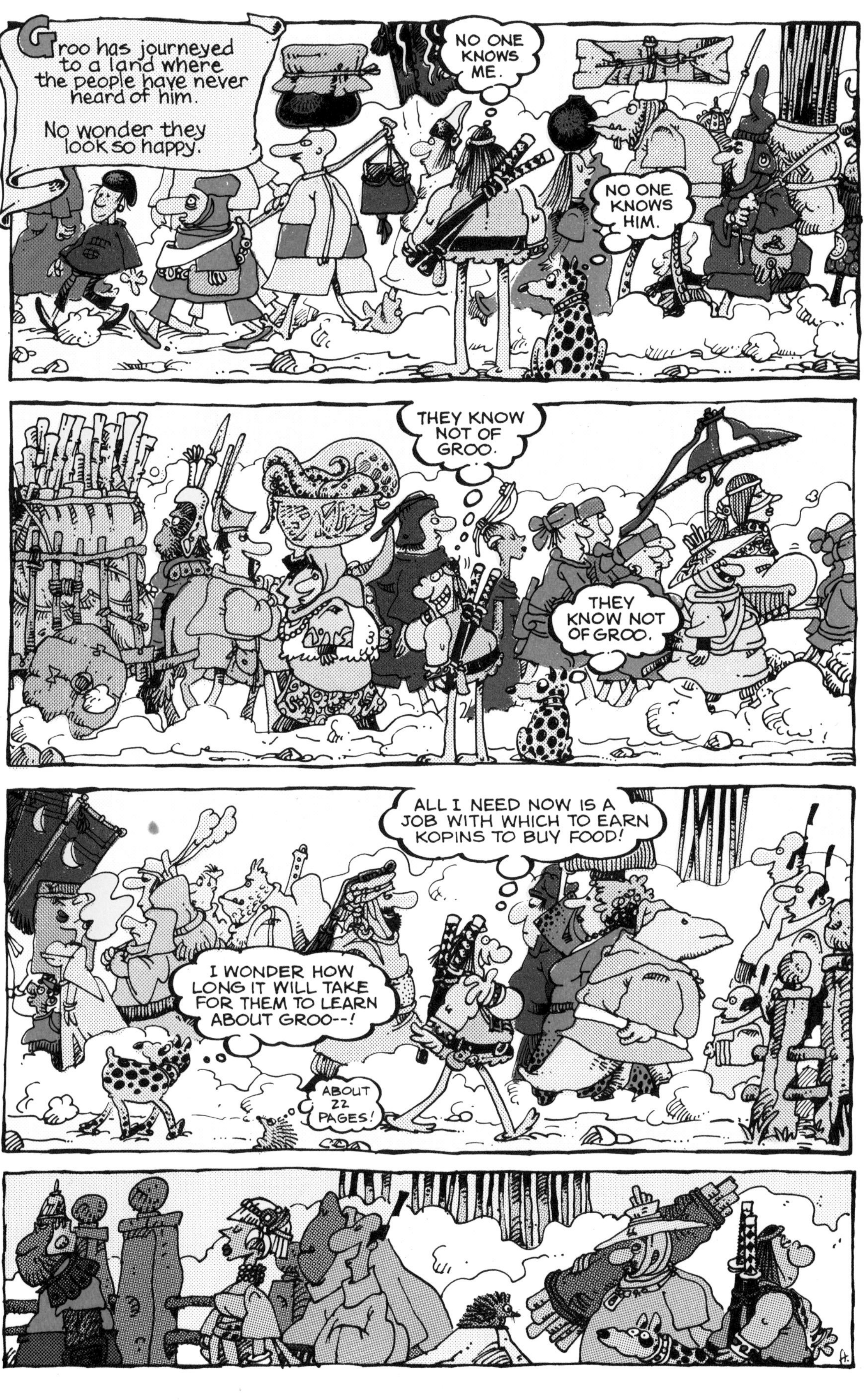
Groo has journeyed to a land where the people have never heard of him.
No wonder they look so happy.
NO ONE KNOWS ME.
NO ONE KNOWS HIM.
THEY KNOW NOT OF GROO.
THEY KNOW NOT OF GROO.
ALL I NEED NOW IS A JOB WITH WHICH TO EARN KOPINS TO BUY FOOD!
I WONDER HOW LONG IT WILL TAKE FOR THEM TO LEARN ABOUT GROO--!
ABOUT 22 PAGES!

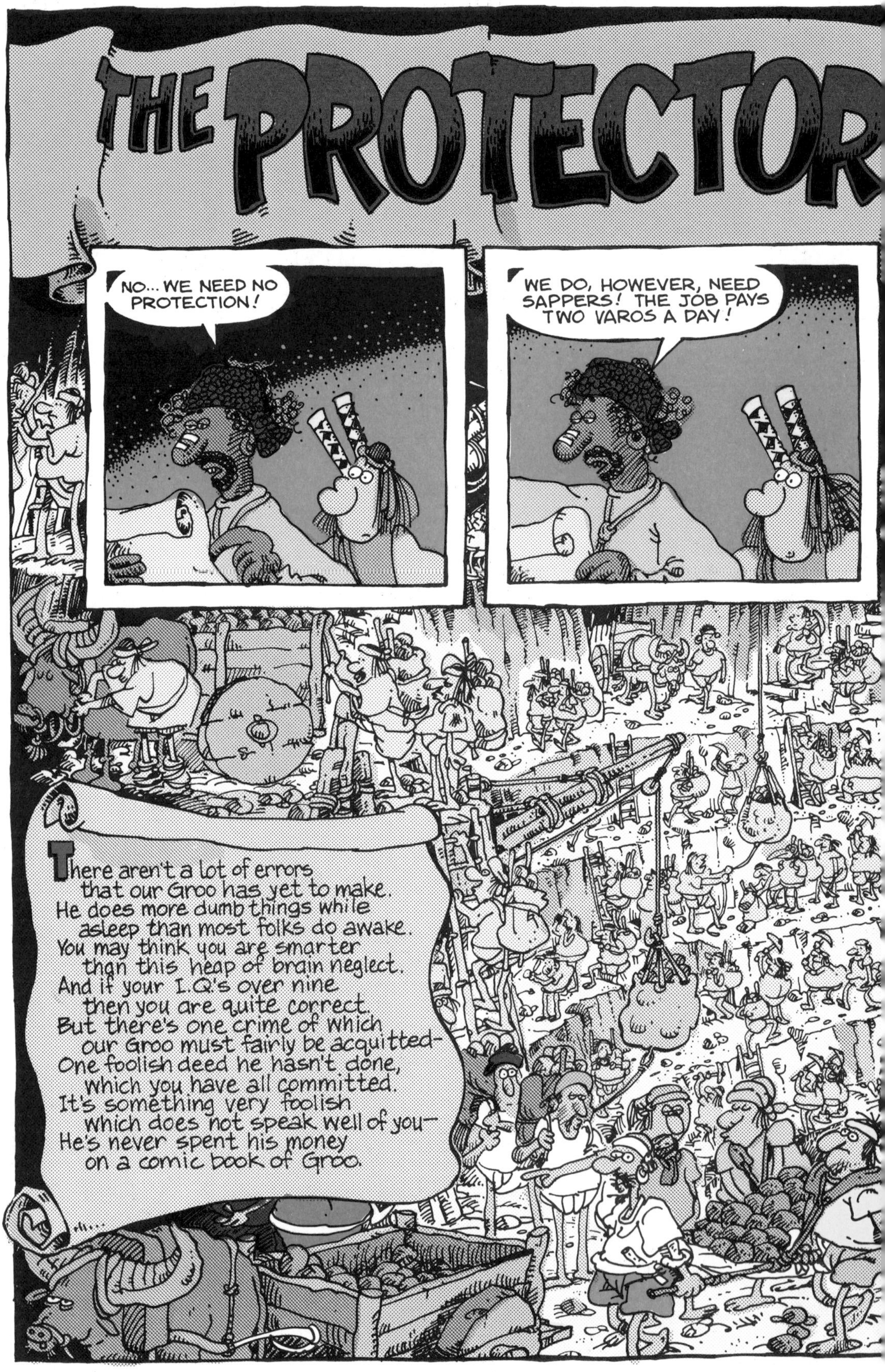
THE PROTECTOR
NO... WE NEED NO PROTECTION!
WE DO, HOWEVER, NEED SAPPERS! THE JOB PAYS TWO VAROS A DAY!
There aren't a lot of errors
that our Groo has yet to make.
He does more dumb things while
asleep than most folks do awake.
You may think you are smarter
than this heap of brain neglect.
And if your I.Q's over nine
then you are quite correct.
But there's one crime of which
our Groo must fairly be acquitted-
One foolish deed he hasn't done,
which you have all committed.
It's something very foolish
which does not speak well of you-
He's never spent his money
on a comic book of Groo.

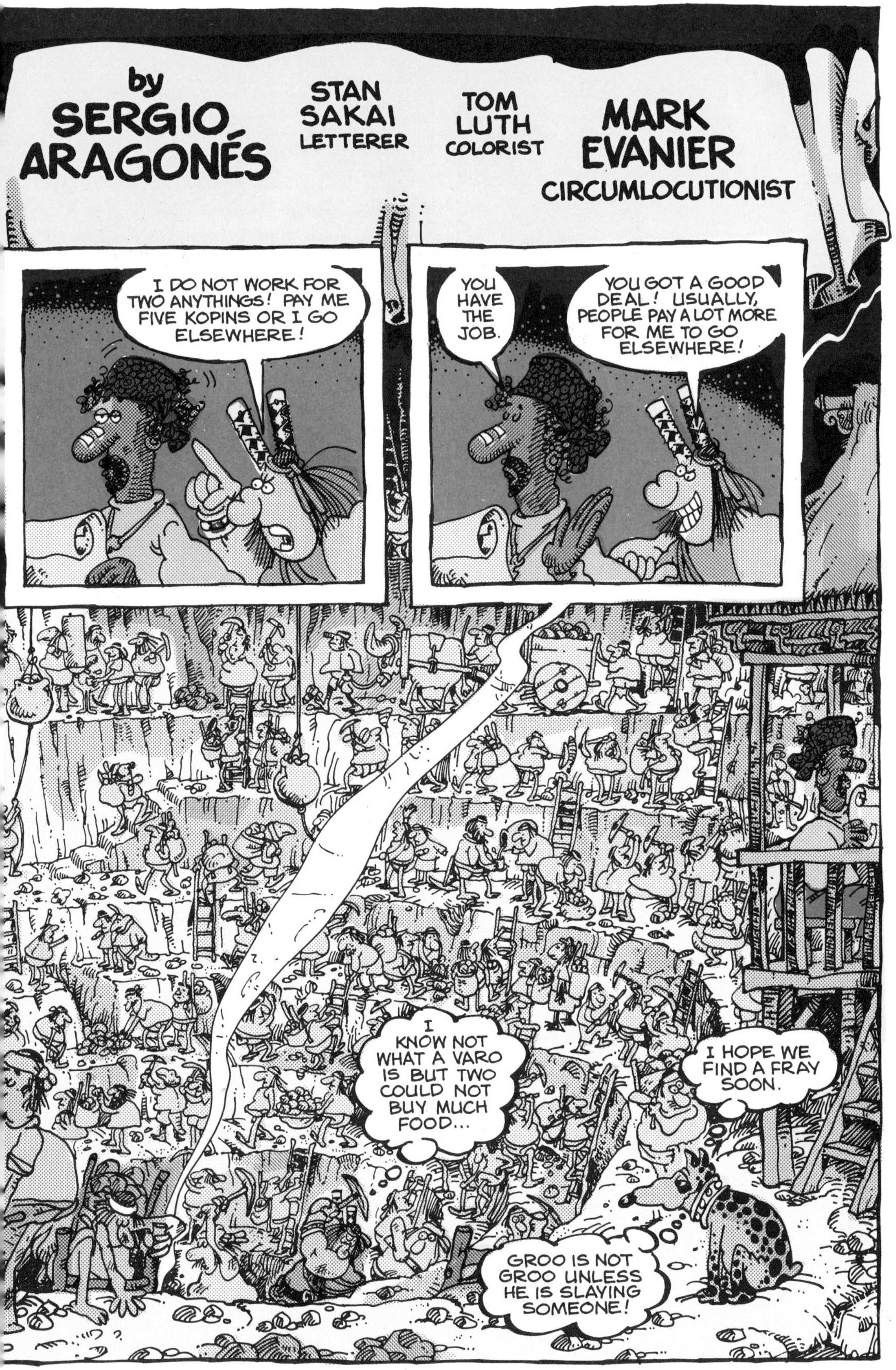
by
SERGIO ARAGONÉS
STAN SAKAI
LETTERER
TOM LUTH
COLORIST
MARK EVANIER
CIRCUMLOCUTIONIST
I DO NOT WORK FOR TWO ANYTHINGS! PAY ME FIVE KOPINS OR I GO ELSEWHERE!
YOU HAVE THE JOB.
YOU GOT A GOOD DEAL! USUALLY, PEOPLE PAY A LOT MORE FOR ME TO GO ELSEWHERE!
I KNOW NOT WHAT A VARO IS BUT TWO COULD NOT BUY MUCH FOOD...
I HOPE WE FIND A FRAY SOON.
GROO IS NOT GROO UNLESS HE IS SLAYING SOMEONE!

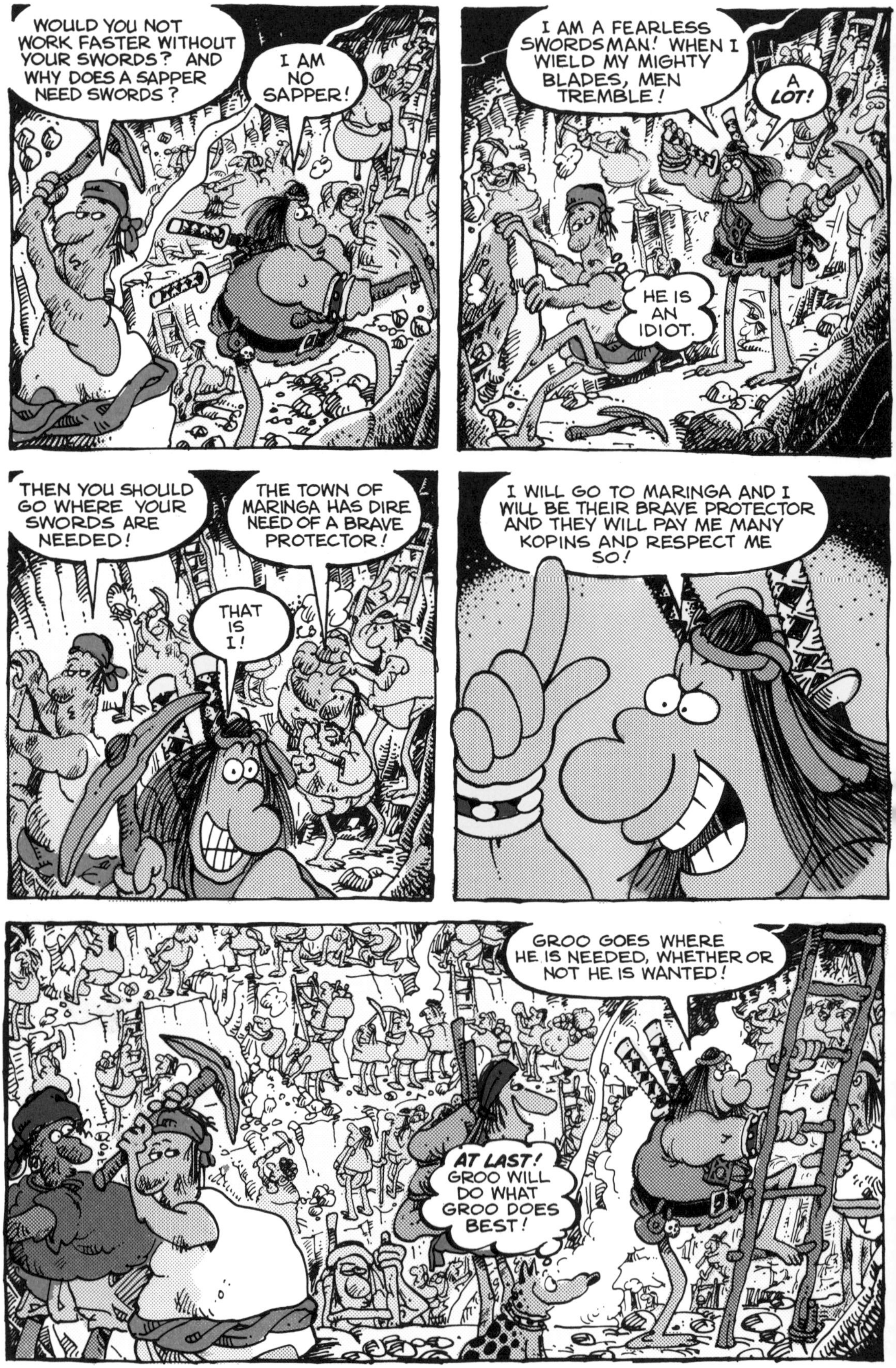
WOULD YOU NOT WORK FASTER WITHOUT YOUR SWORDS? AND WHY DOES A SAPPER NEED SWORDS?
I AM NO SAPPER!
I AM A FEARLESS SWORDSMAN! WHEN I WIELD MY MIGHTY BLADES, MEN TREMBLE!
A LOT!
HE IS AN IDIOT.
THEN YOU SHOULD GO WHERE YOUR SWORDS ARE NEEDED!
THE TOWN OF MARINGA HAS DIRE NEED OF A BRAVE PROTECTOR!
THAT IS I!
I WILL GO TO MARINGA AND I WILL BE THEIR BRAVE PROTECTOR AND THEY WILL PAY ME MANY KOPINS AND RESPECT ME SO!
GROO GOES WHERE HE IS NEEDED, WHETHER OR NOT HE IS WANTED!
AT LAST! GROO WILL DO WHAT GROO DOES BEST!

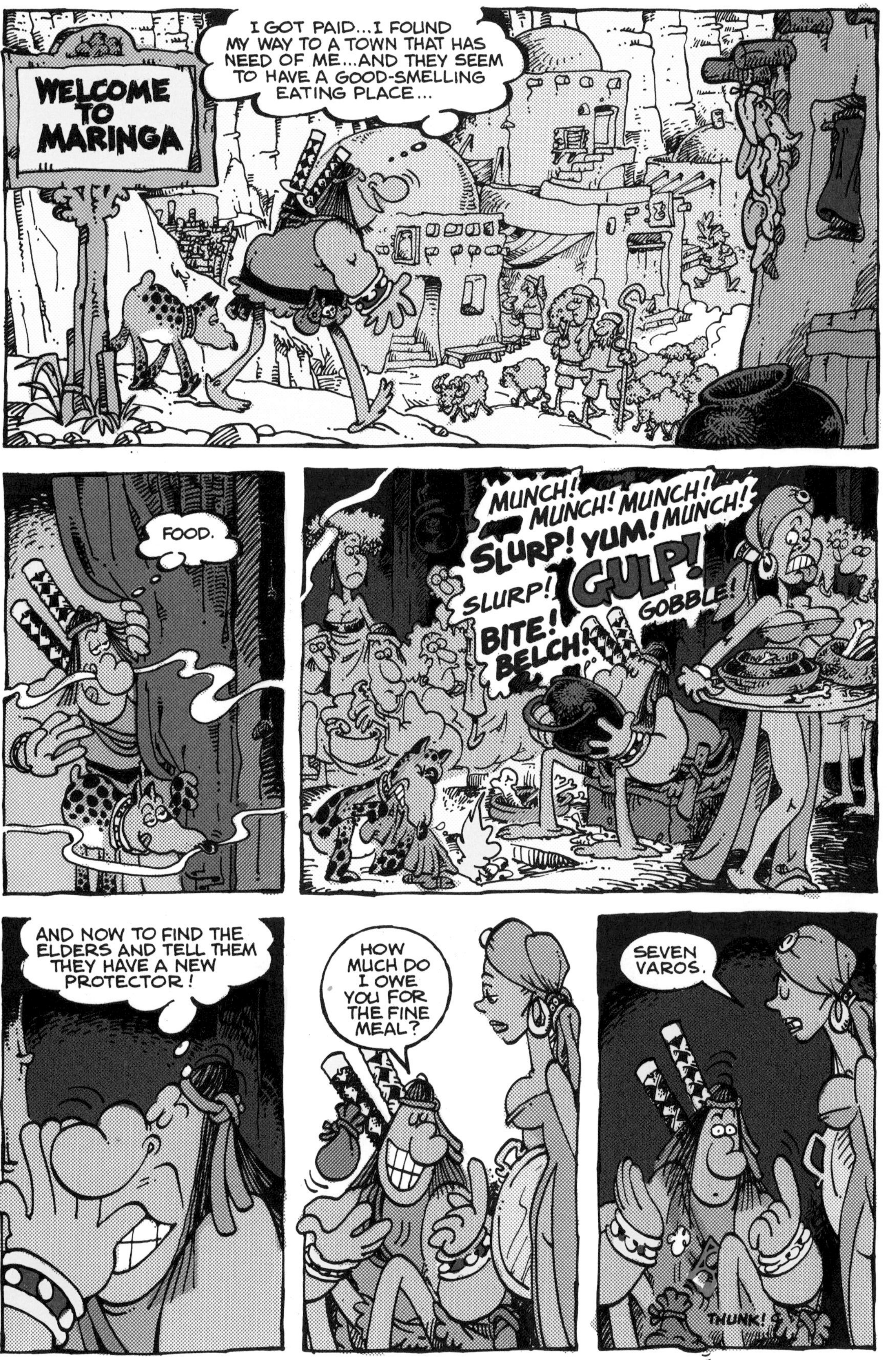
WELCOME TO MARINGA
I GOT PAID...I FOUND MY WAY TO A TOWN THAT HAS NEED OF ME...AND THEY SEEM TO HAVE A GOOD-SMELLING EATING PLACE...
FOOD.
MUNCH! MUNCH! MUNCH!
SLURP! YUM! MUNCH!
SLURP!
GULP!
BITE!
BELCH!
GOBBLE!
AND NOW TO FIND THE ELDERS AND TELL THEM THEY HAVE A NEW PROTECTOR!
HOW MUCH DO I OWE YOU FOR THE FINE MEAL?
SEVEN VAROS.
THUNK!

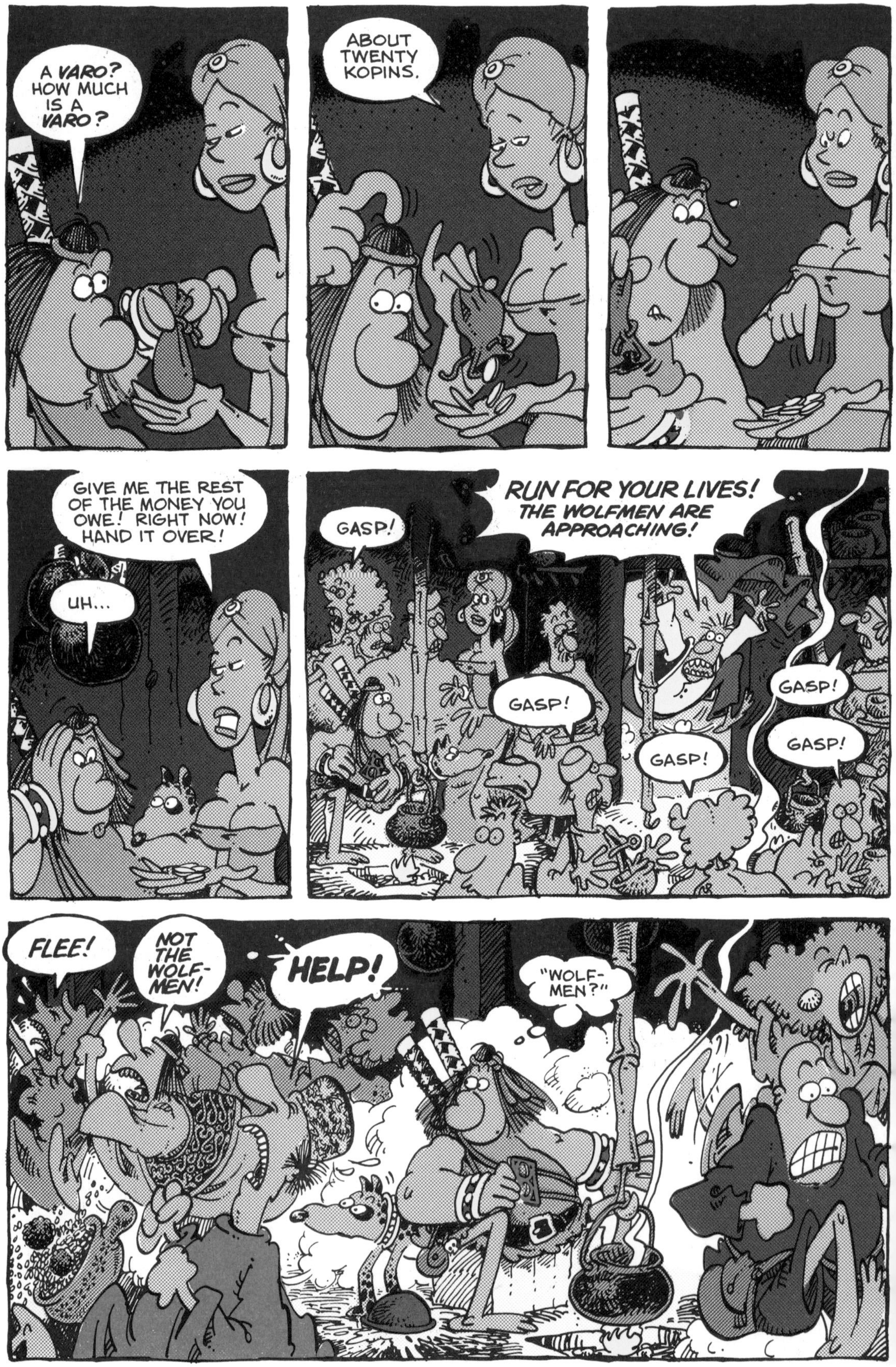
A VARO? HOW MUCH IS A VARO?
ABOUT TWENTY KOPINS.
GIVE ME THE REST OF THE MONEY YOU OWE! RIGHT NOW! HAND IT OVER!
UH...
GASP!
RUN FOR YOUR LIVES! THE WOLFMEN ARE APPROACHING!
GASP!
GASP!
GASP!
GASP!
FLEE!
NOT THE WOLF-MEN!
HELP!
"WOLF-MEN?"

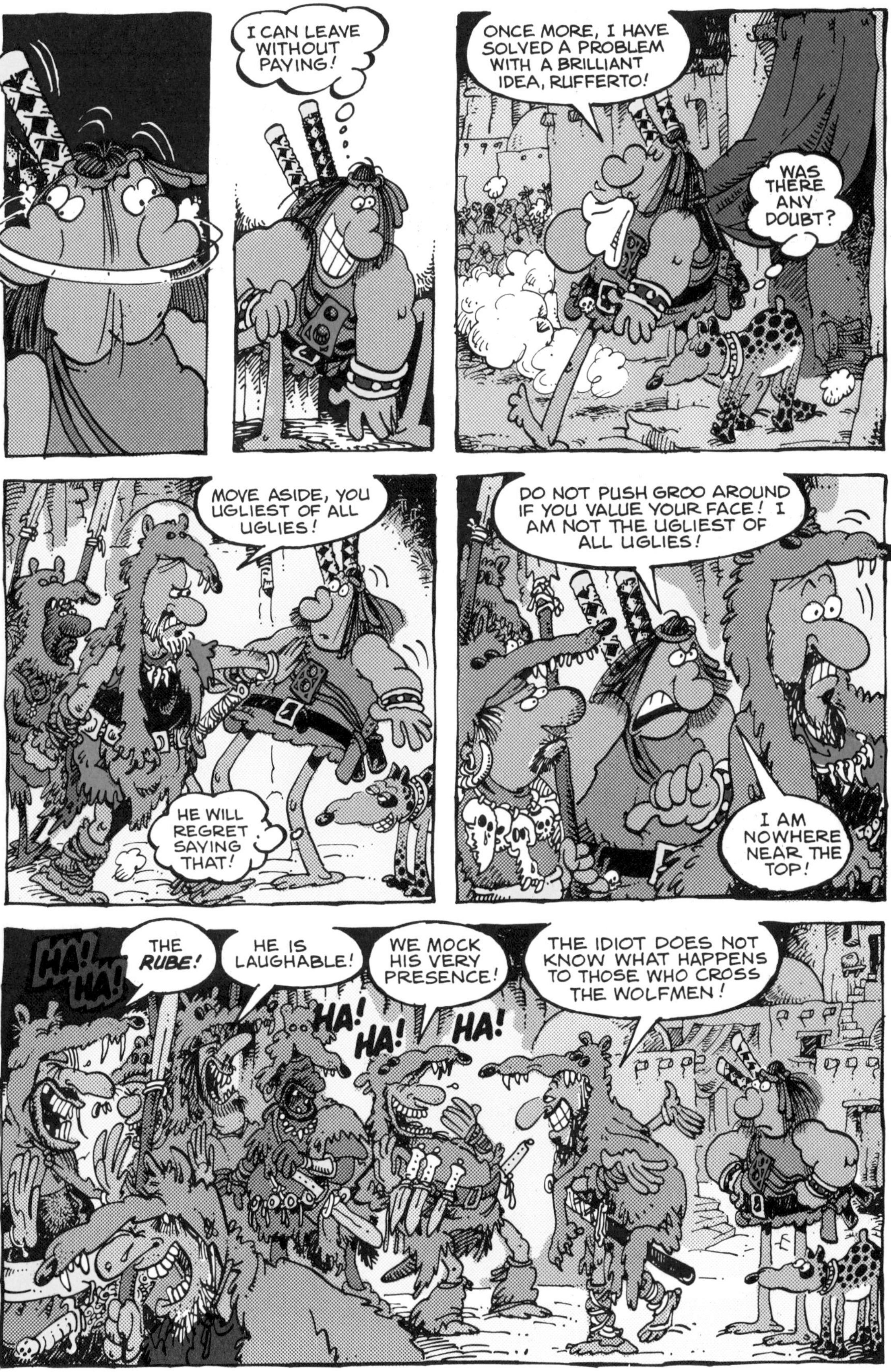
I CAN LEAVE WITHOUT PAYING!
ONCE MORE, I HAVE SOLVED A PROBLEM WITH A BRILLIANT IDEA, RUFFERTO!
WAS THERE ANY DOUBT?
MOVE ASIDE, YOU UGLIEST OF ALL UGLIES!
HE WILL REGRET SAYING THAT!
DO NOT PUSH GROO AROUND IF YOU VALUE YOUR FACE! I AM NOT THE UGLIEST OF ALL UGLIES!
I AM NOWHERE NEAR THE TOP!
HA! HA!
THE *RUBE*!
HE IS LAUGHABLE!
HA! HA!
WE MOCK HIS VERY PRESENCE!
HA!
THE IDIOT DOES NOT KNOW WHAT HAPPENS TO THOSE WHO CROSS THE WOLFMEN!

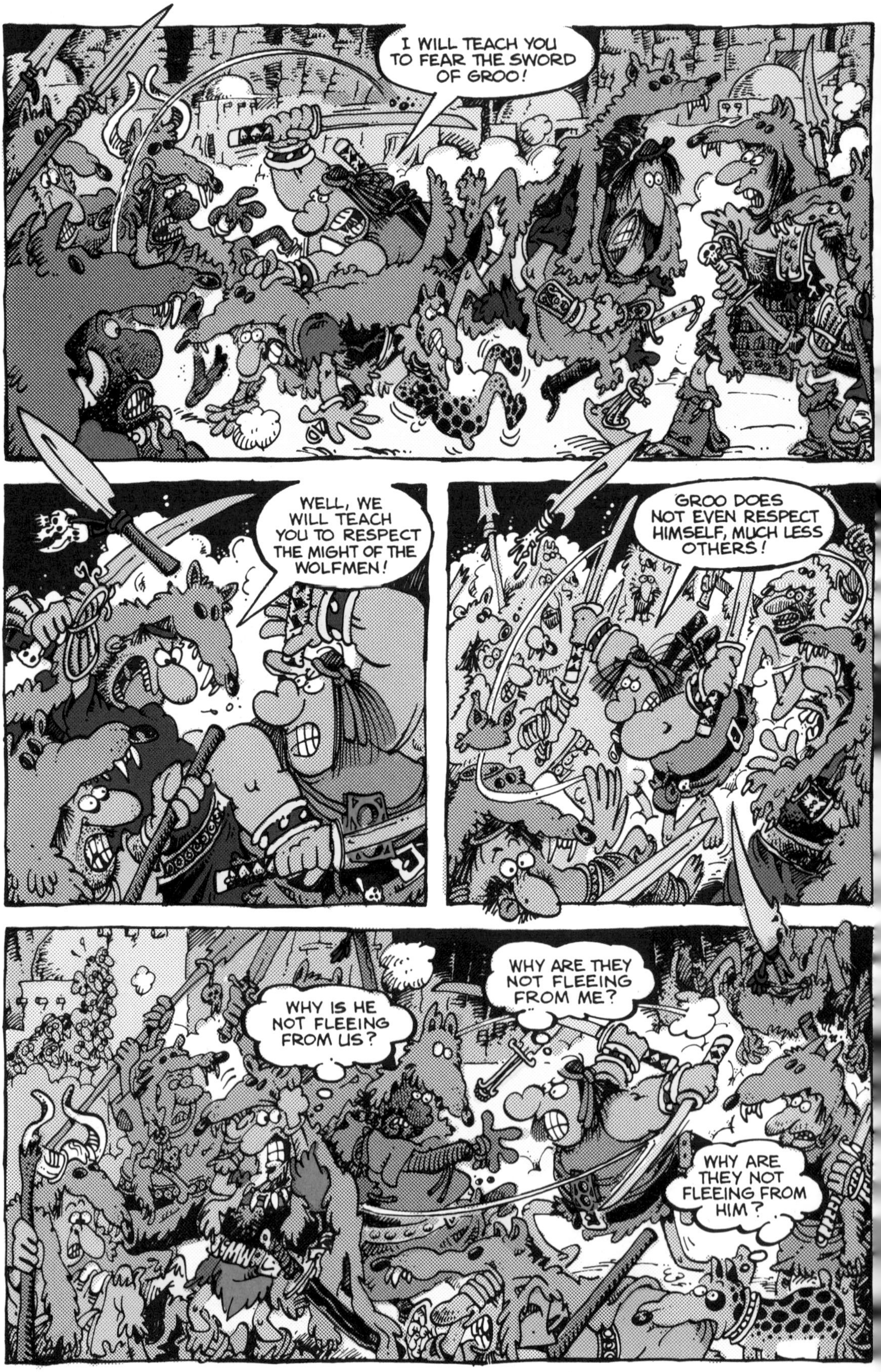
I WILL TEACH YOU TO FEAR THE SWORD OF GROO!
WELL, WE WILL TEACH YOU TO RESPECT THE MIGHT OF THE WOLFMEN!
GROO DOES NOT EVEN RESPECT HIMSELF, MUCH LESS OTHERS!
WHY IS HE NOT FLEEING FROM US?
WHY ARE THEY NOT FLEEING FROM ME?
WHY ARE THEY NOT FLEEING FROM HIM?

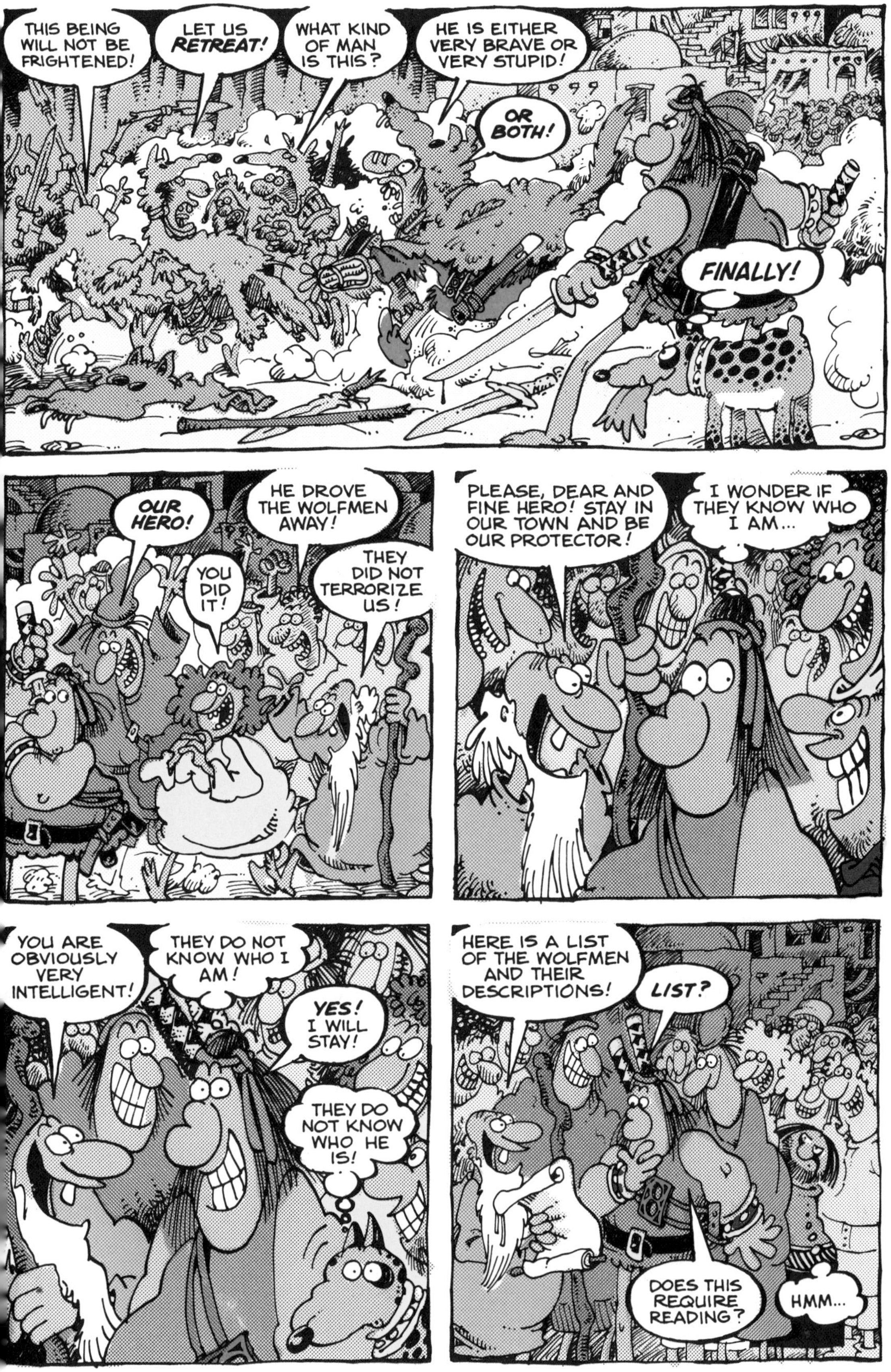
THIS BEING WILL NOT BE FRIGHTENED!
LET US RETREAT!
WHAT KIND OF MAN IS THIS?
HE IS EITHER VERY BRAVE OR VERY STUPID!
OR BOTH!
FINALLY!
OUR HERO!
HE DROVE THE WOLFMEN AWAY!
YOU DID IT!
THEY DID NOT TERRORIZE US!
PLEASE, DEAR AND FINE HERO! STAY IN OUR TOWN AND BE OUR PROTECTOR!
I WONDER IF THEY KNOW WHO I AM...
YOU ARE OBVIOUSLY VERY INTELLIGENT!
THEY DO NOT KNOW WHO I AM!
YES! I WILL STAY!
THEY DO NOT KNOW WHO HE IS!
HERE IS A LIST OF THE WOLFMEN AND THEIR DESCRIPTIONS!
LIST?
DOES THIS REQUIRE READING?
HMM...

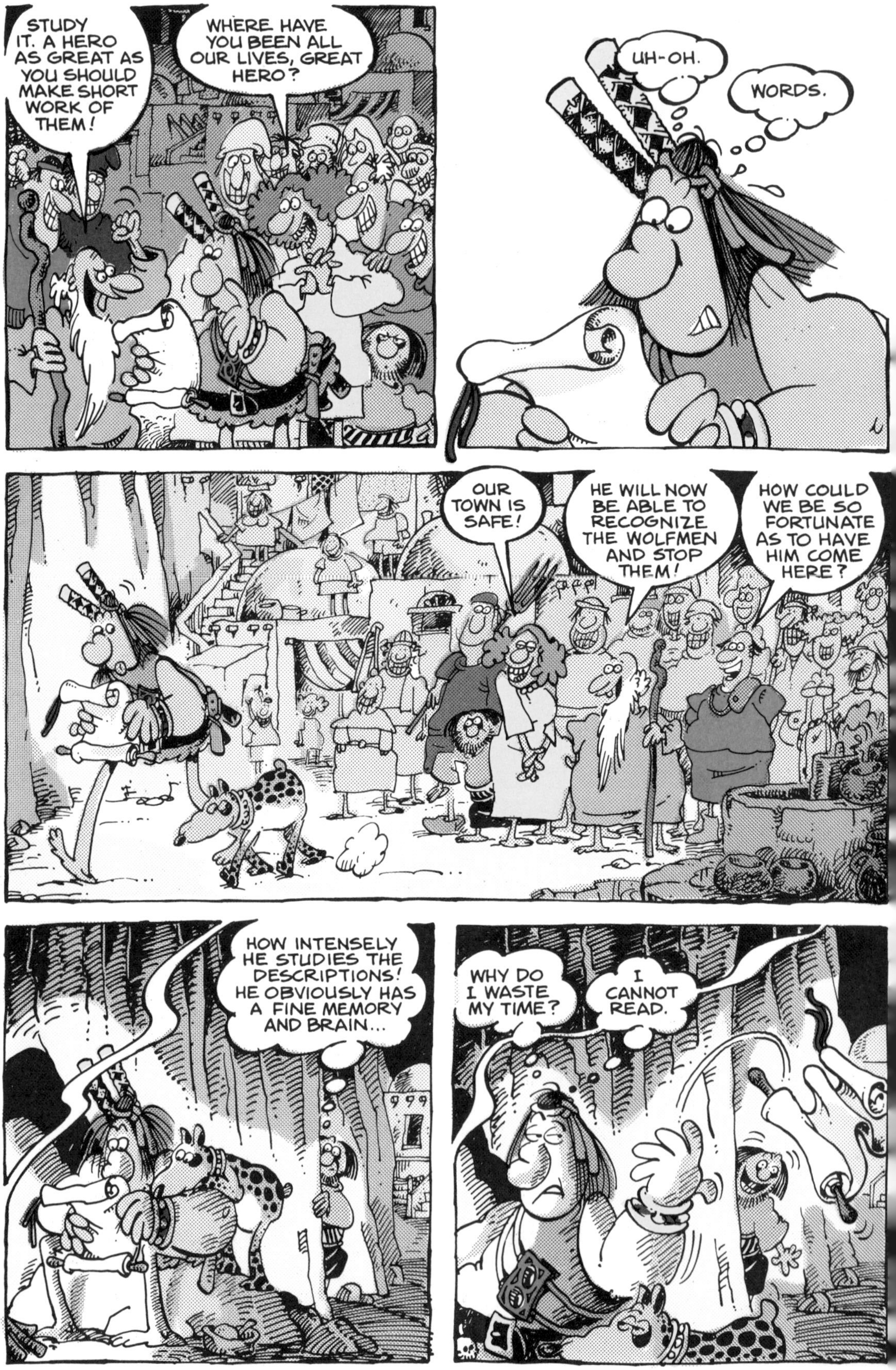
STUDY IT. A HERO AS GREAT AS YOU SHOULD MAKE SHORT WORK OF THEM!
WHERE HAVE YOU BEEN ALL OUR LIVES, GREAT HERO?
UH-OH.
WORDS.
OUR TOWN IS SAFE!
HE WILL NOW BE ABLE TO RECOGNIZE THE WOLFMEN AND STOP THEM!
HOW COULD WE BE SO FORTUNATE AS TO HAVE HIM COME HERE?
HOW INTENSELY HE STUDIES THE DESCRIPTIONS! HE OBVIOUSLY HAS A FINE MEMORY AND BRAIN...
WHY DO I WASTE MY TIME?
I CANNOT READ.

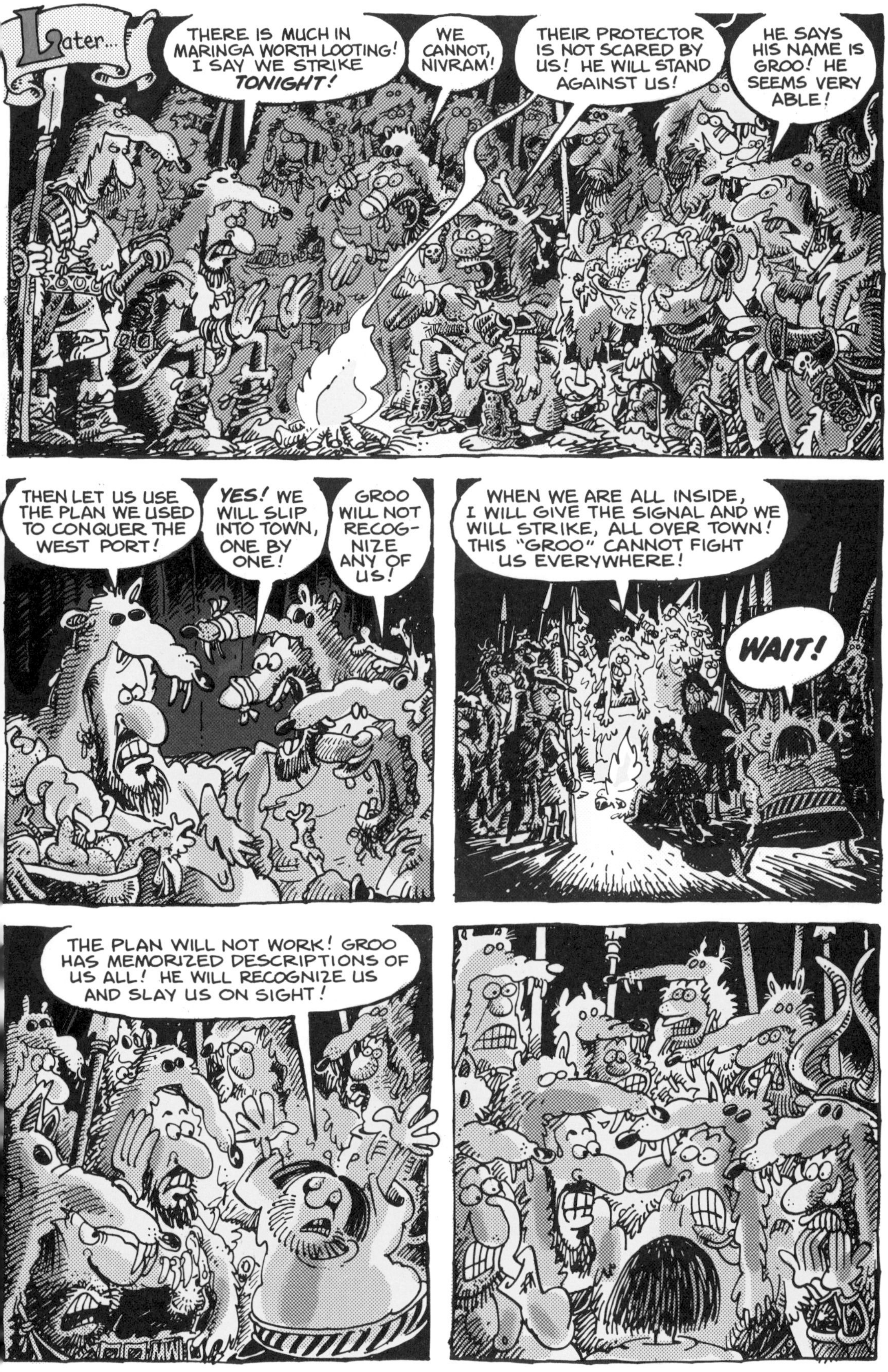

Later...
THERE IS MUCH IN MARINGA WORTH LOOTING! I SAY WE STRIKE *TONIGHT!*
WE CANNOT, NIVRAM!
THEIR PROTECTOR IS NOT SCARED BY US! HE WILL STAND AGAINST US!
HE SAYS HIS NAME IS GROO! HE SEEMS VERY ABLE!
THEN LET US USE THE PLAN WE USED TO CONQUER THE WEST PORT!
YES! WE WILL SLIP INTO TOWN, ONE BY ONE!
GROO WILL NOT RECOG-NIZE ANY OF US!
WHEN WE ARE ALL INSIDE, I WILL GIVE THE SIGNAL AND WE WILL STRIKE, ALL OVER TOWN! THIS "GROO" CANNOT FIGHT US EVERYWHERE!
WAIT!
THE PLAN WILL NOT WORK! GROO HAS MEMORIZED DESCRIPTIONS OF US ALL! HE WILL RECOGNIZE US AND SLAY US ON SIGHT!

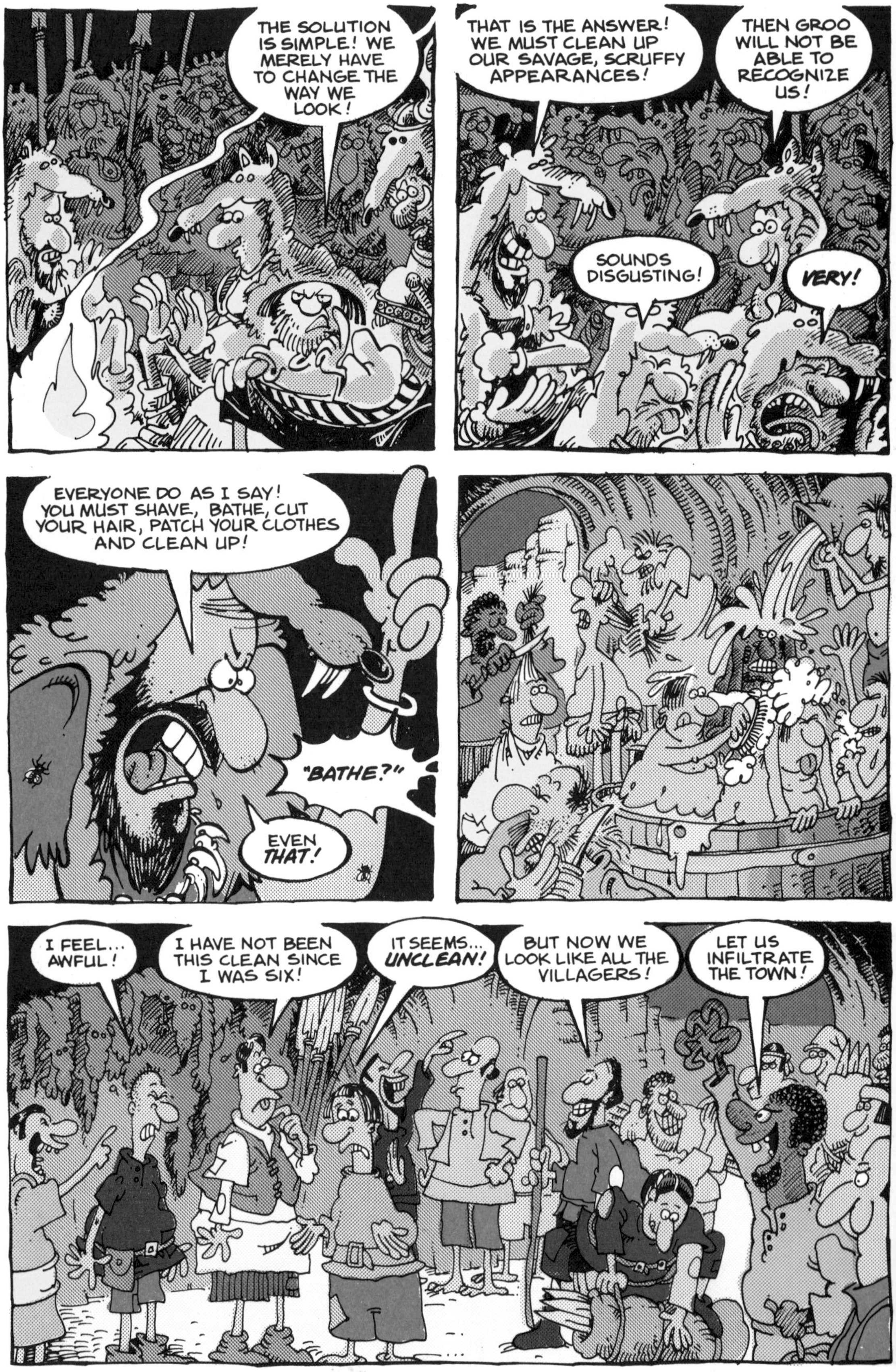
THE SOLUTION IS SIMPLE! WE MERELY HAVE TO CHANGE THE WAY WE LOOK!
THAT IS THE ANSWER! WE MUST CLEAN UP OUR SAVAGE, SCRUFFY APPEARANCES!
THEN GROO WILL NOT BE ABLE TO RECOGNIZE US!
SOUNDS DISGUSTING!
VERY!
EVERYONE DO AS I SAY! YOU MUST SHAVE, BATHE, CUT YOUR HAIR, PATCH YOUR CLOTHES AND CLEAN UP!
"BATHE?"
EVEN THAT!
I FEEL... AWFUL!
I HAVE NOT BEEN THIS CLEAN SINCE I WAS SIX!
IT SEEMS... UNCLEAN!
BUT NOW WE LOOK LIKE ALL THE VILLAGERS!
LET US INFILTRATE THE TOWN!

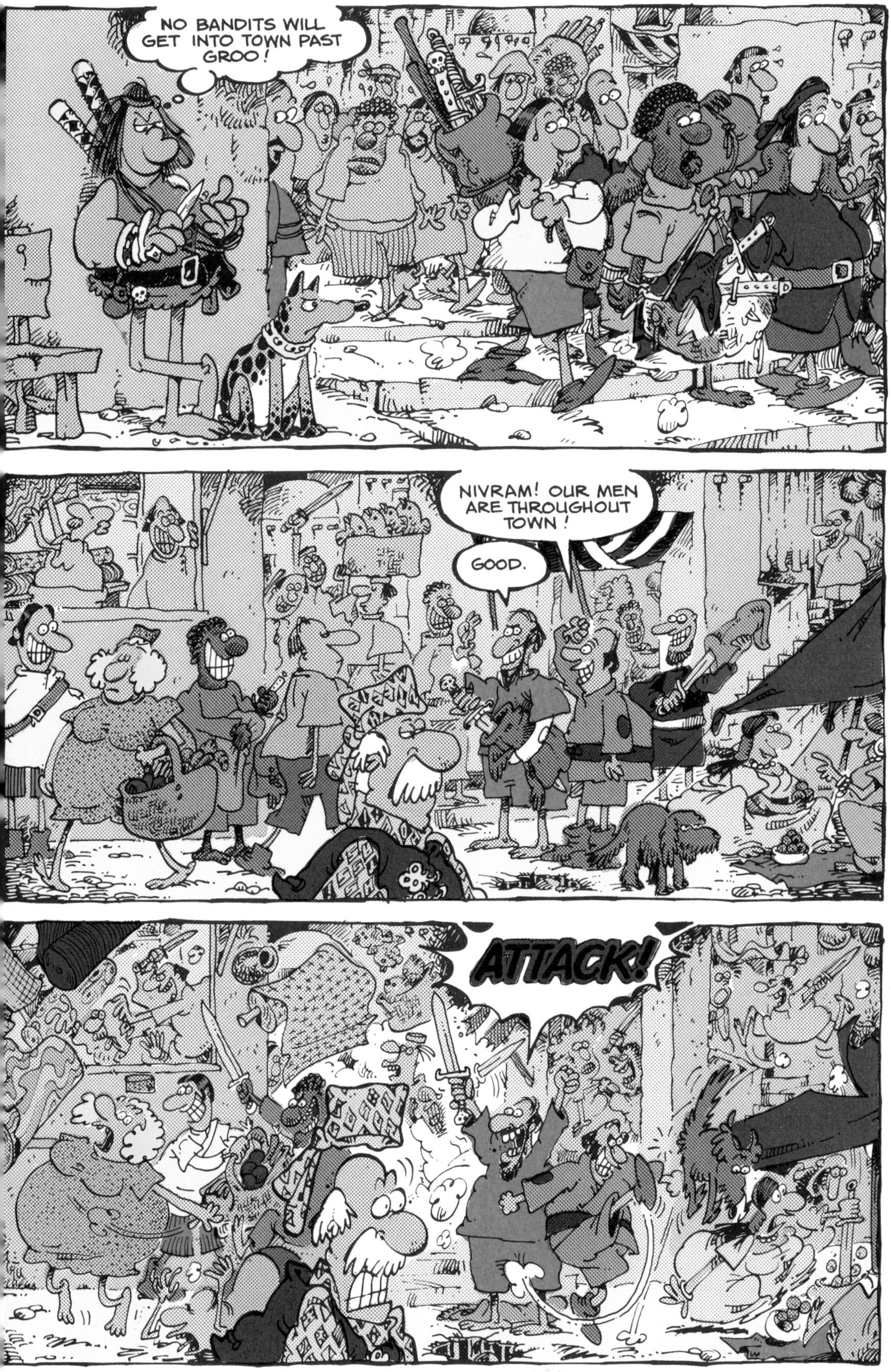
NO BANDITS WILL GET INTO TOWN PAST GROO!
NIVRAM! OUR MEN ARE THROUGHOUT TOWN!
GOOD.
ATTACK!

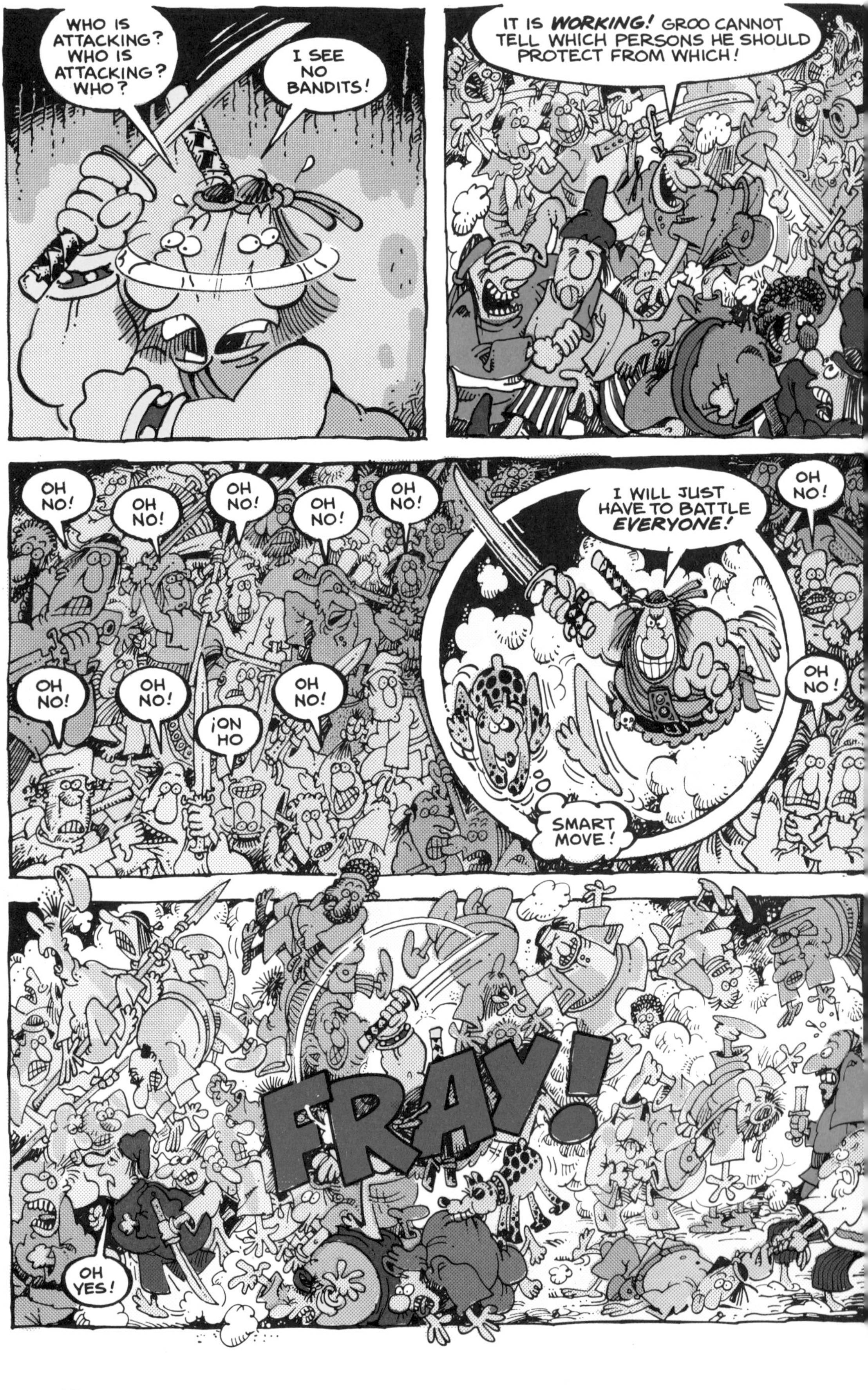
WHO IS ATTACKING? WHO IS ATTACKING? WHO?
I SEE NO BANDITS!
IT IS *WORKING!* GROO CANNOT TELL WHICH PERSONS HE SHOULD PROTECT FROM WHICH!
OH NO!
OH NO!
OH NO!
OH NO!
OH NO!
I WILL JUST HAVE TO BATTLE *EVERYONE!*
OH NO!
OH NO!
OH NO!
¡ON HO
OH NO!
OH NO!
SMART MOVE!
FRAY!
OH YES!

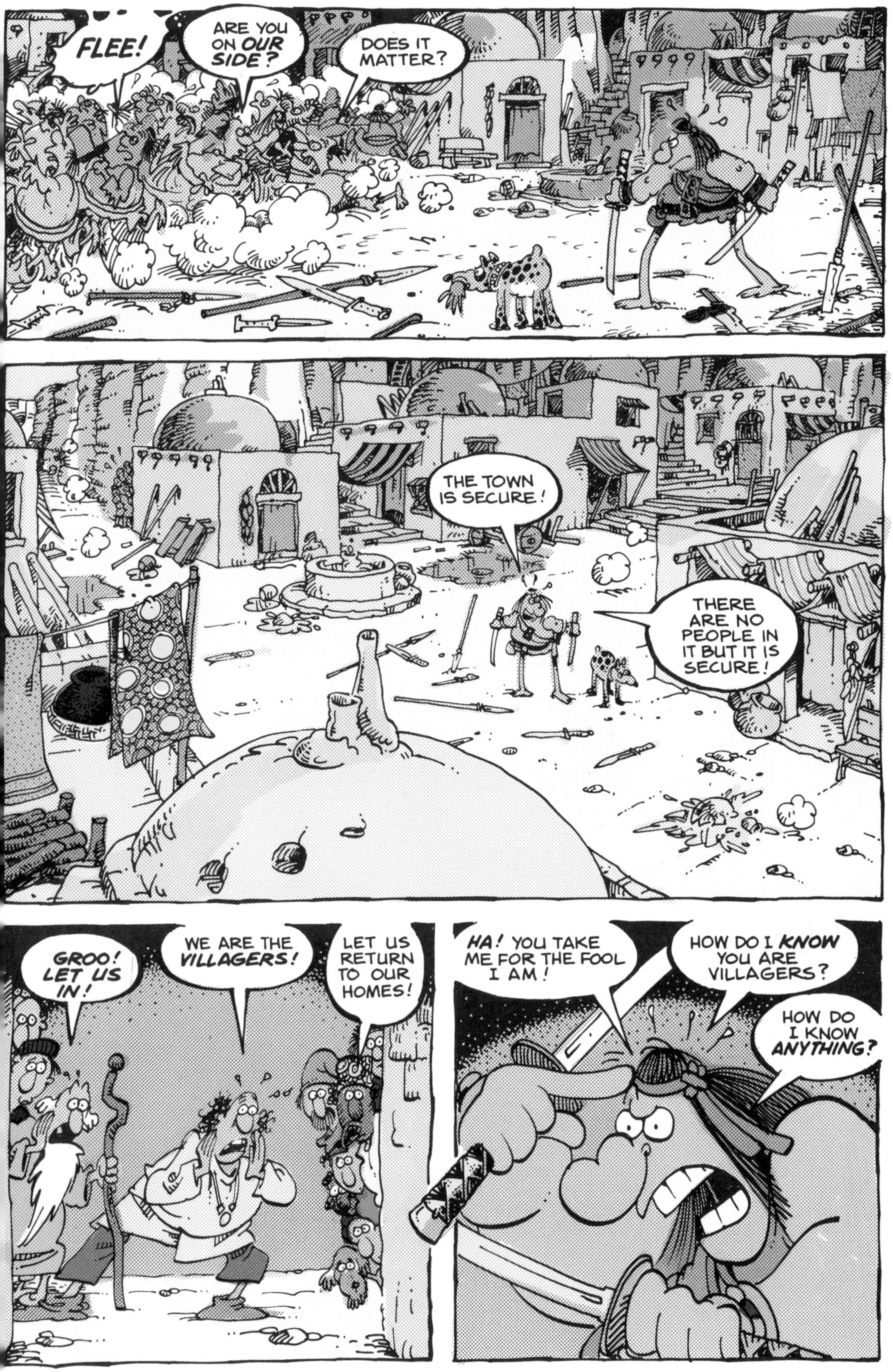
FLEE!
ARE YOU ON OUR SIDE?
DOES IT MATTER?
THE TOWN IS SECURE!
THERE ARE NO PEOPLE IN IT BUT IT IS SECURE!
GROO! LET US IN!
WE ARE THE VILLAGERS!
LET US RETURN TO OUR HOMES!
HA! YOU TAKE ME FOR THE FOOL I AM!
HOW DO I KNOW YOU ARE VILLAGERS?
HOW DO I KNOW ANYTHING?

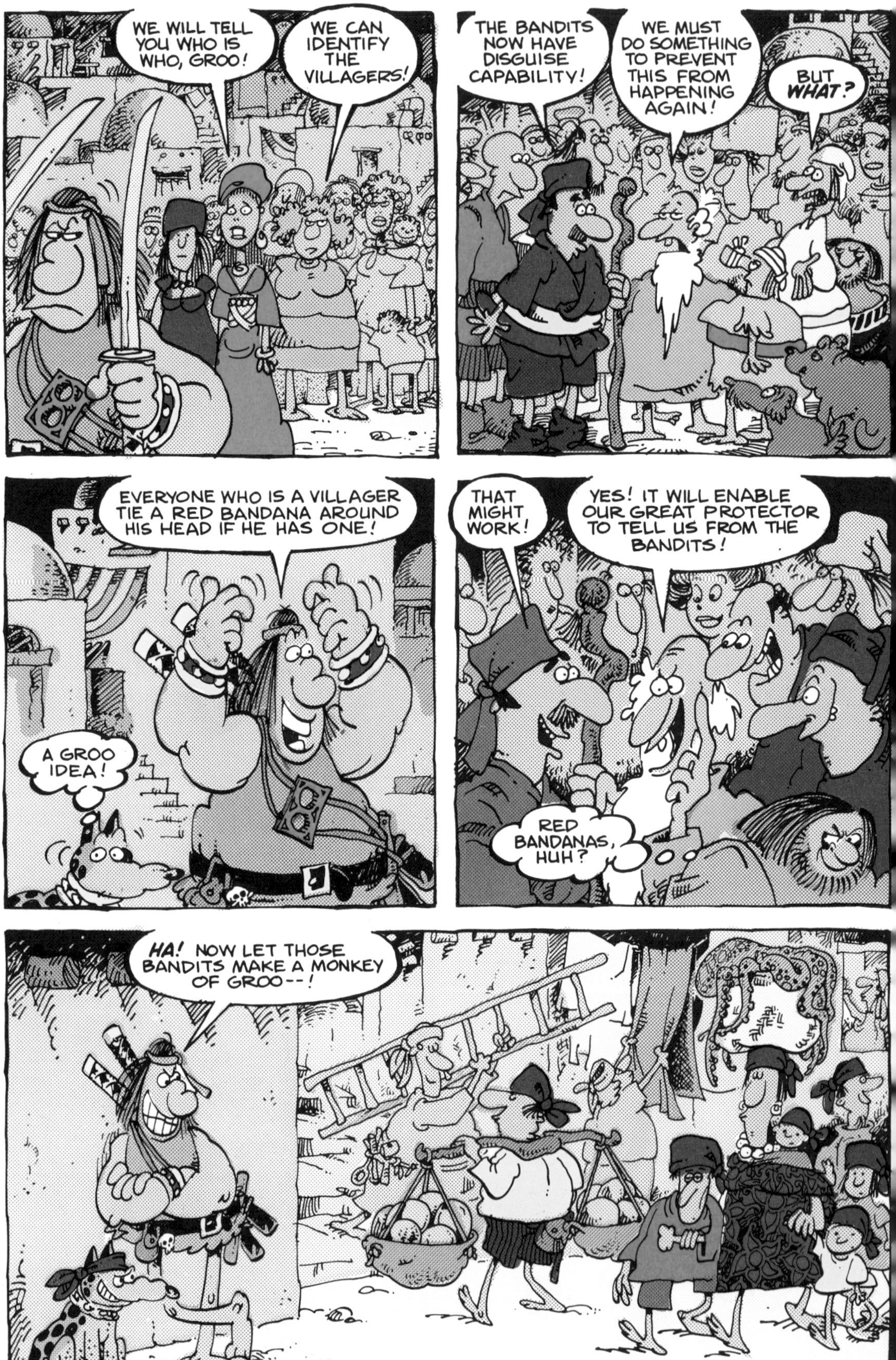
WE WILL TELL YOU WHO IS WHO, GROO!
WE CAN IDENTIFY THE VILLAGERS!
THE BANDITS NOW HAVE DISGUISE CAPABILITY!
WE MUST DO SOMETHING TO PREVENT THIS FROM HAPPENING AGAIN!
BUT WHAT?
EVERYONE WHO IS A VILLAGER TIE A RED BANDANA AROUND HIS HEAD IF HE HAS ONE!
A GROO IDEA!
THAT MIGHT WORK!
YES! IT WILL ENABLE OUR GREAT PROTECTOR TO TELL US FROM THE BANDITS!
RED BANDANAS, HUH?
HA! NOW LET THOSE BANDITS MAKE A MONKEY OF GROO--!

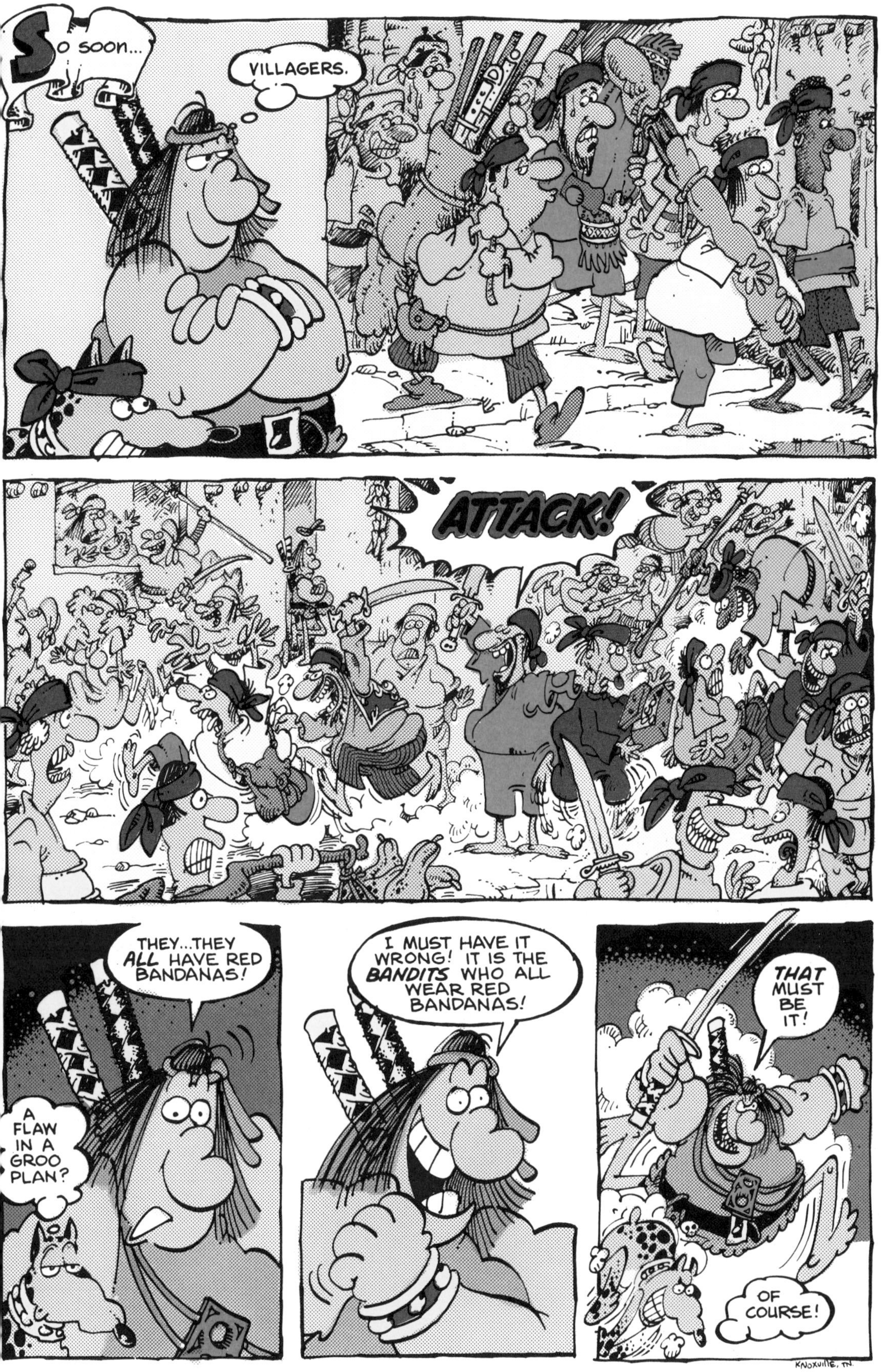
So soon...
VILLAGERS.
ATTACK!
THEY...THEY ALL HAVE RED BANDANAS!
A FLAW IN A GROO PLAN?
I MUST HAVE IT WRONG! IT IS THE BANDITS WHO ALL WEAR RED BANDANAS!
THAT MUST BE IT!
OF COURSE!
KNOXVILLE, TN.

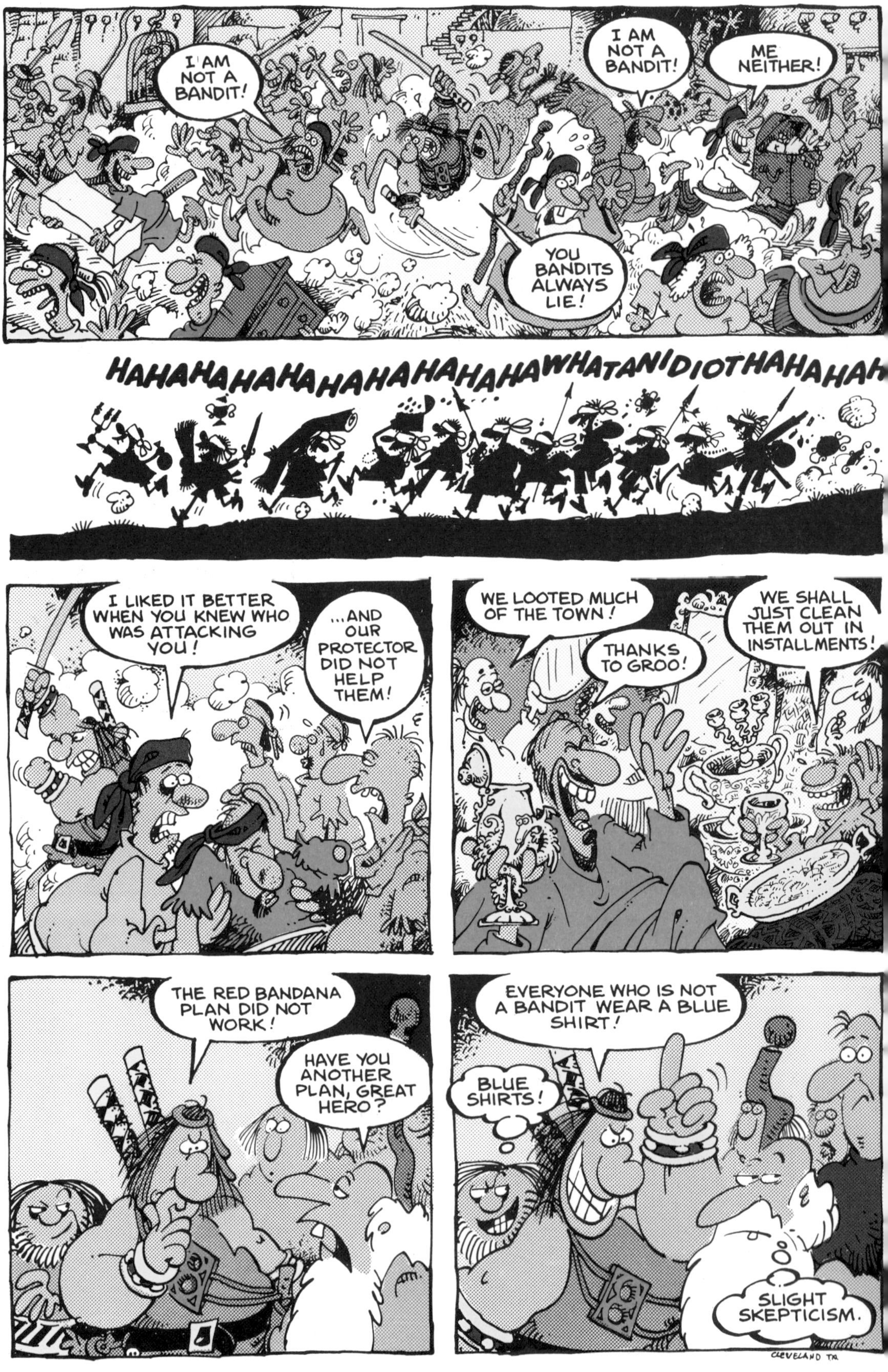
I AM NOT A BANDIT!
I AM NOT A BANDIT!
ME NEITHER!
YOU BANDITS ALWAYS LIE!
HAHAHAHAHAHAHAHAHAHAHAWHATANIDIOTHAHAHAH
I LIKED IT BETTER WHEN YOU KNEW WHO WAS ATTACKING YOU!
...AND OUR PROTECTOR DID NOT HELP THEM!
WE LOOTED MUCH OF THE TOWN!
THANKS TO GROO!
WE SHALL JUST CLEAN THEM OUT IN INSTALLMENTS!
THE RED BANDANA PLAN DID NOT WORK!
HAVE YOU ANOTHER PLAN, GREAT HERO?
EVERYONE WHO IS NOT A BANDIT WEAR A BLUE SHIRT!
BLUE SHIRTS!
SLIGHT SKEPTICISM.
CLEVELAND TX

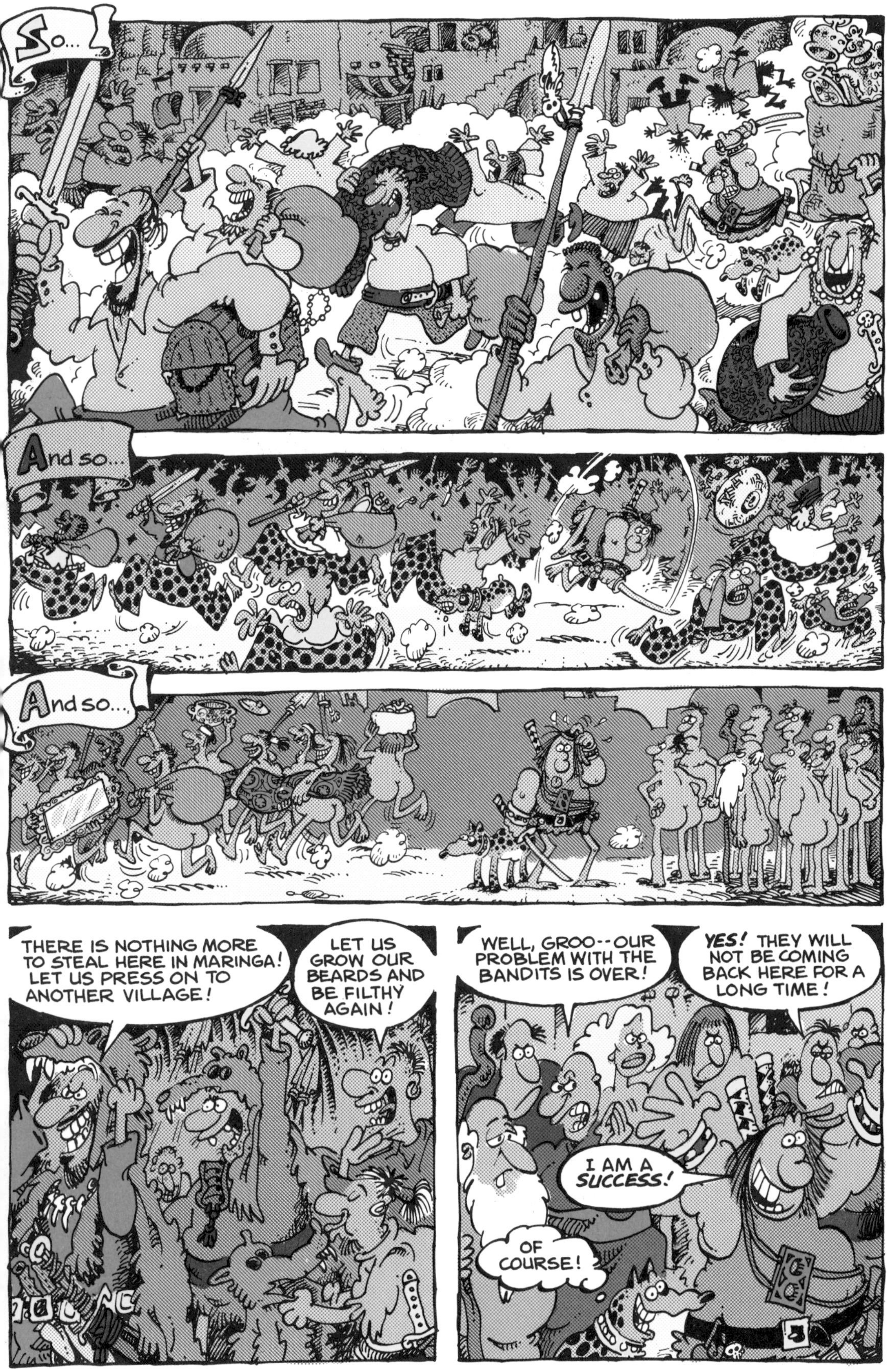
So...
And so...
And so...
THERE IS NOTHING MORE TO STEAL HERE IN MARINGA! LET US PRESS ON TO ANOTHER VILLAGE!
LET US GROW OUR BEARDS AND BE FILTHY AGAIN!
WELL, GROO--OUR PROBLEM WITH THE BANDITS IS OVER!
YES! THEY WILL NOT BE COMING BACK HERE FOR A LONG TIME!
I AM A SUCCESS!
OF COURSE!

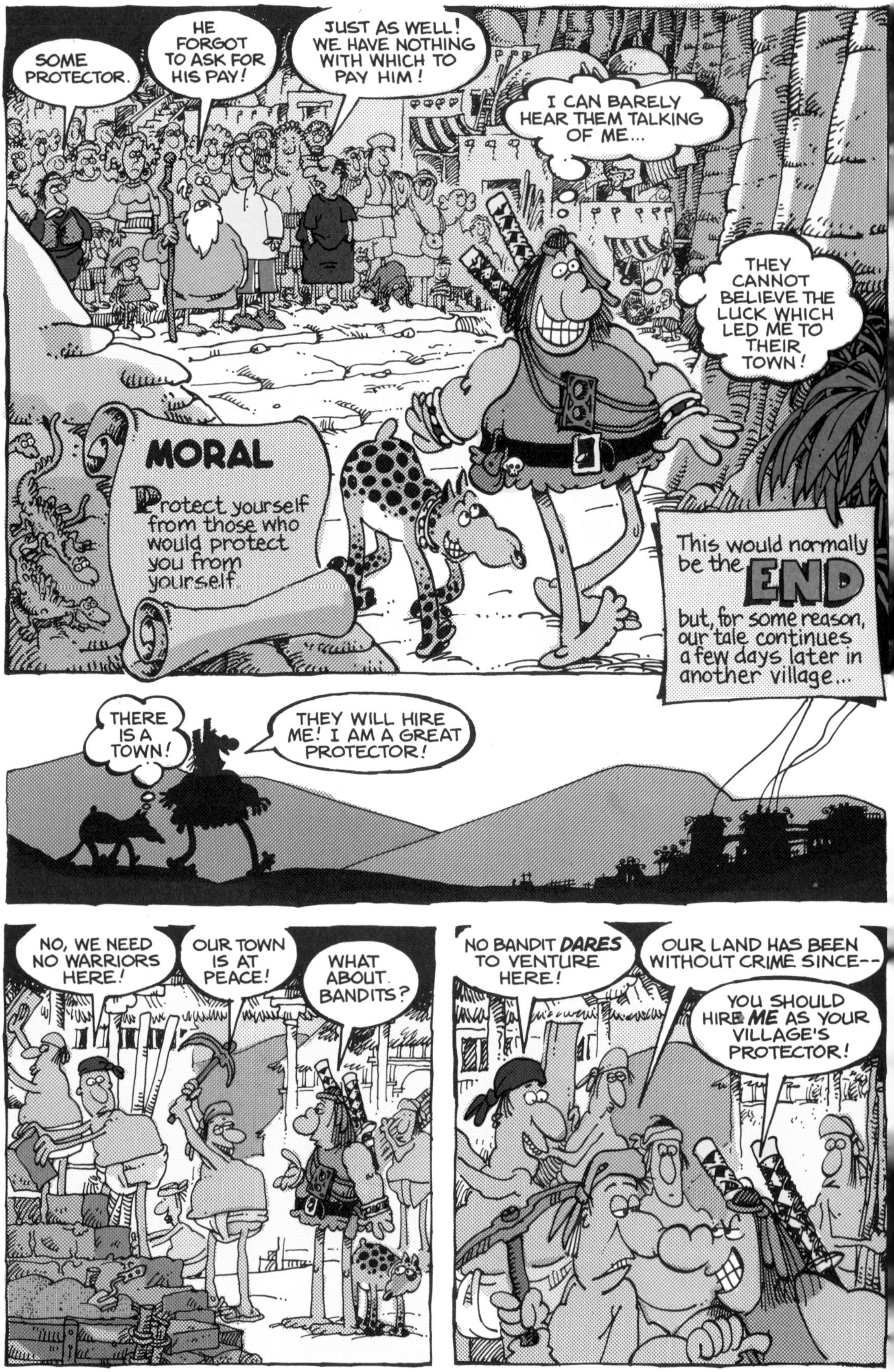
SOME PROTECTOR.
HE FORGOT TO ASK FOR HIS PAY!
JUST AS WELL! WE HAVE NOTHING WITH WHICH TO PAY HIM!
I CAN BARELY HEAR THEM TALKING OF ME...
THEY CANNOT BELIEVE THE LUCK WHICH LED ME TO THEIR TOWN!
MORAL
Protect yourself from those who would protect you from yourself
This would normally be the END but, for some reason, our tale continues a few days later in another village...
THERE IS A TOWN!
THEY WILL HIRE ME! I AM A GREAT PROTECTOR!
NO, WE NEED NO WARRIORS HERE!
OUR TOWN IS AT PEACE!
WHAT ABOUT BANDITS?
NO BANDIT DARES TO VENTURE HERE!
OUR LAND HAS BEEN WITHOUT CRIME SINCE--
YOU SHOULD HIRE ME AS YOUR VILLAGE'S PROTECTOR!

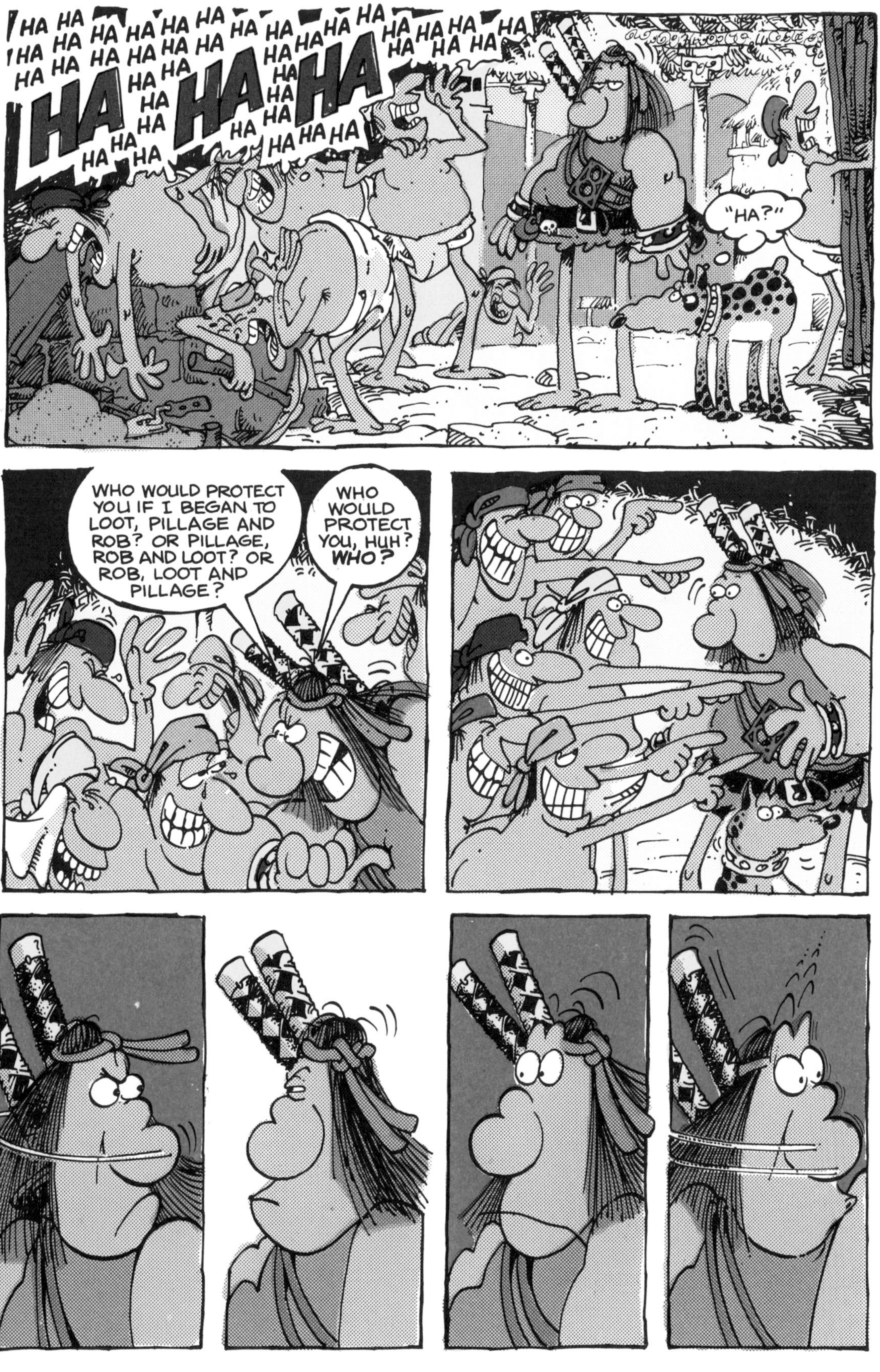
HA HA HA HA HA HA HA HA HA HA HA HA HA HA HA HA HA HA HA HA HA HA HA HA HA HA HA HA HA HA HA HA HA HA HA HA HA HA HA HA HA HA HA HA HA HA HA HA HA
"HA?"
WHO WOULD PROTECT YOU IF I BEGAN TO LOOT, PILLAGE AND ROB? OR PILLAGE, ROB AND LOOT? OR ROB, LOOT AND PILLAGE?
WHO WOULD PROTECT YOU, HUH? WHO?

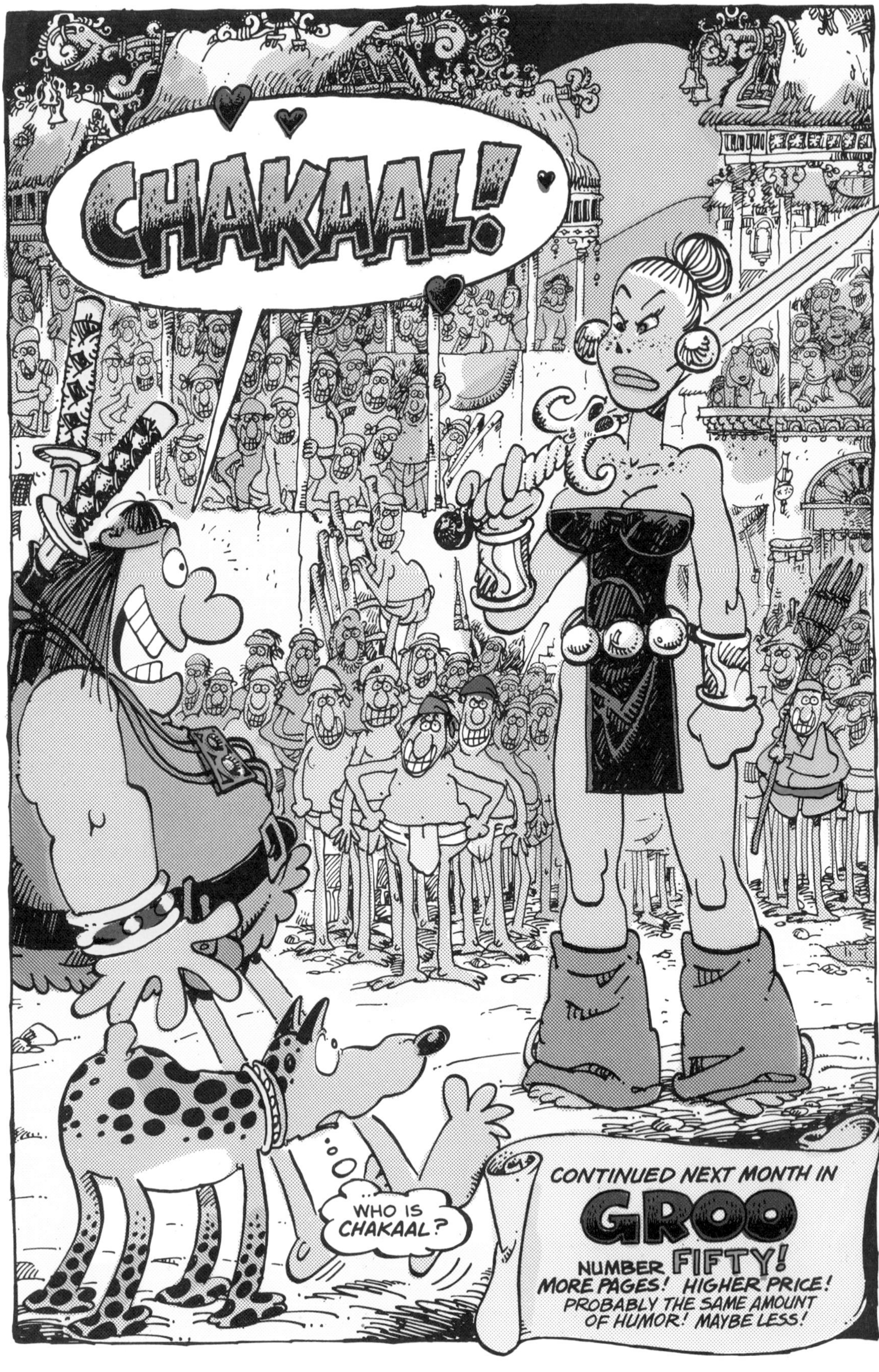
CHAKAAL!
WHO IS CHAKAAL?
CONTINUED NEXT MONTH IN
GROO
NUMBER FIFTY!
MORE PAGES! HIGHER PRICE!
PROBABLY THE SAME AMOUNT OF HUMOR! MAYBE LESS!

THE END OF THE BOOK

This is *The Groo Library,* which means nothing except that we've made it to "L." (Once, when we approached a respected British publisher about putting out *Groo,* he told us to go to "L.") (That's not true, by the way. That's a joke and, now that I think of it, not a very good one.) In case you haven't noticed, there's a certain logic to the names of these volumes.

We started with *The Groo Adventurer* and followed it with *The Groo Bazaar, The Groo Carnival, The Groo Dynasty, The Groo Epoch, The Groo Festival, The Groo Garden, The Groo Houndbook, The Groo Inferno, The Groo Jamboree, The Groo Kingdom,* and now, *The Groo Library.* Next up is *The Groo Maiden*, which is all about Chakaal.

But notice a pattern in those titles? Of course you do, but then you're smart. (Though not *too* smart. My God, look at what you're reading!)

We started these when we were back at Marvel, and the original idea was to call the first one *The Groo Collection, Volume 1* and the next, *The Groo Collection, Volume 2* ...and so on. We are so damn clever. Then someone in the company's marketing division said, "No, you don't want to do that!"

"Why," we asked, "do we not want to do that?"

"Because," they said, "if these books are successful" — and this was uttered with more than a trace of skepticism — "you'll someday be up to Volume 9 or Volume 14 or something. And potential new customers will say to themselves, 'I can't buy Volume 14, inasmuch as I have not the first thirteen volumes. Ergo, I shall purchase something else.'"

We argued back, "But most Groo stories are fully and wonderfully self-contained and one need not have them all to understand any." (The stories in this book and the next are as close as we've ever come to violating that.)

"No, no," the all-wise funnybook marketers insisted. "Folks will see those volume numbers and toss their dollars elsewhere." And since they, the biz folks, seemed to know of what they spoke, we concurred.

"We agree, now that you've explained it," we said — except that it was only I who said that. Sergio can't pronounce "explained." It comes out, "splained." But together we added, "We will have no numbering of any kind on our *Groo* reprint collections."

"No, no, no," proclaimed "they" again. "You don't want to do that because the fans who do start buying them will keep on buying if they're numbered. They'll want to keep their collections complete and it won't seem like a series to be collected if they're not numbered."

"So what you're saying," we said — and at this point, I was the one who was at the disadvantage since, unlike Sergio, I speak only English — "is that they should be numbered but not have numbers on them."

"Precisely," they said. Well, we puzzled that until our puzzlers were sore. Finally, I came up with the idea of the alphabetical names. They tell the die-hard *Groo* collectors (there are such people) which volume this is without announcing to the world that, for example, this is VOLUME TWELVE!!!

And it features, by the way, "Rufferto Reverie," which first appeared in *Groo* #44 (Oct., '88), "Rufferto Reality" (which was in the next issue), and then we jump to "The 300% Solution" from #47 (January of '89) and "The Protector," which first saw print in #49 (March, '89). We're not going precisely in sequence because some stories were continued or connected, but don't worry. Nothing will be omitted. #46 was in the previous collection and #48 will be in *The Groo Nursery,* which is the book after next.

But, getting back to the names: Everyone liked the idea except one guy in Marvel's publicity/promo department who wanted us to figure out 26 titles in advance. "What are you going to do for 'Q'?" he asked. "Or 'X'? And what if we need to go past 'Z'?" At this point, we hadn't even put out *The Groo Adventurer.*

I told him, "'Q' could be *The Groo Quest* " — and it probably will be, we'll see — "And as for 'X,' I dunno. We may never get that far and even if we do, you're putting these out, two a year. We have more than a decade to figure it out. Maybe someone will invent a new word that starts with 'X' in that time."

"And if they don't?"

I said, "How about *The Groo X-Men*? That would sell." He didn't think that was funny and he also felt that things like The *Groo X-travaganza* (or, as Sergio would say, *Stravaganza*) were cheating.

Anyway, before I could get back to him with a better answer, he was fired, probably for asking too many premature questions.

Still, his key concern remains: What will we do for "X"? After "Z," we can just start over again with *The Groo Almanac,* The *Groo Bible* and so on...but what will we call the "X" volume?

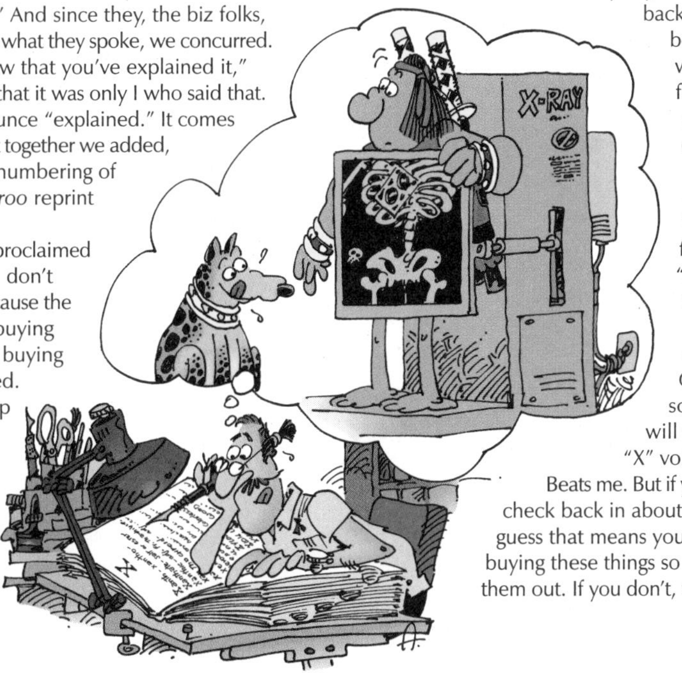
X-RAY

Beats me. But if you want to know, check back in about six years. And I guess that means you'll have to keep buying these things so we have to put them out. If you don't, we'll never know.

— Mark Evanier

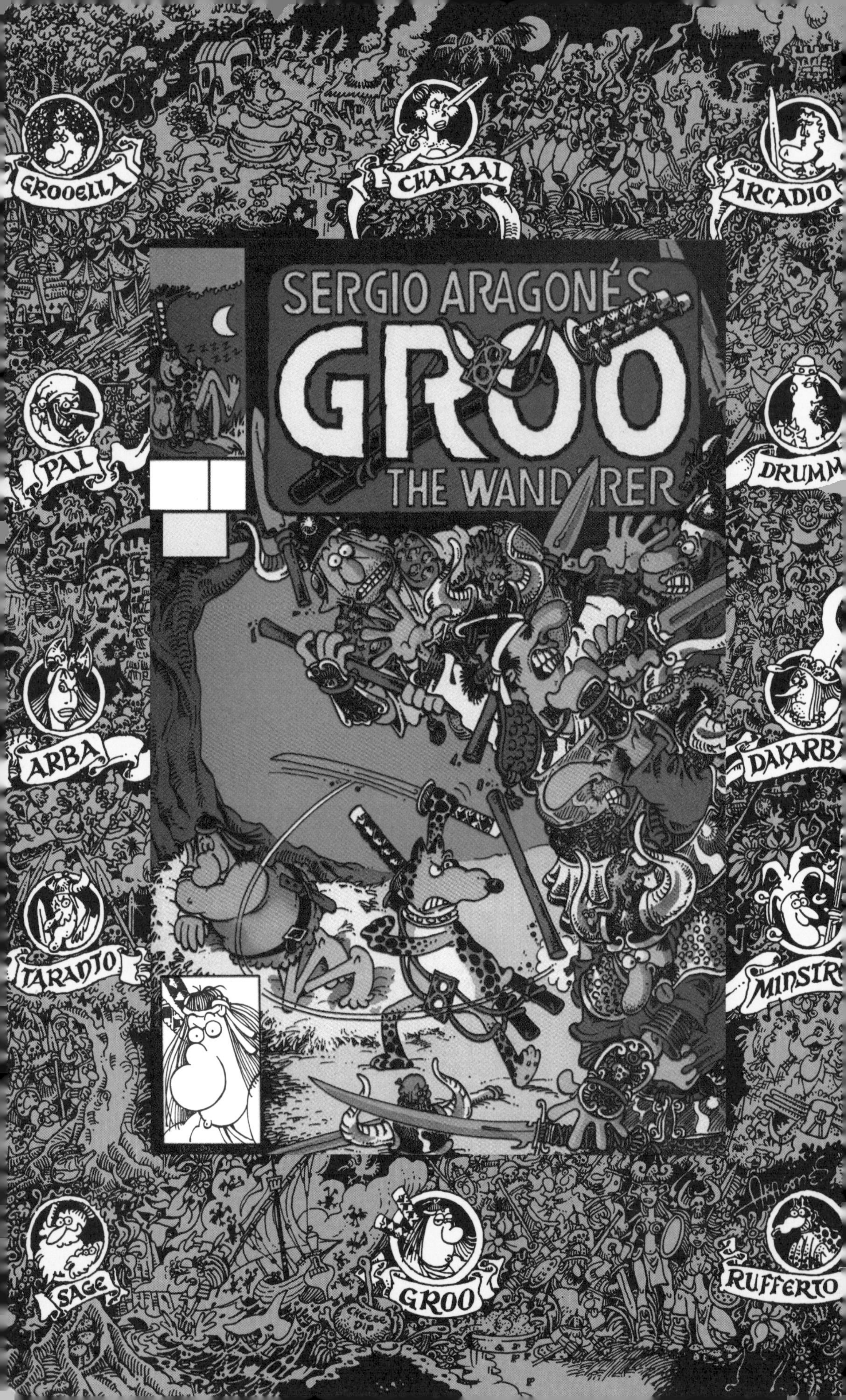

GROOELLA
CHAKAAL
ARCADIO
SERGIO ARAGONÉS
GROO
THE WAND RER
PAL
DRUMM
ARBA
DAKARBA
TARANTO
MINSTR
SAGE
GROO
RUFFERTO
CHEESE DIP

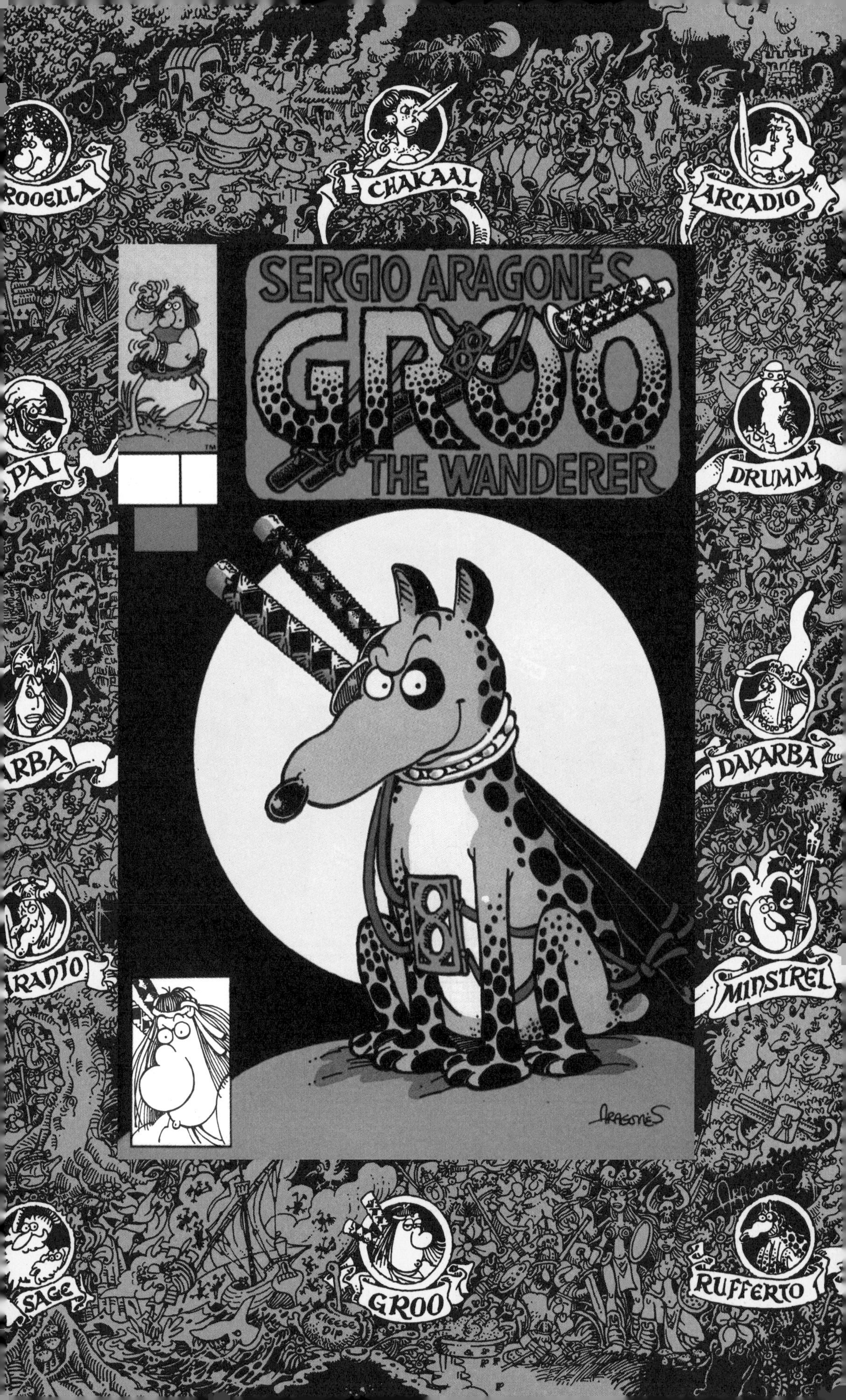
ROOELLA
CHAKAAL
ARCADIO
SERGIO ARAGONÉS
GROO
THE WANDERER
PAI
DRUMM
ARBA
DAKARBA
RANTO
MINSTREL
ARAGONÉS
SAGE
GROO
CHEESE DIP
RUFFERTO

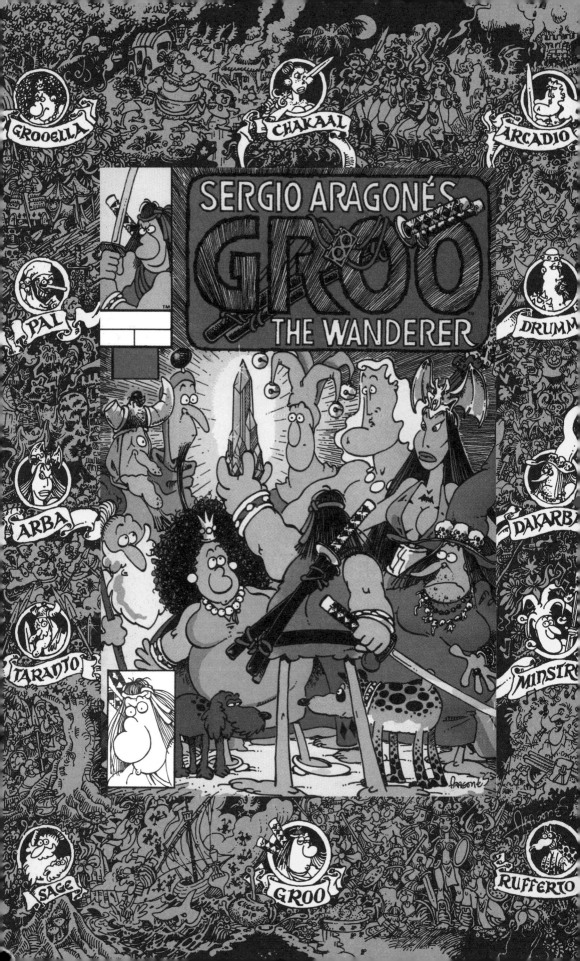

OTHER TRADE PAPERBACKS AVAILABLE FROM DARK HORSE COMICS

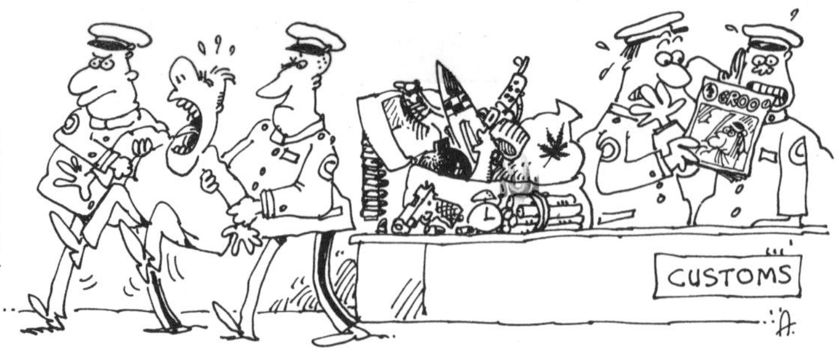
GROO
CUSTOMS

SERGIO ARAGONÉS GROO
Sergio Aragonés
THE GROO HOUNDBOOK
color paperback
ISBN: 1-56971-385-5 $9.95
THE GROO INFERNO
color paperback
ISBN: 1-56971-430-4 $9.95
THE MOST INTELLIGENT MAN IN THE WORLD
color paperback
ISBN: 1-56971-294-8 $9.95
GROO AND RUFFERTO
color paperback
ISBN: 1-56971-447-9 $9.95
THE GROO JAMBOREE
color paperback
ISBN: 1-56971-462-2 $9.95
THE GROO KINGDOM
color paperback
ISBN: 1-56971-478-9 $9.95

SERGIO ARAGONÉS LOUDER THAN WORDS
Sergio Aragonés
B&W paperback
ISBN: 1-56971-343-X $12.95

BOOGEYMAN
Sergio Aragonés
B&W paperback
ISBN: 1-56971-374-X $9.95

MICHAEL MOORCOCK'S ELRIC: STORMBRINGER
P. Craig Russell
color paperback
ISBN: 1-56971-339-7 $17.95

ENO & PLUM
Terry LaBan
B&W paperback
ISBN: 1-56971-265-4 $12.95

FAX FROM SARAJEVO
Joe Kubert
color hardcover
ISBN: 1-56971-143-7 $24.95

FLAMING CARROT
Bob Burden
MAN OF MYSTERY
B&W paperback
ISBN: 1-56971-263-8 $14.95
THE WILD SHALL WILD REMAIN
B&W paperback
ISBN: 1-56971-322-7 $17.95
FLAMING CARROT'S GREATEST HITS
B&W paperback
ISBN: 1-56971-282-4 $17.95
FORTUNE FAVORS THE BOLD
B&W paperback
ISBN: 1-56971-333-2 $16.95

HELLBOY
Mike Mignola
SEED OF DESTRUCTION
with John Byrne
color paperback
ISBN: 1-56971-316-2 $17.95
THE CHAINED COFFIN AND OTHERS
color paperback
ISBN: 1-56971-349-9 $17.95

LAND OF NOD
ROCKABYE BOOK
Jay Stephens
B&W paperback
ISBN: 1-56971-356-1 $13.95

MOEBIUS
ARZACH
color paperback
ISBN: 1-56971-132-1 $6.95
THE MAN FROM THE CIGURI
color paperback
ISBN: 1-56971-135-6 $7.95
EXOTICS
color paperback
ISBN: 1-56971-134-8 $7.95
H.P.'S ROCK CITY
color paperback
ISBN: 1-56971-133-x $7.95
MADWOMAN OF THE SACRED HEART
B&W paperback
ISBN: 1-56971-136-4 $12.95

TOO MUCH COFFEE MAN
Shannon Wheeler
GUIDE FOR THE PERPLEXED
B&W paperback
ISBN: 1-56971-289-1 $10.95
limited-edition hardcover
ISBN: 1-56971-283-2 $49.95

USAGI YOJIMBO
Stan Sakai
SHADES OF DEATH
B&W paperback
ISBN: 1-56971-259-x $14.95
DAISHO
B&W paperback
ISBN: 1-56971-292-1 $14.95
BRINK OF LIFE & DEATH
B&W paperback
ISBN: 1-56971-297-2 $14.95

WHAT'S MICHAEL?
Makoto Kobayashi
MICHAEL'S ALBUM
B&W paperback
ISBN: 1-56971-247-6 $5.95
LIVING TOGETHER
B&W paperback
ISBN: 1-56971-248-4 $5.95
OFF THE DEEP END
B&W paperback
ISBN: 1-56971-249-2 $5.95
MICHAEL'S MAMBO
B&W paperback
ISBN: 1-56971-250-6 $5.95

WOLVERTON IN SPACE
Basil Wolverton
240-page B&W paperback
ISBN: 1-56971-238-7 $16.95

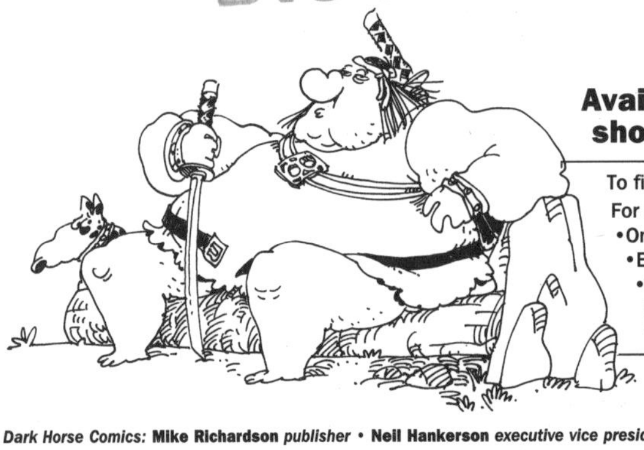

Available from your local comics shop or bookstore!

To find a comics shop in your area, call 1-888-266-4226
For more information or to order direct:
- On the web: www.darkhorse.com
- E-mail: mailorder@darkhorse.com
- Phone: 1-800-862-0052 or (503) 652-9701
Mon.-Sat. 9 A.M. to 5 P.M. Pacific Time

*Prices and availability subject to change without notice

Dark Horse Comics: **Mike Richardson** *publisher* • **Neil Hankerson** *executive vice president* • **Andy Karabatsos** *vice president of finance* • **Randy Stradley** *vice president of publishing* • **Chris Warner** *senior editor* • **Michael Martens** *vice president of marketing* • **Anita Nelson** *vice president of sales & licensing* • **David Scroggy** *vice president of product development* • **Cindy Marks** *director of production & design* • **Mark Cox** *art director* • **Dale LaFountain** *vice president of information technology* • **Kim Haines** *director of human resources* • **Darlene Vogel** *director of purchasing* • **Ken Lizzi** *general counsel*